The Individualist Anarchists

The Individualist Anarchists

AN ANTHOLOGY OF *LIBERTY* (1881-1908)

Frank H. Brooks

EDITOR

With an introduction by the editor

Routledge
Taylor & Francis Group

LONDON AND NEW YORK

First published 1994 by Transaction Publishers

2 Park Square, Milton Park, Abingdon, Oxfordshire OX14 4RN
711 Third Avenue, New York, NY 10017

Routledge is an imprint of the Taylor & Francis Group, an informa business

First issued in paperback 2017

Library of Congress Catalog Number: 93-30303

Library of Congress Cataloging-in-Publication Data
The individualist anarchists : an anthology of Liberty (1881-1908) / edited and
with an introduction by Frank H. Brooks.
    p. cm.
Includes bibliographical references.
ISBN 1-56000-132-1
    1. Anarchism—United States—History. 2. Anarchists—United States—
History. 3. Liberty (Boston, Mass.) I. Brooks, Frank H., 1961- . II.
Liberty (Boston, Mass.)
HX843.I557   1994
320.5'0973—dc20

            93-30303
            CIP

ISBN 13: 978-1-56000-132-4 (hbk)
ISBN 13: 978-1-138-51613-7 (pbk)

Dedicated to Andrea, Jared, and Hanna

Contents

Part III: Social Controversies

Part IV: Strategies for Advancing Anarchism

Preface

It is by now a commonplace that right and left may converge at the extremes. The typical examples of this ideological convergence, however, refer to the similarities of left- and right-wing versions of authoritarianism. Mussolini's trajectory from revolutionary socialist to fascist leader and the awful parallels between Stalinism and Nazism are prominent cases. More recently, New Left activists have become New Right activists. Less commonly cited are those who travel from Right to Left extremism, or those who somehow straddle the divide at the extremes. Often, these extremists are demanding complete liberty, rather than the institution of total authority. Thus, it is anarchism that has the most potential to bridge the gap between right and left libertarians.

That anarchism, notable among ideologies for its almost complete failure to be implemented, is discussed at all is testimony to its intellectual credentials. Yet its singleminded emphasis on liberty conceals a wide variety of anarchist ideologies. Usually considered to be an extreme left-wing ideology, anarchism has always included a significant strain of radical individualism, from the hyperrationalism of Godwin, to the egoism of Stirner, to the libertarians and anarcho-capitalists of today. Bridging the gap between early nineteenth-century individualist anarchism and its resurgence in the late twentieth century is Benjamin Tucker's classic journal of the late nineteenth century, *Liberty*. Bringing together labor reformers, former state socialists, radicalized free traders, free love advocates, and generally individualists of many stripes, *Liberty* was a forum for ideological convergence. The focus of this convergence, however, were Tucker's two "plumb-line" principles: individual sovereignty and equal liberty. Around these principles a talented group of individualist radicals gathered, to discuss the foundation of individual liberty and to measure the various reform proposals of the day.

A fascinating journal, *Liberty* has still to receive the attention it deserves and I feel lucky indeed to be able to present this anthology of writings from its twenty-seven-year run. Editing such an anthology was initially suggested to me by my dissertation advisor, Isaac Kramnick. He directed my research on Dyer Lum, a revolutionary anarchist comrade of the Haymarket defendants who simultaneously promoted individualist economic reforms in *Liberty* and other radical journals, and thus well knew the significance of *Liberty*. I'm not sure Dr. Kramnick suspected, however, just how enjoyable and stimulating the project would be for me. His proposal built upon the intellectual (and material) support I have gotten over the years from the Institute for Humane Studies. Institute scholars such as Leonard Liggio, Walter Grinder, Jeremy Shearmur, and Ralph Raico not only did not scoff at my suspicion that anarchism could be a meeting point of right and left, but insisted that I pursue my suspicion in research. The Institute led me to a number of scholars interested in individualist anarchism, particularly Charles Hamilton, Wendy McElroy, Carl Watner, and Michael Coughlin. Although not directly connected with this project, others have helped me to understand the place of anarchism in the broader scheme of American political culture, especially Blaine McKinley, Lyman Tower Sargent, Bruce C. Nelson, Nick Salvatore, and Michael Goldfield. While at McNeese State University, a number of people have helped to sustain and expand my intellectual and academic interests, namely Cheryl Ware, Tom Fox, Alan Schwerin, Martha Hoskins, Mary Richardson, Jamie Whelan, Judith Haydel, and, of course, my students.

This project could not have been completed without the generous support of a National Endowment for the Humanities Summer Stipend in 1991. Given the content of this book, it seems ironic or, as Proudhon might have put it, paradoxical that such support was offered (or solicited, for that matter), but I am nevertheless sincerely grateful for it.

I am also grateful for the forbearance of Andrea, who had to put up with my thinking out loud and occasional excited ramblings, and for the joy and patience of Jared and Hanna, who had to accept my absence on numerous evenings and weekends. Without the help of all these people, this book would not have been possible, but of course they are not responsible for the uses to which I put their contributions. As befits a project centering on individual liberty, I alone accept that responsibility.

Introduction: Putting *Liberty* in Context

The American individualist anarchist newspaper, *Liberty, Not the Daughter But the Mother of Order* (1881–1908), edited by Benjamin R. Tucker, was "the longest-lived of any radical periodical of economic or political nature in the nation's history and certainly one of the world's most interesting during the past two centuries." It provided "a forum for native American radicalism . . . which earned the admiration of H.L. Mencken, George Bernard Shaw and Walt Whitman."[1] Besides the writings of its editor, *Liberty* published writers of high quality, including Bernard Shaw and Vilfredo Pareto, as well as a host of lesser-known individualists. The recent resurgence of interest in anarchism has led to renewed appreciation for Tucker and his journal. *Liberty* is now generally acknowledged to have been the most important anarchist periodical to appear in the United States: "It is impossible to overemphasize the influence *Liberty* had over the development of libertarian thought in America"; "arguably the finest libertarian periodical ever published in the English language."[2] Benjamin Tucker's own writings, after appearing in *Liberty*, were reprinted as pamphlets and in book form and have recently surfaced in anthologies of anarchism.[3] Modern libertarians have been particularly interested, so much so that Stephen Newman, an analyst of libertarianism, refers to Tucker and his followers as their "true culture heroes."[4] Libertarians trying to reappropriate the radical thrust of classical liberalism naturally find historical allies in the individualists of late nineteenth-century America. Tucker and the contributors to *Liberty* confronted the early development of the centralized American state and the complicity of mainstream liberalism in this development by discussing and criticizing laissez-faire economics, political reforms, and such theoretical issues as natural rights. Their critiques of reformers' reliance on the state have become newly relevant as the welfare state is increasingly criticized and Soviet-style communism continues to fragment.

Yet to locate *Liberty*'s significance merely in its prophetic criticisms dramatically curtails and ultimately distorts the nature of the ideology it helped to define. *Liberty* was not just a treasure trove of protolibertarianism, but the culmination of fifty years of radical individualism and labor reform. The preeminent analyst of American individualist anar-

1

chism, James J. Martin, refers to Tucker's newspaper as "theoretical anarchism matured."[5] Even recognizing its historical roots, however, is insufficient, for *Liberty* also reflected, and participated in, the dramatic political and intellectual changes occurring around the turn of the century. The same newspaper that popularized the decades-old theories of Josiah Warren, Pierre-Joseph Proudhon, and Max Stirner was also one of the first American journals to print works by and about Bernard Shaw, Friedrich Nietzsche, and Henrik Ibsen. Tucker and his associates wrote perceptively about the Russian nihilists of the 1880s and the French bombthrowers of the 1890s, the development of anarchist communism, reformers such as Henry George and Edward Bellamy, and the temptations of Populist politics. Rooted in a radical past, reacting to (if not notably shaping) a dramatic present, and bearing lessons for the future, *Liberty* must be considered in several temporal contexts.

As the topics indicated above show, *Liberty* also cannot be constrained by its obvious connections to American life or to liberal theory. Although individualist anarchism was nowhere larger in scale than in the United States, the anarchism expressed in *Liberty* owed only a general debt to individualist thinkers in America such as Thoreau or Jefferson and a substantial debt only to one American thinker, Josiah Warren.[6] The major intellectual influences were British, French, and German: the "law of equal freedom" from Herbert Spencer, mutualist economics (especially the mutual bank) from Pierre-Joseph Proudhon, and egoist ethics from Max Stirner. *Liberty*'s connection to liberalism is also more apparent than real, or rather more critical than thankful. Individualist anarchism shared liberalism's concern with individual liberty, but took that to extremes that liberals could not contemplate. For instance, under the influence of Proudhon, the labor theory of property became a critique of state-enforced property rights, while, under the influence of Stirner, contract became the basis for creating "rights," not the mechanism for enforcing preexisting natural rights. The economic and political fixations of classical liberalism were transcended in *Liberty* as it went beyond even J.S. Mill and Mary Wollstonecraft in addressing the problems of women, children, and education in individualist terms.

Thus, if one examines *Liberty* closely, a complex, interesting, and potentially confusing phenomenon emerges: an American newspaper with European sensibilities and concerns, an individualist organ whose primary concern was with the "labor problem," and an anarchist project that aimed not to destroy the state, but rather, in Proudhon's suggestion, to dissolve it within a transformed economy. The standard selections from Benjamin Tucker's work only hint at this complexity, while his own anthology, *Instead of a Book*, represents only the first twelve years of *Liberty*'s publication and, as James Martin points out, is unacceptable as a representative collection because "significant material was omitted from its contents."[7]

The present anthology is designed to convey the breadth of *Liberty*'s concerns, while also indicating its historical roots and contemporary relevance. To this end, it has been organized topically into four parts reflecting the major concerns discussed in *Liberty* and also paralleling disciplinary boundaries in the humanities and social sciences. Of course, the anthology might have been organized so as to directly reflect the roots and relevance, or to present the articles in strict chronological fashion. The former alternative would, however, have involved rather arbitrary editorial decisions, while the latter might have restricted the audience to historians. As it stands, this anthology attempts to summarize a newspaper whose concerns were not only political, but also economic and cultural, not only philosophical, but also practical and strategic. The first part examines the "political theory" of individualist anarchism, particularly its connections to ideologies such as liberalism and socialism, and such classic controversies in political theory as human nature and the maintenance of social order. Part two is given over to the economic reforms advocated by *Liberty*. This involved the abolition of state-created monopolies, notably the money and land monopolies, and the establishment of free competition. By such reforms, workers would receive the full product of their labor, for the individualist anarchists considered exploitation to be the product of state interference, not of capitalism. Part three addresses the social and cultural implications of anarchist principles of equal liberty and contract. Thus, free love was to replace marriage and women were to become economically and socially independent, while literature should be free of censorship and should frankly reflect social reality. Children posed a conundrum, however, and a bitter debate ensued over whether children had rights, or were the property of their mother before becoming independent beings. The fourth part deals with a dilemma facing all radical ideologies: "what is to be done?" The individualist anarchists, relativist, tolerant, and antiauthoritarian, did not have a uniform strategy. Most, however, emphasized agitation and passive resistance over communes, unions, and boycotts, and opposed voting and revolutionary violence in virtually all conceivable situations.

Liberty and American Individualist Anarchism

While *Liberty* was the most interesting and significant of American anarchist newspapers, it was neither the first one nor the only one in existence at the time. The first explicitly anarchist newspaper in the United States, *The Peaceful Revolutionist*, was published fifty years before by Josiah Warren. Even Warren, however, was not the first reformer to demonstrate anarchistic tendencies. Religious dissidents like Anne Hutchinson exhibited such tendencies already in the seventeenth century, and political radicals such as Thomas Paine verged on anarchism in their thoroughgoing liberal critiques of government. Analysts of American anarchism such as Reichert, Schuster, DeLeon, and Rocker[8] have made much of these early roots of the anarchist movement. However, American anarchism, like its European counterpart, is best seen as a nineteenth-century development, an ideology that, like socialism generally, responded to the growth of industrial capitalism, republican government, and nationalism. Although this is clearest in the more collectivistic anarchist theorists and movements of the late nineteenth century (Bakunin, Kropotkin, Malatesta, communist anarchism, anarcho-syndicalism), it also helps to explain anarchists of early- to midcentury such as Proudhon, Stirner and, in America, Warren. For all of these theorists, a primary concern was the "labor problem"—the increasing dependence and immiseration of manual workers in industrializing economies. Thus, as James Martin insists, while it is interesting to point out anarchist tendencies in religious and political radicalism, American anarchism as a movement and an ideology was primarily directed toward economic reform and thus did not come into its own (in Europe or America) until the 1830s, when Warren and Proudhon began developing the theory.[9]

The initial concerns of American anarchism were money and land reform, issues that were addressed by antebellum anarchists such as Warren, William B. Greene, Stephen Pearl Andrews, and Joshua K. Ingalls. Their concerns were part of the broader labor movement and continued to be promoted after the Civil War in the New England Labor

Reform League. In the 1870s, anarchists were also prominent in the "free love" movement, which criticized the institution of marriage (with its legal and social barriers for women) and insisted on the availability of birth control. It was into this milieu that Benjamin Tucker, born in 1854 near New Bedford, Massachusetts, was introduced. Raised in a liberal Unitarian environment and falling under the spell of Victoria Woodhull (a controversial free-love speaker, member of the First International, and spiritualist), Tucker met several of the antebellum anarchists at meetings of the New England Labor Reform League. He began to write for *The Word*, edited by Ezra Heywood (an officer of the NELRL and a free-love activist), and became its associate editor in 1875. By December of 1876, however, Tucker resigned from the *Word*, complaining that it was more interested in love reform than labor reform. He established his own newspaper, the *Radical Review*, which in its short run (1877–78), featured articles by most of the major American anarchists. He quit his own venture in order to take charge of the *Word* when Heywood was jailed for running afoul of the rampaging censor, Anthony Comstock, in August 1878. Between 1879 and 1881, however, Tucker was not directly engaged in anarchist publishing, working instead as a journalist in Boston.

Tucker continued to work at least part-time as a mainstream journalist throughout the period that he published *Liberty*, whose first issue came out on August 6, 1881. From the beginning, *Liberty* was under the firm editorial direction of Tucker, who sought to make it a "plumb-line" journal of individualist anarchism:

> It may be well to state at the outset that this journal will be edited to suit its editor, not its readers. He hopes that what suits him will suit them; but if not, it will make no difference. No subscriber, or body of subscribers, will be allowed to govern his course, dictate his policy, or prescribe his methods. *Liberty* is published for the very definite purpose of spreading certain ideas, and no claim will be admitted on any pretext of freedom of speech, to waste its limited space in hindering the attainment of that object.[10]

Actually, this statement was more bark than bite, for Tucker allowed a wide variety of views to be expressed in *Liberty*, always reserving, and often exercising, his editorial right to criticize, amplify, or clarify any that did not suit him. Tucker's theoretical views were probably mature by the time he began publishing *Liberty*, but there is still a discernible hardening of the "plumb-line" over the years. Partly this was because

Tucker's own attitudes became more fixed, but the radical movement also underwent significant changes. For this reason, *Liberty*'s stable of writers also shifted several times over the years, reflecting the broader shifts in the reform, radical, and anarchist movements.

In the first three or four years, there was considerable ideological fluidity in *Liberty*, as the socialist and labor parties that had been active in the late 1870s gave way to a smaller radical movement overall, but one with a growing anarchist tendency. In 1881, *Liberty* was officially designated as the English-language journal of a nascent anarchist federation.[11] Although not controlled by this federation, Tucker allowed wide, and often sympathetic, coverage of anarchism's various tendencies, notably to the communist anarchism of Kropotkin. *Liberty* was also quite favorable to quasianarchistic movements such as the Russian nihilists and the Irish No-Rent movement.

By the time of the Pittsburgh organizing congress of the International Working-People's Association (the anarchist successor of the First International) in 1883, however, Tucker had become estranged from the organized anarchist movement. *Liberty* began to sharpen its line against the left of the anarchist movement, insisting on the inviolability of private property and criticizing the authoritarianism that it saw as inherent in communism. By the mid-1880s, there were several major anarchistic newspapers in the field, in several languages. On the west coast, Burnette Haskell published *Truth*, a rather confusing amalgam of Marxism and anarchism. In Kansas, Moses Harman published *Lucifer, the Light Bearer*, a free-love paper with significant anarchist leanings. In Chicago, the English-language paper of the IWPA, the *Alarm*, supplemented a German-language paper, the *Chicagoer Arbeiter-Zeitung* and a Bohemian paper, *Budoucnost*. In Detroit, Robert Reitzel was publishing *Der Arme Teufel* and in New York, Johann Most published *Freiheit*. Of course, Ezra Heywood continued to publish the *Word*. In this expanded universe of anarchist journalism, Tucker tried to define individualist anarchism more narrowly in order to distinguish it from its cousins, or in some cases, its pretenders. This process was hastened by the uproar surrounding the Haymarket incident in 1886. Although the fatal bombing of a police contingent about to break up an anarchist meeting in Chicago brought unprecedented interest in anarchism, the public tended to identify anarchism with violent, foreign, communistic bombthrowers. Tucker and his writers tried to differentiate individualist anarchism theoretically, economically, and strategically from the "Chicago anarchism" represented by the defendants in the Haymarket case.

By 1888 or so, a third stage in the "plumb-line" had been reached, where the theoretical uniqueness and consistency of individualist anarchism had been established, but still had to be defended against narrower, and more theoretical, objections. Typically, these objections were raised by reformers, such as Hugh Pentecost, editor of *Twentieth Century*, who claimed to be anarchists, or by individualists, such as Wordsworth Donisthorpe or Auberon Herbert, who were almost anarchists. Other objections came from those who were not convinced by details of *Liberty*'s economic reforms, such as Hugo Bilgram's criticisms of the theory of money it espoused. Still others objected to the implications of the egoist theory of ethics which had effectively become doctrine in *Liberty* in the mid-1880s. In short, *Liberty* after 1888, with the exception of reactions to incidents such as Alexander Berkman's attempted assassination of Henry Frick or to newly emerging movements such as Populism or Bellamy's Nationalism, became primarily a theoretical journal for clarifying the fine points of individualist anarchism. The only major exception to this trend was Tucker's growing interest in European avant-garde literature and drama, which were increasingly discussed in *Liberty* and sold by Tucker in his capacity as a publisher and bookseller.

These shifts in *Liberty*'s emphases must be borne in mind when considering the arguments in any particular selection from *Liberty*. For example, articles on the strategy of "propaganda by deed" differed significantly, from sympathetic accounts of Russian nihilists in the early 1880s to more critical assessments of *attentats* in the 1890s and beyond.

One must also consider differences in emphasis due to the authors writing in *Liberty*. On theoretical, strategic, and rhetorical matters, Tucker's writers often deviated widely from the editor. The best example of this would be the changing relationship between Tucker and his protégé, Victor Yarros. Having emigrated from the Ukraine in the early 1880s, Yarros settled in New England and was initially attracted to the collectivist anarchists beginning to organize at that time. However, under Tucker's influence, he became one of the most prominent of the individualist anarchists writing for *Liberty*. In the mid-1880s, he was an advocate of both egoistic ethics and Spencerian sociology, but by the late 1880s, he had diverged from Tucker on the former and became the primary interpreter (and critic) of Spencer for the individualist anarchists.

By the early 1890s, after he had moved to Chicago, he also began to differ from Tucker on strategic matters, taking a more opportunistic stance toward election-related agitation in particular. Eventually, Tucker and Yarros drifted apart completely, so much so that Yarros disavowed anarchism altogether.[12]

Other writers were not so dramatic in their shifts, but contributed greatly to the variety and interest of *Liberty*.[13] In the first stage of its publication, *Liberty* published many writers with backgrounds in the antebellum anarchist movement as well as many labor-oriented journalists. The former category includes Lysander Spooner, the venerable and radical lawyer best known for his demolition of the Constitution and of slavery from the vantage point of natural law and consent, and Joshua King Ingalls, the longtime land reformer. The latter included Joseph Labadie, a Detroit unionist who advocated broad cooperation between labor and radical activists and who wrote a column entitled "Cranky Notions." Henry Appleton, writing as "X," was a Providence, Rhode Island journalist and a forceful critic of collectivism, who eventually broke with *Liberty* because it did not offer enough of a positive program of reform. E.C. Walker, of Valley Falls, Kansas, promoted the issues of free love and birth control, both in *Liberty* and in his own newspaper, *Lucifer, the Light Bearer*. Another Walker, James. L (writing as "Tak Kak" to conceal his identity as the editor of the *Galveston News*), was the most forceful advocate of egoism in *Liberty*, although its readers were first introduced to Stirner by George Schumm, a German immigrant and close friend of Tucker's in Boston. In the later years, Tucker published frequent contributions from John Beverley Robinson, an anarchist with pacifist leanings, and Steven Byington, one of the few professing Christians in the movement, and a tireless activist who initiated the "Anarchist Letter-Writing Corps" and translated Stirner's *The Ego and Its Own*. This brief survey of *Liberty*'s writers suggests the breadth of concerns and the nature of the activists drawn to individualist anarchism. It also shows that individualist anarchism was not confined to New England, as the epithet "Boston anarchists" (first applied by the collectivist Burnette Haskell) suggests.

However, the other label given to these individualist radicals, "philosophical anarchism," may fit somewhat better. This term came into currency around the time of Haymarket and was a favorite insult of the collectivist anarchists, who meant to characterize *Liberty*'s adherents as do-nothing, armchair anarchists, whose class origins belied their alleged sympathies with the working class. The ambivalence of Tucker to unions (and the outright hostility of some of his writers), as well as the individualists' allegiance to many of the tenets of antebellum labor reform and, more generally, to a (truly) free-market economy, led many workers and collectivist anarchists to suspect them as petit-bourgeois. Another nail in this coffin was their professed admiration for Proudhon and Stirner, two victims of Karl Marx's withering criticism.

Was individualist anarchism a "petit-bourgeois" ideology? Although a loaded question, it is worth considering in order to gain further insight into *Liberty*'s character. Certainly many of the writers for the paper were neither wage workers nor capitalists, but rather small proprietors and skilled artisans. However, this is not notably different from the case of many labor papers of the day, for those who have some economic security as well as leisure for reading and thinking are the ones most likely to become active, particularly in reform or radical journalism. A better way of getting at this provocative question is to consider the readership of *Liberty*. Tucker's paper probably never had more than about one thousand subscribers, although its influence was widely felt.[14] Tucker did not leave any subscription lists and the characteristics of its readers can only be inferred from several pieces of evidence.[15] The only substantial glimpse into *Liberty*'s readership comes in an article Tucker wrote around the time of President McKinley's assassination, "Are Anarchists Thugs?"[16] The ludicrous theories of Cesare Lombroso (that anarchists and criminals were easily identified by their physiognomy) were current and Tucker took pains to indicate that his readership was quite respectable. He claimed that America's anarchists included "scores" of lawyers and physicians, "at least three professional librarians," "numerous teachers," "one or two college professors," "a large number of journalists," "perhaps a dozen inventors," as well as engineers, architects, bankers, brokers, manufacturers, merchants, government clerks, artists, "farmers by the score," "workmen in every craft," and "one or two millionaires." Discounting Tucker's intent, it remains clear that *Liberty*'s appeal, in class terms, was broad (excluding perhaps only the least skilled of wage workers). Whether the majority of its readers were professionals, artisans, or "petit-bourgeois" is impossible to tell, but the prominence of these categories in Tucker's list suggests that the appeal of *Liberty* among the "proletariat" was probably quite limited.

Whatever its class, sectional, historical, or ideological characteristics, one thing remains: *Liberty* provides one of the richest sources for interesting, sophisticated, provocative, and, yes, occasionally hair-splitting and arcane, writing on issues that continue to be vital today. Although much has changed in society, politics, and the economy since the turn of the century, the theoretical rigor and penetrating insights of *Liberty* make it relevant not merely to historians of intellectual trends and reform. It is also helpful to those grappling with the legacy, rather than the threat, of communism. For those trying to understand the temptations of democratic politics and its tendency to intervene in all realms of life, *Liberty* is significant. For those seeking a principled defense of individual liberty against its many enemies, *Liberty* is essential. The three short lines of John Hay's poetry that began every issue of *Liberty* sum up its mission:

> For always in thine eyes, O Liberty!
> Shines that high light whereby the world is saved;
> And though thou slay us, we will trust in thee.

Notes

1. James J. Martin, *Men Against the State: The Expositors of Individualist Anarchism in America, 1827–1908*, Colorado Springs: Ralph Myles, 1970 (DeKalb, Illinois, 1953), p. 208; George Woodcock, *Anarchism: A History of Libertarian Ideas and Movements*, Harmondsworth: Penguin, 1962, p. 434.
2. William O. Reichert, *Partisans of Freedom. A Study in American Anarchism*, Bowling Green: Bowling Green University Popular Press, 1976, p. 145; Wendy McElroy, "Benjamin Tucker, Individualism, and *Liberty: Not the Daughter but the Mother of Order*," *Literature of Liberty*, IV:3 (1981), p. 7.
3. Benjamin R. Tucker, *Individual Liberty*, C.L. Swartz, ed., New York: Vanguard Press, 1972 (1926); Benjamin R. Tucker, *Instead of a Book; By a Man Too Busy to Write One*, 2nd ed., New York: Benjamin R. Tucker, 1897 (reprinted New York: Arno Press, 1972); Benjamin R. Tucker, *State Socialism and Anarchism and Other Essays*, Colorado Springs: Ralph Myles, 1970; Benjamin Tucker, selections from "State Socialism and Anarchism" and "The Relation of the State to the Individual," in Leonard I. Krimerman and Lewis Perry, eds., *Patterns of Anarchy*, New York: Anchor Books, 1967, pp. 61–69, 251–259; Benjamin R. Tucker, "State Socialism and Libertarianism [Anarchism]," in Irving L. Horowitz, ed., *The Anarchists*, New York: Dell, 1964, pp. 169–182.
4. Stephen L. Newman, *Liberalism at Wits' End: The Libertarian Revolt Against the Modern State*, Ithaca: Cornell University Press, 1984, p. 24. See also the writings of economists such as Murray Rothbard and Gordon Tullock as well as, more specifically, Carl Watner, "Benjamin Tucker and His Periodical *Liberty*," *Journal of Libertarian Studies*, I:4 (1977), pp. 307–318; Carl Watner, "Benjamin Tucker's *Liberty*," *Reason*, 10:12 (1979), pp. 36–38; Richard P. Hiskes, "Community in the Anarcho-Individualist Society: The Legacy of Benjamin Tucker," *Social Anar-*

chism, October 1980, pp. 41–52; and Michael E. Coughlin, Charles H. Hamilton, and Mark A. Sullivan, eds., *Benjamin R. Tucker and The Champions of Liberty: A Centenary Anthology*, St. Paul: Michael E. Coughlin, n.d. [1986]. Several dissertations have also appeared on Benjamin Tucker: Irving Levitas, "The Unterrified Jeffersonian, Benjamin R. Tucker: A Study of Native American Anarchism as Exemplified in His Life and Times," Ph.D.: New York University, 1974; David Ebner, "The Ideology of the Individualist Anarchist in America," Ph.D.: New York University, 1968; Dale Allen Johnston, "An American Anarchist: An Analysis of the Individualist Anarchism of Benjamin R. Tucker," Ph.D.: University of New Mexico, 1974.

5. Martin, *Men Against the State*, chapter 8.
6. A number of writers have insisted that anarchism is peculiarly suited to America, for example Voltairine de Cleyre, "Anarchism and American Traditions," in Alexander Berkman, ed., *Selected Works of Voltairine de Cleyre*, New York: Mother Earth Publishing Co., 1914; Rudolf Rocker, *Pioneers of American Freedom: Origin of Liberal and Radical Thought in America*, Arthur Briggs, trans., Los Angeles: Rocker Publications Committee, 1949; Eric Foner, "Radical Individualism in America: Revolution to Civil War," *Literature of Liberty*, I:3 (1978), pp. 5–31; David DeLeon, *The American as Anarchist: Reflections on Indigenous Radicalism*, Baltimore: Johns Hopkins University Press, 1978; Eunice Minette Schuster, *Native American Anarchism*, New York: Da Capo Press, 1970 (originally published in *Smith College Studies in History*, 17 (1931–32).
7. Martin, *Men Against the State*, p. 271.
8. Reichert, *Partisans of Freedom*; Schuster, *Native American Anarchism*; DeLeon, *The American as Anarchist*; Rocker, *Pioneers of American Freedom*. For a more specific case, see Lewis Perry, *Radical Abolitionism: Anarchy and the Government of God in Antislavery Thought*, Ithaca: Cornell University Press, 1973.
9. Martin, *Men against the State*, introduction.
10. *Liberty*, August 6, 1881, p. 1.
11. Paul Avrich, *The Haymarket Tragedy*, Princeton: Princeton University Press, 1984, p. 60.
12. Martin, *Men against the State*, pp. 234–241; Yarros, "Philosophical Anarchism: Its Rise, Decline and Eclipse," *American Journal of Sociology*, XLI (January 1936), pp. 470–483.
13. Martin, *Men against the State*, pp. 241–261.
14. Charles H. Hamilton, "The Evolution of a Subversive Tradition," in Coughlin et al., eds. *Benjamin R. Tucker and the Champions of Liberty*, p. 10.
15. The earliest list is a subscription for aid to Russian Nihilist prisoners and exiles, begun on March 18, 1882. This of course would give a rather-too-broad picture of *Liberty*'s readership. Another list are those who subscribed for Tucker's compilation, *Instead of a Book*, in 1893. Unfortunately, this lists only names, cities, and number of books subscribed for. Byington's descriptions of the Letter-Writing Corps between 1894 and 1897 offer some fleeting glimpses, but only of course of the activists among the readers (and the most literate of them at that).
16. January 1899 (XIII:9, #359), pp. 3–4.

PART ONE

The Political Theory of Individualist Anarchism

1

General Theories of Individualist Anarchism

Liberty's editorial stance was based on two principles that constituted a "plumb-line" by which individualist anarchism would be measured, and by which all other reform schemes would be criticized. These two basic principles were individual sovereignty and equal liberty. The basis of anarchist society was to be the sovereign individual who would recognize that her own liberty could not be absolute, but had to be limited by an equal amount of liberty for other individuals. Only by making liberty equal for all could all individuals enjoy liberty and none be enslaved.

On these two building blocks, the theory of individualist anarchism was developed over the course of *Liberty*'s run. From them flowed definitions of government ("invasion," or the use of force against the non-invasive), visions of anarchist society (voluntary contracts between free individuals for all social needs, including defense against aggressors), and proposals for radical economic reforms that would attack state-maintained monopolies. They also served as the touchstone for individualist anarchists' responses to events and reform proposals that arose between 1881 and 1908. Strikes, assassinations, and elections, liberals, socialists, and communists were all measured by the "plumb-line" of these two principles and most were found to be crooked in one way or another. Although the plumb-line was employed primarily as a critical weapon by Tucker, it nevertheless had substantive and positive aspects, which also emerged in a variety of articles. Before considering the theoretical relationship of individualist anarchism to liberalism and socialism (chapters two and three), or the implications of this theory for economic reform (part two), social reform (part three), and strategy (part four), it is essential to get some general sense of individualist anarchism as a political theory.

The first two selections in this chapter, from 1882 and 1885, fit into a period when *Liberty*'s theoretical articles evinced a broad view of anarchism, the first portraying anarchism as the logical conclusion of consent theories, and the second embracing elements of more collectivistic anarchism. However, the third selection, Tucker's classic "The Relation of the State to the Individual," draws the lines firmly, distinguishing individualist anarchism from other forms of anarchism and radicalism. The last two selections address some of the analytical fine points of individualist anarchism. The last selection in particular considers issues that continue to concern modern libertarians, minimal statists, and anarcho-capitalists.

Further Reading in Liberty

Two extended essays in the early years of *Liberty* showcased writers with a "tendency" toward individualist anarchism: A) Auberon Herbert, "A Politician in Sight of Haven," July 26, 1884 (II:21, #47), pp. 7–8 (continues #48–50). B) Edmund Burke, "A Vindication of Natural Society," October 25, 1884 (III:1, #53), p. 7 (continues #54–59). Both of these are available elsewhere, for example from Liberty Classics in Indianapolis.

A biographical article by A.L. Ballou called "A Retrospect" (April 19, 1890, VII:1, #157, p. 3) is interesting for its description of his odyssey through various reform camps on the road to anarchism. In his far from atypical case, these included Universalism, freethought, free love, Greenbackism, and communism. Tucker's view of anarchism is further clarified in an exchange with Henry Appleton: "L'Etat, c'est l'Ennemi," February 26, 1887 (IV:16, #94), pp. 4–5, 8.

Finally, several series tried to present an overview of individualist anarchism for general propaganda purposes. From shortest to longest, these are: A) Stephen Byington, "What Anarchism Means," October 1897 (XIII:6, #356), p. 5. B) Victor Yarros, "An Anarchistic View of the Social Problem," June 7, 1890 (VII:3, #159), pp. 4–7. C) Thomas P. Perkins, "Political Duty: A Confession of Skepticism," July 2, 1892 (VIII:46, #228), pp. 2–3 (continues #229–231). D) William Bailie,

"Problems of Anarchism," January 7, 1893 (IX:19, #253), p. 1 (continues #254–267, 271, 272, 276, 279).

A. "Anarchism and Consent"—Benjamin Tucker[*]

One of the common rhetorical strategies of radicals has been to link their ideas to central documents of American politics, the Declaration of Independence being a particular favorite. In 1883, the International Working-People's Association, an anarchist federation, quoted the Declaration in its Pittsburgh Manifesto to justify revolution. Here, a year earlier, the Declaration's invocation of consent is turned against the American government and indeed against government in general.

The author of this unsigned editorial is unkown, although in the absence of compelling textual evidence, it must be assigned to Tucker. However, it bears the unmistakable impact of Lysander Spooner, an anarchist lawyer whose critique of the Constitution revolved around the concept of consent.[1]

The Declaration of Independence is probably the most "communistic" document that ever obtained celebrity among good "law-and-order" people on both continents. It contains numerous internal evidences to show that, were Thomas Jefferson living to-day, he would be a pronounced Anarchist. It is no wonder that Sir Henry Maine quotes its reputation among aristocratic circles of its day as a chimera of generalities imbibed by Jefferson through familiar contact with French atheists.

The above-named document declares that "governments derive their just powers from the consent of the governed." It therefore follows that, when any individual is governed by a government without his or her consent, that government is exercising unjust powers, and is a usurpation. And yet, in the government subsequently instituted under the Constitution one-half of the people (the women) were denied representation at the onset, while, under the ban of slavery and other constitutional bars, the number permitted to express consent or dissent was in the aggregate cut down to less than one-tenth of the whole people. To what a ridiculous farce do Jefferson's glittering generalities reduce themselves at the first touch of common sense!

---

[*] December 9, 1882 (II:5, #31), p. 2.

It was never seriously contemplated by the founders of this government that it should be a government of consent. The framers of the Constitution could not have even meant that the will of a majority should stand as consent, for they disfranchised a majority of the people to start with. Allowing that the majority principle stood with them for consent, they must have had plainly in view a *majority of the minority*, which involves a stroke of *reductio ad absurdum* for the vaunted majority-rule idea, not very comforting to Fourth of July patriots.

Force is the essence of all positive governmental institutions. Under any conceivable interpretation of Jefferson's talk about the consent of the governed, every existing government is outlawed beyond recovery, and the "just powers" vanish into thin air.

The only pretext on which the defender of political government can make existing usurpations float upon consent is to assert that going to the polls and voting, bearing arms, paying taxes, serving on juries, etc., are presumptive evidences that those who do so consent to the institutions under which they live.[2] As well might it be argued that, in accepting the offer of a highwayman to toss one's last penny to see whether the robber should take it or leave it, the victim thereby consents to the highwayman's occupation. As the only alternative against extortion, a man may go to the polls and vote against the proposed levy of a corrupt ring of political jobbers, recognizing the ballot-box only on grounds of expediency, as a sinking man might hug a filthy pile in the dock. An Anarchist may pay taxes to escape going to jail, or sit in a jury-box to save a friend, in accordance with his rating of the costs of given offences against his principles.[3]

But behind all these accidents of fate, the Anarchist puts this bottom question to government and its defenders: *By what right am I thrust into the alternative of recognizing the machinery of the State as the only chance left me of rescuing my life, liberty, and possessions from invasion?* To argue the right of consent in response to this question is utterly ridiculous. To argue the right of might is to use the argument of a professional robber. How will the defender of the State answer it, then?

The State is a pure usurpation. The individual is coerced for his own good,—somebody outside of himself being set up an authoritative judge of what is for his own good. He is thus put in the same moral dock as were the victims of the Inquisition. This scheme will continue to work finely for the oppressor until the political victim turns around and applies the same argument to the inquisitor. The Anarchist, however, proposes to coerce the agents of the State no further for their own good than to see to it that they step down and out, go home and mind their own business, and leave Liberty, consent, and natural selection to crystallize society into an organization that shall conform to natural law. If the inquisitors refuse to go home peaceably, and among the accidents of the war for Liberty some of them consequently get hurt "for their own good," they, as Christians, can do no more than enter it upon the profit-and-loss account of an All-Wise Providence.

B.   "The Beliefs of Anarchists"—"An English Anarchist"[*]

This selection, with its critique of law and its discussions of prisons and education, gives some sense of the breadth of anarchist concerns. It also indicates the cross-fertilization of European and American anarchism that always characterized Liberty, *and of collectivist and individualist anarchism that was beginning to wane by the mid-1880s. Citing Bakunin, Whitman, and Spencer, it culminates in the argument that anarchism is a hybrid of individualism and socialism, a position similar to Tucker's definition of anarchism as libertarian socialism.*

It passes as a truism that public opinion—the expression of the collective moral sense—is the real sovereign of today. Its sanction has replaced the old religious sanctions as a moral restraint. Law is supposed but to give voice to its mandates, and deliberative assemblies to be its humble servants. It is admitted that the voice is muffled and unintelligible, and that the servants are treacherous and remarkably ineffective; but it is supposed that Democracy can change all that by judicious lopping and enlargement. In that supposition we Anarchists do not agree. We believe,—not only what all thinkers already admit, that a large proportion of the misery of mankind is attributable to bad Government,—but that Government is in itself essentially bad, a clumsy makeshift for the rule of each man by his own reason and conscience, which, in the present stage of civilization, has served its turn.

The idea of government sprang in barbarous times from the authority of the leader in war, and the patriarchal rule of the head of the family; it grew up in the superstition born of the fears of an ignorant age; and on

---

[*] October 3, 1885 (III:15, #67), p. 7. Originally appeared in London Justice.

the brute instincts and childishness, the ignorance and fears of mankind it has prospered ever since, until progress began slowly and surely to cut away the ground under its feet.

Whilst government was viewed as a divinely appointed arbiter in the affairs of the uninspired commonalty, it was naturally deemed its duty to watch over its subjects in all their relations, and provide, not only for their protection from all force or fraud but its own, but for their eternal welfare. But now that government and law are looked on as mere conveniences, forms destitute of sanctity, and possessing no authority but such as the aggregate of the nation are pleased to allow, it may be worth considering if the collective life of the community cannot find expression in some fashion less costly in time, wealth, and human freedom . . .

We believe opinion to be the real and inevitable expression of collective existence in civilized communities, and that its natural outlets in the public press, in literature and art, in societies, meetings, voluntary combinations of all sorts, and social intercourse are amply sufficient to enable it to act as a binding and corrective force in a society relieved from privileges and private property. Even now it is the strongest deterrent from crime; even now its punishment is the bitterest, its reward the highest, and its rule of conduct the most absolute for the average mortal. Yet, unfortunately, its sense of right and wrong is continually blunted and falsified by the action of the authorized exponent of justice. At the present day law is supposed in the abstract to represent the moral sense of the community as against its immoral members. Practically it cannot do so. Public morality is continually fluctuating, and, by changing as fast as its want of dignity will admit, law cannot keep up with it, and only succeeds in stereotyping the mistakes from which opinion is just shaking itself free, and fitting old precedents upon new conditions, where naturally they look absurd and do mischief. Being framed to suit a variety of cases, no two of which are alike, it is actually unjust in every one, and, moreover, becomes so complicated that, after all the efforts of a specially trained class to expound it, its awards are uncertain and mysterious to all concerned. The modes of punishment are necessarily brutal and degrading, not only to those who suffer, but to those who inflict them, and its attempts to enforce contracts and settle disputes cause at least as much suffering as they avert. Law stands, and—from what experts say of the difficulties of reform—must ever stand, hopelessly in the way of morality, rendering a higher conception of it impossible to the mass of mankind, and consequently to the public opinion which represents them.[4]

When the collective moral sense is relieved of the incubus of law, it may still be unjust in many instances, but its injustice will take a less permanent form and one more capable of rectification, whereas its sense of justice may be perpetually widened and increased by the growth of knowledge and human sympathy. Certainly, judging from its present influence, it will be strong enough to serve as a restraint upon those individuals who refuse to respect the rights of others. But when Society has ceased deliberately to condemn certain of its members to infamy and despair from their birth, there are both physical and moral grounds for the belief that the "criminal classes" will cease to exist. Crime will become sufficiently rare to give the mass of the population courage to face the fact that moral depravity, like madness, is a terrible affliction, a disease to be carefully treated and remedied, not punished and augmented by ill-treatment. We know this now, but we are too cowardly or too Pharisaical to admit it.

Prevention, however, is better than cure, and the surest mode of securing virtuous citizens, as well as healthy public opinion, is by a sound system of education. The rough discipline of the Revolution will clear the air of many prejudices, and serve to raise men's minds to a higher conception of justice and of duty, but it is on the training of children that the future of society mainly depends. I wish I could quote the fine passages in which Michael Bakounine outlines the Anarchist theory of education in his "Dieu et l'Etat," but that would be trespassing too far upon your space. Suffice it to say, that Anarchism considers that the one end and aim of education is to fit children for freedom. Therefore it teaches, firstly, that intellectual training should be scientific, cultivating the reason and leading it to understand and recognize the immutability of the laws of nature, and to conform to them in all things, taking knowledge of them for rule and guide in place of the arbitrary enactments of men; and, secondly, that moral training, starting with the necessary absolute authority, should proceed by the gradual removal of restraints, and by the inculcation of personal dignity and responsibility, respect for others, and the worship of truth and justice for their own sake, to form free men and women filled with reverence and love for the freedom of their fellows. This view of the subject is familiar also to readers of Mr. Herbert Spencer.

The creed of Anarchism is the cultus of Liberty, not for itself, but for what it renders possible. Authority, as exercised by men over their fellows, it holds accursed, depraving those who rule and those who submit, and blocking the path of human progress. Liberty indeed is not all, but it is the foundation of all that is good and noble; it is essential to the many-sided advance of man's nature, expanding in numberless and ever-conflicting directions, which Walt Whitman likens to the weather, "an infinite number of currents and forces, and contributions and temperatures, and cross purposes, whose ceaseless play of counterpart upon counterpart brings constant restoration and vitality." For is not the tendency of all rules and organizations to stiffen into set shapes, destitute of life and meaning, one of the chief causes of social deterioration?

Viewed in relation to the thought waves of our times, the strength of Anarchism seems to us to lie in its full recognition and acceptance of two lines of thought, which, though their respective champions delight to pose them as in hopeless conflict, are uniting to bring about the social revolution, i.e. Individualism and Socialism. It ignores neither the splendid triumphs of Individualism in thought and action, nor the need for brotherly association which Mazzini considered years ago as the primary necessity of modern Europe; but it holds that the longing for freedom, and the growing sense of the dependence of each on all, the responsibility of all for each, are advancing side by side, and that one cannot be sacrificed to the other without provoking a violent reaction. Therefore do Anarchists oppose all measures which tend to increase the power and influence of governments, even if their immediate result seem [sic] to be an improvement in the condition of the people.

C.   "The Relation of the State to the Individual"[*]
—Benjamin Tucker

Given initially as a public address, this is one of the best short sketches of individualist anarchism and hence has been frequently anthologized.[5] It touches upon major themes of Liberty *(and of this anthology), such as science, progress, economic reform, strategic issues, and egoism. It*

* November 15, 1890 (VII:15, #171), pp. 5–7. Tucker's note: An address delivered before the Unitarian Ministers' Institute at the last annual session in Salem, Mass., October 14, 1890, at which addresses on the same subject were also delivered by Rev. W.D.P. Bliss, from the standpoint of Christian Socialism, and President E. Benjamin Andrews, of Brown University, from the standpoint of State regulation.

indicates the central importance of thinkers like Spencer, Proudhon, and Spooner. Finally, Tucker's style as a writer and editor is shown by his insistence on precise terminology in order to clearly define the issues; as one of his critics put it, Tucker's mind was "essentially formal, legal, political."[6]

Presumably the honor which you have done me in inviting me to address you today upon "The Relation of the State to the Individual" is due principally to the fact that circumstances have combined to make me somewhat conspicuous as an exponent of the theory of Modern Anarchism,—a theory which is coming to be more and more regarded as one of the few that are tenable as a basis of political and social life. In its name, then, I shall speak to you in discussing this question which either underlies or closely touches almost every practical problem that confronts this generation. The future of the tariff, of taxation, of finance, of property, of women, of marriage, of the family, of the suffrage, of education, of invention, of literature, of science, of the arts, of personal habits, of private character, of ethics, of religion, will be determined by the conclusion at which mankind shall arrive as to whether and how far the individual owes allegiance to the State.

Anarchism, in dealing with this subject, has found it necessary, first of all, to define its terms. . . . Take the term "State," for instance, with which we are especially concerned today. It is a word that is on every lip. But how many of those who use it have any idea of what they mean by it? And, of the few who have, how various are their conceptions! We designate by the term "State" institutions that embody absolutism in its extreme form and institutions that temper it with more or less liberality. We apply the word alike to institutions that, besides aggressing, to some extent protect and defend. But which is the State's essential function, aggression or defence, few seem to know or care. Some champions of the State evidently consider aggression its principle, although they disguise it alike from themselves and from the people under the term "administration," which they wish to extend in every possible direction. Others, on the contrary, consider defence its principle, and wish to limit it accordingly to the performance of police duties. Still others seem to think that it exists for both aggression and defence, combined in varying proportions according to the momentary interests, or maybe only whims, of those happening to control it. . . . Seeking, then, the elements common to all the institutions to which the name "State" has been applied, [the

Anarchists] have found them two in number: first, aggression; second, the assumption of sole authority over a given area and all within it, exercised generally for the double purpose of more complete oppression of its subjects and extension of its boundaries. That this second element is common to all States, I think, will not be denied,—at least, I am not aware that any State has ever tolerated a rival State within its borders; and it seems plain that any State which should do so would thereby cease to be a State and to be considered as such by any. The exercise of authority over the same area by two States is a contradiction. That the first element, aggression, has been and is common to all States will probably be less generally admitted. . . . Now, what is aggression? Aggression is simply another name for government. Aggression, invasion, government are interconvertible terms. The essence of government is control, or the attempt to control. He who attempts to control another is a governor, an aggressor, an invader; and the nature of such invasion is not changed, whether it is made by one man upon another man, after the manner of the ordinary criminal, or by one man upon all other men, after the manner of an absolute monarch, or by all other men upon one man, after the manner of a modern democracy. On the other hand, he who resists another's attempt to control is not an aggressor, an invader, a governor, but simply a defender, a protector; and the nature of such resistance is not changed whether it be offered by one man to another man, as when one repels a criminal's onslaught, or by one man to all other men, as when one declines to obey an oppressive law, or by all other men to one man, as when a subject people rises against a despot, or as when the members of a community voluntarily unite to restrain a criminal. This distinction between invasion and resistance, between government and defence, is vital. Without it there can be no valid philosophy of politics. Upon this distinction and the other consideration just outlined, the Anarchists frame the desired definitions. This, then, is the Anarchistic definition of government: the subjection of the non-invasive individual to an external will. And this is the Anarchistic definition of the State: the embodiment of the principle of invasion in an individual, or a band of individuals, assuming to act as representatives or as masters of the entire people within a given area. As to the meaning of the remaining term in the subject under discussion, the word "individual," I think there is little difficulty. Putting aside the subtleties in which certain metaphysicians have indulged, one may use this word without danger of being misunderstood . . .

Now comes the question proper: What relations should exist between the State and the individual? The general method of determining these is to apply some theory of ethics involving a basis of moral obligation. In this method the Anarchists have no confidence. The idea of moral obligation, of inherent rights and duties, they totally discard. They look upon all obligations, not as moral, but as social, and even then not really as obligations except as these have been consciously and voluntarily assumed. If a man makes an agreement with men, the latter may combine to hold him to his agreement; but, in the absence of such agreement, no man, so far as the Anarchists are aware, has made any agreement with God or with any other power of any order whatsoever. The Anarchists are not only utilitarians, but egoists in the farthest and fullest sense. So far as inherent right is concerned, might is its only measure. Any man, be his name Bill Sykes[7] or Alexander Romanoff, and any set of men, whether the Chinese highbinders or the Congress of the United States, have the right, if they have the power, to kill or coerce other men and to make the entire world subservient to their ends. Society's right to enslave the individual and the individual's right to enslave society are only unequal because their powers are unequal. . . [8]

If this, then, were a question of right, it would be, according to the Anarchists, purely a question of strength. But, fortunately, it is not a question of right: it is a question of expediency, of knowledge, of science,—the science of living together, the science of society. The history of humanity has been largely one long and gradual discovery of the fact that the individual is the gainer by society exactly in proportion as society is free, and of the law that the condition of a permanent and harmonious society is the greatest amount of individual liberty compatible with equality of liberty. The average man of each new generation has said to himself more clearly and consciously than his predecessor: "My neighbor is not my enemy, but my friend, and I am his, if we would but mutually recognize the fact. We help each other to a better, fuller, happier living; and this service might be greatly increased if we would cease to restrict, hamper and oppress each other. Why can we not agree to let each live his own life, neither of us transgressing the limit that separates our individualities?" It is by this reasoning that mankind is approaching the real social contract, which is not, as Rousseau thought, the origin of society, but rather the outcome of a long social experience, the fruit of its follies and disasters. It is obvious that this contract, this social law, developed to its perfection, excludes all aggression, all violation of equality of liberty, all invasion of every kind. Considering this contract in connection with the Anarchistic definition of the State as the embodiment of the principle of invasion, we see that the State is antagonistic to society; and, society being essential to individual life and development, the conclusion leaps to the eyes that the relation of the State to the individual and of the individual to the State must be one of hostility, enduring till the State shall perish.

"But," it will asked of the Anarchists at this point in the argument, "what shall be done with those individuals who undoubtedly will persist in violating the social law by invading their neighbors?" The Anarchists answer that the abolition of the State will leave in existence a defensive association, resting no longer on a compulsory but on a voluntary basis, which will restrain invaders by any means that may prove necessary. "But that is what we have now," is the rejoinder. "You really want, then, only a change of name?" Not so fast, please. Can it be soberly pretended for a moment that the State, even as it exists here in America, is purely a defensive institution? Surely not, save by those who see of the State only its most palpable manifestations,—the policeman on the street-corner. And one would not have to watch him very closely to see the error of this claim. Why, the very first act of the State, the compulsory assessment and collection of taxes, is itself an aggression, a violation of equal liberty, and, as such, vitiates every subsequent act, even those acts which would be purely defensive if paid for out of a treasury filled by voluntary contributions. How is it possible to sanction, under the law of equal liberty, the confiscation of a man's earnings to pay for protection which he has not sought and does not desire? And, if this is an outrage, what name shall we give to such confiscation when the victim is given, instead of bread, a stone, instead of protection, oppression? To force a man to pay for the violation of his own liberty is indeed an addition of insult to injury. But that is exactly what the State is doing. Read the "Congressional Record"; follow the proceedings of the State legislatures; examine our statute-books; test each act separately by the law of equal liberty,— you will find that a good nine-tenths of existing legislation serves, not to enforce that fundamental social law, but either to prescribe the individual's personal habits, or worse still, to create and sustain commercial, industrial, financial, and proprietary monopolies which deprive labor of a large part of the reward that it would receive in a perfectly free market. "To be governed," says Proudhon, "is to be watched, inspected, spied, directed, law-ridden, regulated, penned up, indoctrinated, preached at, checked, appraised, sized, censured, commanded, by beings who have neither title nor knowledge nor virtue. To be governed is to have every operation, every transaction, every movement noted, registered, counted, rated, stamped, measured, numbered, assessed, licensed, refused, authorized, indorsed, admonished, prevented, reformed, redressed, corrected. . . ." And I am sure I do not need to point out to you the existing laws that correspond to and justify nearly every count in Proudhon's long indictment. How thoughtless, then, to assert that the existing political order is of a purely defensive character instead of the aggressive State which the Anarchists aim to abolish!

This leads to another consideration that bears powerfully upon the problem of the invasive individual, who is such a bugbear to the opponents of Anarchism. Is it not such treatment as has just been described that is largely responsible for his existence? I have heard or read somewhere of an inscription written for a certain charitable institution:

> "This hospital a pious person built,
> But first he made the poor wherewith to fill't"

And so, it seems to me, it is with our prisons. They are filled with criminals which our virtuous State has made what they are by its iniquitous laws, its grinding monopolies, and the horrible social conditions that result from them. We enact many laws that manufacture criminals, and then a few that punish them. Is it too much to expect that the new social conditions which must follow the abolition of all interference with the production and distribution of wealth will in the end so change the habits and propensities of men that our jails and prisons, our policemen and our soldiers,—in a word, our whole machinery and outfit of defence,—will be superfluous? That, at least, is the Anarchists' belief. It sounds Utopian, but it really rests on severely economic grounds.

D.　"A Business Government"—John Beverley Robinson[*]

The general case for anarchism was made on both constructive and critical grounds in Liberty. *One of the best examples of the latter is this*

---

[*] November 17, 1894 (X:14, #300), pp. 2-3. See also the long-running, ironically-titled series,

excerpt from a longer article advocating a "government" run along business principles, what today probably would be called privatization of government services.[9] In this excerpt, Robinson imagines the opposite of privatization, the assumption by government of monopoly control over a particular economic sector, in this case, insurance.

. . . How is it possible that government, as it is today, should be otherwise than corrupt? Conceive, if you please, a business concern conducted as government is conducted. Or conceive government as it is, turned into a business concern. Suppose, for example, all the other functions of government abolished, and the function of life-assurance assumed instead.

In the first place, all existing life-insurance concerns would be prohibited and abolished, so that no standard of competition would remain by which we could judge of the quality of the insurance offered to us by government.

We should all have to take it, whether we liked it or not, . . . in fact, we should be regarded as "disloyal" if we even entertained an opinion that the governmental insurance was not the best possible.

Our premiums would be taken, if not paid, by the summary proceeding of selling our property and appropriating the amount demanded. There would be a vast crowd of insurance officials elected every year, with absolute power, when once they were elected, to fix the amount of premiums to be taken and to determine the mode of their expenditure. Under these circumstances the Great American Insurance Company would become very much what the Great American Republic is now.

The officials, knowing that their tenure of office and emolument depended more upon getting votes than upon doing their work, would inevitably make getting votes their business, as would those who had formerly had their places and wanted to get them again. Two parties, the Ins and the Outs, would alternate in running the concern, and both would be compelled for the preservation of their life to run it more for their own benefit than for the economical insurance of other people. Each would have to put up a part of his emoluments to pay for the operation of getting votes, and, as long as there were plenty of men out of work and hard up,

---

"Beauties of Government," (first appearing February 24, 1894 (IX:47, #281), pp. 6–7), which compiled news items and letters demonstrating the follies of government.

votes could be bought and would be bought by subscription, of the Ins to keep their places, of the Outs to get them.

Doubtless this would be wrong, but it would be inevitable.

The amount of premiums to be collected would be as great as the officials dared to make it; the insurance would be as inefficient as they dared to make it. Being without the commercial check of bargaining, the customer not being able to refuse to buy, nothing but the fear of popular revulsion, throwing them out of their places, would restrain the exactions of the officials. All sorts of plausible pretexts for establishing new places and increasing the payroll and the premium fund would be invented.

Lavish expenditure upon buildings and other plant would be encouraged and admired by the insured as evidence of the greatness of the Great American Insurance Company. When the danger point in the amount of premiums demanded was approached, recourse would be had to bonds, thus skilfully making the running expenditure seem trifling, when really it was enormously increased; even deficiency bonds to meet the running expenses would be issued.

It is easy to see that a business carried on in this way would at once degenerate into a nest of corruption, as governments everywhere tend to degenerate.

The only remedy will be found to be placing the governments on a business footing,—giving their members the commercial privilege of refusing to buy the wares offered at their pleasure.

E. "Anarchy or Government"
—Victor Yarros and William Salter

By the early 1890s, the basic principles of individualist anarchism had been repeatedly articulated in Liberty *and theoretical articles tended to distinguish it from very similar political theories, in particular the "Individualism" of Wordsworth Donisthorpe.[10] Donisthorpe held a position akin to today's "minimal statists," for whom the primary, perhaps only, justifiable functions of government are defense (external) and protection (internal), and for which taxation can legitimately be made compulsory.[11] By contrast, the individualist anarchists called for "voluntary taxation" and "voluntary defense associations."[12]*

In this selection, Victor Yarros, one of the most frequent contributors to Liberty *and for a time its associate editor, takes on an extended critique of anarchism by William Salter.*[13] *Yarros' articles, Salter's response, and Yarros' rejoinders run to at least 20,000 words, although this was neither the first nor the last time that such an extended debate occurred in Liberty. These excerpts from the debate focus on the question of whether government can coerce individuals to contribute either service or money for the provision of internal protection. This raised questions about ethics, the nature of society, the legitimacy of majority rule, and the law of equal freedom.*

Yarros[*]

. . . Anarchy is defined, not as absence of all physical compulsion, but absence of physical compulsion of the *non-aggressive*. Individuals would *not* be left to do as they choose. They would be left to do as they choose only within certain limits,—those of equal freedom. Criminals or invaders would be restrained or punished by voluntary organizations for defence, and only non-aggressive persons would be exempt from interference. In other words, Anarchy is synonymous with liberty for *all*, not with liberty for some; and [Tolstoyan] non-resistance would mean a state in which some could aggress upon others without any danger of physical punishment[14] . . .

Mr. Salter refers with mild approval to the suggestion "of competition between governments" and the abolition of police monopolies. He admits that it "might be an ideal arrangement if, in the same territory, we could have a choice of governments" and "were bound to none of them," but is inclined to regard the idea as somewhat fanciful. "Voluntary government may be even a contradiction in terms," he remarks. Yes, it certainly is a contradiction in terms, but the difficulty is of Mr. Salter's own making. The organizations in question would not be voluntary governments (since government is an organization which coerces the non-invasive into membership and allegiance), but simply voluntary associations for purposes of defence. Between *these* and liberty there is certainly no incongruity, always remembering that by liberty is meant equal liberty, liberty for all.

Why, seeing that the presumption is always on the side of liberty, should government deal with private wrongs? If society is not threatened

---

[*] "Anarchy or Government," February 22, 1896 (XI:21, #333), pp. 2-3; March 7, 1896 (XI:22, #334), pp. 2-3; March 21, 1896 (XI:23, #335), pp. 2-3.

by external enemies, why should government come to the aid of individuals injured by members of the same society, instead of leaving each
to be his own protector? Mr. Salter, putting these questions, proceeds to
justify governmental interference, and to argue that liberty is utterly
impossible in the premises.

To answer the question, says Mr. Salter, it is necessary to define
society. A society is, of course, made up of individuals, "yet any number
of individuals do not of themselves make a society. It is not one individual
and another and another and so on, but these conceived of as somehow
fitting together, making a unit, a body, an organism." These individuals
make up a whole, "with ties to one another and more or less conscious
of them, feeling that in some sense they belong to one another, that they
are not mere *units*, but *members together* of a somewhat beyond their
individual selves."

Suppose we accept all this, what follows? Mr. Salter tells us that, in
the light of this conception of society, the question of how a private injury
becomes a matter of public concern may be said to answer itself. For "it
would hardly be going beyond the bounds to say that a society in which
this was not the case would not be a real society. If a wrong to any one
individual excites no resentment in the minds of the rest, there is not
properly a society, but simply an aggregate of individuals—the social
bond does not exist." If, then, we take the social standpoint, "then may
a society interfere to protect the lives and property of its members: may,
not because individuals wish it to interfere, not on the basis of any
hocus-pocus of elections or of an imaginary social compact, but because
in the nature of the case it must interfere or have the right to interfere,
else it ceases to be a society, a real whole, a true social body" . . .

Now, we entirely agree with Mr. Salter that society is a thing to be
preserved. Anarchism is not intended as an attack upon the social
principle, but upon governmentalism. That protection against internal
invasion is essential to the preservation of society is admitted, but to
contend, as we do, that there are better ways of attaining this end than
the governmental way is clearly not to attack society. Society would cease
to exist if life and liberty were not protected against invasion, external or
internal; but it would not cease to exist if the governmental method were
abandoned.

What does Mr. Salter mean, in the last analysis, when he asserts that
society, in virtue of being society, has the right to interfere for the

protection of individuals? Nothing else than that protection is essential to all who desire to pursue happiness and live free lives. Now, we contend that, whenever society interferes in the governmental way,—the way of compulsory taxation and compulsory protection,—more evil is accomplished than good, and society, instead of being strengthened, is weakened by such interference. . .

Mark the difference between Mr. Salter's method and the Anarchists' method. The latter, recognizing the necessity and propriety of protection against internal aggression, would have voluntary defensive associations organized by the citizens for the purpose. Expediency would teach them whether it is better to have one large association, or a number of cooperating small associations. A non-resistant, or a person who preferred to take his chances, would not be compelled to belong to the defensive organization. It is certainly absurd to pretend that the recognition of the right of individual secession would destroy society, for not only would the defensive associations protect their own members, but they would also be justified in restraining those who aggressed upon non-members, provided they perceived danger to themselves in suffering the aggressors to go scot free. The non-members would have no claim on the associations, and they would not interfere to punish invaders of the former's rights unless their own interests demanded it. Mr. Salter's method, on the other hand, involves this: that a *majority* of the society organize what they call a government, force the kind of protection they please upon the minority; and tax willing and unwilling alike. So, because *society* has the right to suppress crime, the majority claim the right to say what crime is, what protection is, what the expense shall be, and what the methods shall be. By what hocus-pocus do the majority become the sole mouthpiece of "society," and the minority their slaves? Mr. Salter must realize that he who says government says majority and no individual secession, and he who says liberty says Anarchism. . .

Mr. Salter will doubtless admit that no private association can impose its schools, aesthetic notions, religion, or hygiene upon outsiders. It can insist upon being left alone and having its rights respected, but it can go no farther. But a majority is only a group of individuals, and the hocus pocus of government does not give, from an ethical point of view, any more rights than other voluntary associations possess. How can it impose *its* protection, education, aesthetics, etc., on the minority? What right has it to speak for "society," when society means all of us, majority *and* minority? . . .

Salter [*]

. . . Right and wrong are measured by the welfare of the tribe or community; to force individuals to defend the community is (unless the individuals have conscientious scruples against war) no wrong; and they themselves would feel it to be no wrong, however they might *dislike* the compulsion. . .

I am aware that a difficulty does seem to arise in having the *majority* act for the tribe,—i.e. in deciding when danger exists and war is necessary . . . Undoubtedly it would be better if social action could be unanimous; for, though I do not consider liberty an absolute good, as some "philosophical Anarchists" seem to, I do consider it a good, and the only justification for ever disregarding it is in case some greater good is to be attained. But, practically speaking, unanimity is an ideal rarely attained. The question, then, is whether it is better that a society should act with something short of unanimity rather than not act at all . . .

This question runs back into the more ultimate question whether such things as societies, properly speaking, exist (for, if they exist, it goes without saying that they may defend themselves and act for their welfare). Are there any such things, it may be asked; is there ever anything more than a lot of individuals living alongside of one another? . . .

Whether there *are* any societies or not, there have been various groups of people at different times in the history of the world who have *conceived* themselves as societies,—i.e. as somehow bound to one another, as forming in some sense a unity; and they have acted accordingly. They have lived and fought and perhaps died as groups. Mr. Yarros speaks of the "community," or, "logically speaking," the "majority." He is mistaken. If the community were, logically speaking, the "majority," it would not be the community at all, for no majority makes the community; on the numerical basis it is only all who make the community. But, truly and logically speaking, the majority-vote or any other controlling influence in the community is simply the means by which the community as such comes to act at all. If the community could not act in some such way, it would not act. A majority vote is simply a practical necessity,—

---

[*] "Mr. Yarros on 'Anarchy and Government,'" May 2, 1896 (XI:26, #338), pp. 6–8.

that is all. Hence the language about the minority being "enslaved" and all that loses its relevance . . .

Mr. Yarros appears to think there is a certain arbitrariness in making "social action" and "government" practically synonymous. But by "social action" I mean the action of the society, and all action of the society, so long as there is not unanimous agreement to it, involves the essence of government. On the other hand, mere majority action is not social action; if it does not bind the minority, but only themselves, it is a purely anarchistic, not a governmental, or properly social, procedure. There is really no social action- i.e., action of a society—that is not a governmental action, in the present state and imperfection of human evolution.

Yarros[*]

. . . Now, I entirely agree with Mr. Salter that "right and wrong are measured by the welfare of tribe or community." and that "in its origin conscience was a social sentiment." This is the Darwinian, or, rather, evolutionary, view of ethical sentiments and conceptions, but it is wholly consistent with the doctrine of individual sovereignty; and Mr. Salter is simply guilty of question-begging when, after stating this proposition regarding the *meaning* of right and wrong, or the *origin* of social sentiments, he immediately assumes that it is right for "the community" to force an individual to defend it, regardless of his own feelings in the matter. The conclusion does not follow from the premise. It is true that everything is wrong which is injurious to the community, and that everything is right which is beneficial and necessary to the community. But whether a thing is or is not necessary and beneficial to the community is itself a question. As I have repeatedly insisted, the Anarchistic position, the demand for absolute non-interference with the non-aggressive, rests precisely on the contention that such conduct is in the highest degree advantageous to the community, and that the society which will respect equality of liberty and decline to force non-invasive individuals into cooperation even for purposes of defensive war will be happier, freer, more stable and harmonious and progressive, than any other society. We assert that individual sovereignty is the essential condition of *social* well-being, and that coercion of the non-invasive individual is injurious

---

* "Mr. Salter's Defense," May 16, 1896 (XII:1, #339), pp. 2-4; May 30, 1896 (XII:2, #340), pp. 2-3; June 13, 1896 (XII:3, #341), pp. 2-4.

and demoralizing to the community as a whole. The difference, then, between Mr. Salter and myself is that he assumes certain things to be necessary and beneficial to society which I hold to be injurious and fatal to it, and not at all with reference to the meaning of right and wrong, or the origin of social sentiments . . .[15]

Properly understood, the interests of the individual and the aggregate are identical. The aggregate has no existence apart from the existence of the units. Society is happy, prosperous, and free only when its members are happy, prosperous, and free. Society, I repeat, is a scientific abstraction; there are only individuals. But the conditions of happiness are the same for all of them, or for all except those under-developed persons whose instincts or impulses are predatory. When we insist, then, on right and just conduct, we insist on that which is beneficial and necessary for all, and no subjection or subordination is contemplated. Societies exist only because they are agencies or means of individual progress. Men surrender nothing in entering society; that ancient fallacy is exploded. They gain in every way by the social relation. They are what they are in consequence of social conditions. Society is simply indirect cooperation for material, intellectual, and moral development, and, if it ceased to subserve individual needs, it could not survive; men would simply abandon the social state.

If these propositions are sound, there is no antagonism between social and individual interests. That alone is good for "society" which is good for all its members. To ask any number of individuals to sacrifice themselves for "society"—that is, for the rest of the membership—is to deprive them of every motive for wishing to lead a social life. The individual has no need for society, if it does not tend to increase his happiness.

But how about the invasive, the men with predatory proclivities? it may be asked. A moment's reflection shows that they are not required to sacrifice or subordinate themselves to society. They are merely required to respect the limits which *everybody* is bound to observe, the limits imposed by associative life. He is allowed as much liberty as his neighbor or fellow-member, and prevented only from infringing upon the rightful liberty of others. In no sense can this be called subordination. It is unfortunate for him that he is underdeveloped, and that his sentiments are anti-social; but he is required to refrain only from pursuing courses of conduct inconsistent with the liberty of other men. He is denied nothing which anybody else is permitted to enjoy . . . [16]

Of course, I cannot really admit, even in Mr. Salter's sense, that the only method by which society can act is majority rule. How about monarchies, absolute and constitutional? How about oligarchies and plutocracies? How about governments by the wise and educated? Each of these forms is ready to assert that the system it favors is the best method by which social action can be effected, and there is absolutely no difference in principle between those governments and majority government. . . . Not only, therefore, is it not true that majority rule is the "only" method by which social action can be effected (I am speaking from Mr. Salter's point of view), but it is by no means established that it is better than some of the other methods that have been favored by governmentalists . . .

I agree with Mr. Salter that societies are more, much more, than a lot of individuals situated alongside of one another, and I am sure that in the course of evolution the ties that bind individuals will grow stronger rather than weaker. But Mr. Salter begs the whole question when he assumes that, unless the majority is permitted to use coercion for certain purposes, there is no sense of unity, no true social existence. It is precisely this assumption which I emphatically deny. Life under the same conditions, exchange of thought, social, industrial, and other relations, and all the thousand and one factors and influences that are brought into play by the existence of individuals alongside each other necessarily produce that feeling of unity and solidarity which is characteristic of society. Will men cease to cooperate, directly and indirectly, for economic, social, artistic, and political purposes when invasion is done away with and individual sovereignty, within the limits of equal freedom, recognized? Certainly not; and, since this cooperation makes men social and produces the sentiments of unity and solidarity, Anarchism does not fail to provide for the perpetuation of society and the satisfaction of social needs. Mr. Salter seems to think that "sovereign individuals" cannot form a society. This is the old fallacy which identified individualism with separatism and isolation. On the contrary, it is only sovereign individuals that can make a true society, since their bonds are exclusively moral and civilized. Slaves and master do not make a society; "free and equal" beings do. To say that the moment you deny to the majority the right to use force for any other purpose than the enforcement of equal freedom you abolish society, or reduce it to something less than it is to-day, is to imply that force makes society,—which is absurd.

Notes

1. Spooner published frequently in the early years of *Liberty*, under the pseudonym of "O" and under his own name, as well as in Tucker's earlier journal, *The Radical Review*. His reputation was well established as a forceful abolitionist and critic of the Constitution. In the latter capacity, he argued that no one had ever really had the opportunity to consent unequivocally to the American government and thus that it was illegitimate. He was also a forceful advocate of juries reclaiming their traditional power to pass on questions of law as well as of fact. This argument was condensed by Victor Yarros in "Free Political Institutions: Their Nature, Essence, and Maintenance. An Abridgement and Rearrangement of Lysander Spooner's 'Trial by Jury," *Liberty*, June 8, 1889 (VI:16, #146), pp. 2–3 (continued in #147–153).
2. This passage bears considerable resemblance to Lysander Spooner' argument in *No Treason: The Constitution of No Authority*, Boston: Lysander Spooner, 1870 (Colorado Springs: Ralph Myles, 1973, 1980).
3. See chapter 13, especially the selection "Tactical Voting," for more on the "expediency" of voting.
4. This critique of law and punishment parallels Peter Kropotkin's writings. See particularly his essays "Law and Authority" and "Prisons and Their Moral Influence on Prisoners" in either Emile Capouya and Keitha Tompkins, eds. *The Essential Kropotkin*, New York: Liveright, 1975, or Roger N. Baldwin, ed., *Kropotkin's Revolutionary Pamphlets*, New York: Dover, 1970 (New York: Vanguard, 1927).
5. See, for example, Leonard I. Krimerman and Lewis Perry, eds., *Patterns of Anarchy*, New York: Anchor Books, 1967, pp. 251–259.
6. J. William Lloyd, "Loyalty and Liberty for the Human," *Liberty*, February 8, 1896 (XI:20, #332), p. 6.
7. Bill Sikes, in Dickens' novel *Oliver Twist*, was the brutal leader of a band of trained thieves.
8. At this point, Tucker cites Max Stirner's book, *The Ego and His Own*.
9. According to Tucker's definition (as he reminds his readers in a footnote to this article), this would not be "government" at all because individuals could choose whether to purchase the services.
10. See, in particular, Donisthorpe's articles "Individualism: A System of Politics," *Liberty*, December 28, 1889 (VI:23, #153), pp. 6–7 and the long and humorous story "The Woes of an Anarchist," *Liberty*, January 25, 1890 (VI:24, #154), pp. 6–7.
11. See Robert Nozick, *Anarchy, State, and Utopia*, New York: Basic Books, 1974.
12. See, for example, Stephen T. Byington, "What Anarchism Means," *Liberty*, October 1897 (XIII:6, #356), p. 5. Originally appeared in the Cleveland *Reformer*.
13. William M. Salter, *Anarchy or Government? An Inquiry in Fundamental Politics*, New York: T.Y. Crowell and Co., 1895. Salter was one of the primary figures in the "Society for Ethical Culture."
14. See Benjamin Tucker, "Mr. Levy's Maximum," *Liberty*, November 1, 1890 (VII:14, #170), p. 4 for a similar argument, i.e. that anarchists aim not for absolute liberty, or the maximum of individual liberty, but for equal liberty.

15. On this point, Benjamin Tucker entered one of his characteristic editorial dissents. Although he and Yarros continued to work for similar aims throughout the time that *Liberty* was published, after about 1890, they had agreed to disagree on the theoretical basis of ethics, Tucker retaining his Stirnerite egoism, while Yarros shifted to "evolutionary ethics" and its concept, expressed here, that an objective standard of right and wrong was possible. In his dissent ("Mr. Yarros' Ethics in His Way," #339, p. 4), Tucker repeats the egoist version of "right and wrong" already set out in "The Relation of the State to the Individual" above). For more on egoism and ethics, see chapter two.

16. Again, Tucker dissented and his comments are worth quoting: "I must except to his [Yarros'] statement that to coerce the invasive is not to require their subordination. Coercion of the invasive is not tyranny, to be sure; on the contrary, it is defence against tyranny. But he who successfully defends himself against a tyrant subordinates the tyrant's wishes to his own, just as truly as the successful tyrant subordinates his victim. Anarchism is not the doctrine of no subordination; it is the doctrine that none but the invasive should be subordinated. To say that restraint upon the predatory does not subordinate their instincts to those of the non-predatory, or to society if you will, is to deceive oneself with words." ("Mr. Yarros' Ethics in His Way")

2

Critique of the Liberal Legacy

The theoretical connections between individualist anarchism and liberalism seem obvious. While liberalism called for individual liberty and a limited state, individualist anarchism called for individual sovereignty and no state. In economics as well as in politics, individualist anarchism seemed to be the logical extreme of liberalism. George Bernard Shaw put this succinctly: "*laissez-faire*, in spite of all the stumblings it has brought upon itself by persistently holding the candle to the devil instead of to its own footsteps, is the torchbearer of Anarchism."[1] However, this picture is too simplistic for several reasons. First of all, socialism was at least as influential as liberalism on the character of individualist anarchism, particularly in terms of economics. Secondly, there was little actual discussion of classical liberalism in the pages of *Liberty*: Locke barely appears and more contemporary liberals were usually derided as conservatives.[2] One exception was J.S. Mill, who was cited primarily for his economic theories (with a strong preference for his later, more socialistic writings) rather than for political works such as "Representative Government," "On the Subjection of Women," or even for "On Liberty."[3] The more significant exception was Herbert Spencer, whose works enjoyed considerable vogue in popular and anarchist circles in the 1880s. Spencer had provided the classic formulation of one of the building blocks of individualist anarchism, the law of equal freedom and, at least in his earlier works, seemed to have strong anarchist tendencies. By the late 1880s, however, the individualist anarchists argued that he had betrayed his earlier radicalism by providing a defense of the bourgeoisie and the status quo. Finally, the word "liberal" in *Liberty* typically referred to religious liberals, those who attacked ecclesiastical authority in the name of some individualistic form of religion, much as political liberals sought to limit political authority for the sake of individuals. This use of the term is indicated in the first selection from Tucker.[4]

In actuality, then, "liberalism" per se was not a major topic in *Liberty*, but the issues it raised, particularly as it evolved in the nineteenth century, were. The individualists saw themselves as more consistent and radical than liberals in applying the logic of liberalism and criticized liberals for not having the courage of their convictions. Specifically, they saw themselves as more "progressive," that is, more in line with contemporary intellectual trends. This explains much of their ambivalence to Spencer. They had adopted his argument that society progressed from militancy (centralized authority, reliance on coercion, and social relations defined by status) to industrialism (decentralized authority, cooperation, and contract relationships).[5] But even more significant to the anarchists was Spencer's "sociological" method, that is, his exhaustive, "scientific" study of human and animal societies. This had become the only legitimate way to study society, far superior to the "theological" and "metaphysical" methods of earlier centuries.[6]

This, however, created a dilemma for the individualist anarchists. Spencer had developed the "law of equal freedom" and its anarchistic corollary "the right to ignore the state" in his first book, *Social Statics*, which was not characterized by any "scientific" method, but was rather a moralistic critique of utilitarianism. While the anarchists approved of Spencer's methodological shift from this book to his later books, they emphatically disapproved of the increasingly authoritarian and conservative conclusions that he drew. The dilemma was not so much a crisis of faith in Spencer, though there were some elements of that (as indicated in the Tucker and Kelly selections on Spencer), but a more general theoretical crisis, in which developments in anarchist theory paralleled developments in Spencer's theory, in liberalism, and in political thought generally. Most generally, the dilemma was: if principles of social order (or reform) could not be legitimately grounded in divine sanctions, or unequivocally based on rational deductions, then could the scientific method provide a foundation? If so, what principles did it recommend? As Victor Yarros' critique of Spencer's "Justice" (excerpted here) shows, many of the anarchists believed that science could provide a foundation, but that the principles Spencer (and all advocates of the state) recommended were wrong because they were partial, cowardly, or inconsistent.

Specifically, the anarchists had to find "scientific" arguments to bolster the two building blocks of their ideology: individual sovereignty and equal liberty. Equal liberty in itself was not problematic, for few seriously disputed that sociology would recommend equal liberty as an operating principle for a modern society. The problem was whether (or rather, how) sovereign individuals would recognize equal liberty and put it into practice (i.e. by accepting limits on their own freedom). Three basic alternatives emerged. The first position was that egoistic individuals would adopt the constraints posed by equal liberty purely out of self-interested considerations. Although grounded in the rather "metaphysical" theories of Max Stirner, the egoists (Tak Kak, J. B. Robinson, and, for a time, Yarros) insisted that egoism was "realistic." This position was immediately and forcefully opposed by the advocates of evolutionary "ethics," who insisted that egoism would tear an anarchist society apart, but that this was not really a problem, since human evolution had created a moral sentiment (Kelly) or an expanding body of "rights" (Lum) that would restrain the destructiveness of egoism. Tucker articulated a hybrid position, suggesting that "rights" could be created (they were neither inherent, nor evolved) through contracts between egoistic individuals. Through self-interest, moral sentiments, or contract (all significant motivations in liberal theory, of course), individuals would remain sovereign and a stateless society would be characterized by equal liberty.

In time, however, the egoist position became the predominant one; as Tucker put it in 1892: "most Anarchists are Egoists."[7] This occurred despite the loss of several major writers for *Liberty* over the issue and the shift of Yarros to evolutionary ethics. It is probably attributable to Tucker's own sympathy, as well as the forceful arguments of Walker and Robinson and the influence of Tucker's close friend, George Schumm, who had studied under Stirner and who translated many passages from Nietzsche for *Liberty* in the 1890s.[8] In any case, *Liberty* at the end of the century was paralleling broader developments in Western philosophy, with its increasingly critical, subjective, and minimal approach, perhaps best exemplified here by the long selection on egoism by the German writer, E. Horn.

Further Reading in Liberty

In addition to the selections here, a good short summary of *Liberty*'s view on Spencer is S.R., "Spencer and Political Science," February 1904 (XIV:18, #380), p. 2. S.R. also wrote on Spencer's disavowal of his "right to ignore the state" in "Spencer as His Own Critic," June 1904 (XIV:21, #383), p. 2. Victor Yarros wrote extensively on Spencer and some of his additional articles are cited in the headnote to his selection here, but two from 1894 convey Yarros' sense of exasperation with Spencer: "Spencer's Injustice to Anarchism," February 24, 1894 (IX:47, #281), pp. 3–4 and "Are We Fit for Freedom?" April 7, 1894 (IX:50, #284), p. 2. In addition, Yarros subjected William Graham Sumner to a similar criticism: "The Bourgeoisie's Loyal Servants," February 12, 1887 (IV:15, #93), p. 4.

The debate on egoism was massive, but several classics that couldn't be included are: (1) Tucker, "The Philosophy of Right and Wrong," October 29, 1881 (I:7, #7, pp. 2–3; (2) Tak Kak, "What is Justice?" and "Killing Chinese" March 6, 1886, (III:25, #77), p. 8 [and Tucker's response]; (3) Tak Kak, "Egoism," April 9, 1887 (IV:19, #97), pp. 5–7; (4) J.M.L. Babcock, "Egoism and Its Opposite," November 5, 1887 (V:7, #111), p. 7; (5) J.B. Robinson, "The Limits of Governmental Interference," August 15, 1891 (VIII:10, #192), pp. 3–4; (6) J.B. Robinson, "The Land of the Altruists," August 10, 1895 (XI:7, #319), p. 3; (7) J.B. Robinson, "Ethics," December 1897 (XIII:7, #357), pp. 6–8.

Another set of articles, digressing from a debate on whether children are property (see chapter 9), attempted to define the relative importance of self-interest and sympathy in establishing and maintaining defensive associations: Tucker, "What Is Property?" October 5, 1895 (XI:11, #323), pp. 3–4; Stephen T. Byington, "The Defensive Contract," November 2, 1895 (XI:13, #325), pp. 6–7; Tucker, "Defense of Whom and by Whom?" #325, pp. 3–5.

A.   "The Root of Despotism"—Benjamin Tucker[*]

This brief selection illustrates the line that Tucker took on religion, even in its "liberal" forms. Many anarchists had backgrounds in free thought or "liberal" denominations such as the Unitarians or Quakers.

---

[*] August 20, 1881 (I:2, #2), pp. 6–7.

Indeed, the earliest anarchist tendencies in America cropped up among radical dissenters such as Anne Hutchinson in the 1600s. The Abolitionist movement also had its share of anarchistic religious radicals.[9] *By the 1880s, however, most anarchists considered religion to be an outdated and immoral superstition, and one that reinforced authority. Here, Tucker describes, with much the same argument and invective as Bakunin, the parallels between religious and political authority.*[10]

The purpose of Liberty, boiled down to its ultimate essence, is the abolition of authority. But, until the reader has come into accord with our philosophy, he must not misunderstand what we mean by the abolition of authority. The reason of the writer of this article is (to him) authority; otherwise it would be foolishness for him to write.

But the writer of this article is an individual. He can set up whatever gods he chooses (for himself) as authority. Yea, he may offer whatever these gods dictate to him for the consideration of his fellow-men. If he makes a god of his reason, he may worship that god to his heart's content, and submit to the letter to the authority of that god. And he may give that god a tongue through the press, the pulpit, and the rostrum. He may set him up on every corner, and call him holy, infallible, and all-wise.

Thus far he has violated no man's liberty. He begins to be a despot and a public enemy only when he imposes that god upon others by force. See how it is under our advanced democratic institutions. A man starts out campaigning for his god. He convinces some, bribes others, and swindles enough more till he secures what he calls a majority. But, when he gets so far, he recollects that a certain fiction possesses the masses, viz., "the majority must rule." He thereupon drops the methods of peace and persuasion, and proceeds to saddle his god upon the minority by force.

Now, what Liberty proposes to abolish is all these gratuitous fictions by which any and all gods, theological, political, and social, are saddled by force upon unwilling shoulders. That toppling theological colossus who has straddled humanity for centuries had first to be "boycotted" and unseated from those who are tired of his weight. Now that he feels the pillars giving way and begins to quake, a swarm of ecclesiastical parasites and priestly dead-beats, from the pope down, are beginning to dress their wings and look for new roosts. Not that Liberty has anything against the Christian God *per se*. It simply asks that Jewish usurper to stand on his own merits, pay his own bills, and stop sitting down on people who do not want his company.

The dangerous fiction, crowned God, which makes an authority out of the Jewish usurper theologically, has its exact counterpart in that fiction which sets up the State as an authority politically. God is the supreme being for the plundering purposes of the ecclesiastic. The State is the supreme being for the plundering purposes of the politician. The saving grace which perpetuates the whole swindle lies in the ability to keep the masses drugged with superstitious reverence for that fiction of authority which keeps the double-headed monster alive.

Liberty denies the authority of anybody's god to bind those who do not accept it through persuasion and natural selection. Liberty denies the authority of anybody's State to bind those who do not lend voluntary allegiance to it. Liberty denies the authority of anybody's "public opinion," "social custom," "consensus of the competent," and every other fashionable or scholarly despot, to step between the individual and his free option in all things. In short, it sets up the standard of uncompromising rebellion against authority, meaning by authority any coercive force not developed spontaneously and naturally out of the constitution of the individual himself or herself.

We of course believe in forces. Nature is made up of forces. But we want native, healthy, spontaneous forces in social life, not arbitrary, extraneous, usurping forces. And we believe in authority too, when authority is made to mean that which is sifted through reason and made welcome by choice. The thing that we have gone into defensive warfare with is that usurping aggressor which proposes to saddle its forms and fictions upon us without our consent, and make us its slaves under the many cunning guises which have made history a bloody record of the brutality practised by the few upon the ignorance and helplessness of the many.

B.   "The Sin of Herbert Spencer"—Benjamin Tucker[*]

This is probably the most succinct, and earliest, of the major critiques of Spencer in Liberty. *That Tucker should have written this, and little else, about Spencer is unsurprising, since his debt to Spencer was more rhetorical than intellectual. Although Spencer did clearly articulate and*

---

[*] May 17, 1884 (II:16, #42), pp. 4–5.

justify the law of equal freedom and offer pungent critiques of state action, he was hardly unique in this, so Tucker showed little hesitation in criticizing Spencer when his rhetoric began to seem less useful for promoting individualist anarchism.[11]

Tucker's two major themes here, that Spencer is a partisan of the bourgeoisie and that this contradicts his earlier radicalism, are expanded by Kelly and Yarros in the next two selections.

Liberty welcomes and criticises in the same breath the series of papers by Herbert Spencer on "The New Toryism," "The Coming Slavery," "The Sins of Legislators," &c, now running in the "Popular Science Monthly" and the English "Contemporary Review."[12] They are very true, very important, and very misleading. They are true for the most part in what they say, and false and misleading in what they fail to say. Mr. Spencer convicts legislators of undeniable and enormous sins in meddling with and curtailing and destroying the people's rights. Their sins are sins of commission. But Mr. Spencer's sin of omission is quite as grave. He is one of those persons . . . who are making a wholesale onslaught on Socialism as the incarnation of the doctrine of State omnipotence carried to its highest power. And I am not sure that he is quite honest in this. I begin to be a little suspicious of him. It seems as if he had forgotten the teachings of his earlier writings, and had become a champion of the capitalistic class. It will be noticed that in these later articles, amid his multitudinous illustrations (of which he is as prodigal as ever) of the evils of legislation, he in every instance cites some law passed, ostensibly at least, to protect labor, alleviate suffering, or promote the people's welfare. He demonstrates beyond dispute the lamentable failure in this direction. But never once does he call attention to the far more deadly and deep-seated evils growing out of the innumerable laws creating privilege and sustaining monopoly. You must not protect the weak against the strong, he seems to say, but freely supply all the weapons needed by the strong to oppress the weak. He is greatly shocked that the rich should be directly taxed to support the poor, but that the poor should be indirectly taxed and bled to make the rich richer does not outrage his delicate sensibilities in the least. Poverty is increased by the poor laws, says Mr. Spencer. Granted; but what about the *rich* laws that caused and still cause the poverty to which the poor laws add? That is by far the most important question; yet Mr. Spencer tries to blink it out of sight.

C.   "Mr. Spencer and Socialism—Gertrude B. Kelly[*]

For Kelly, one of the few women contributors to Liberty, *Spencer had "sold out." His allegiance to the bourgeoisie and his abandonment of his earlier radicalism were intimately connected. Her sympathy for the working class, and consequent criticism of Spencer for the lack thereof, were not unusual in* Liberty. *As will become clear in the next chapter, many of its writers considered the "labor problem" paramount and found capitalists in the present economic order to be at fault. Nevertheless, they (and Kelly) maintained their commitment to individual liberty and, thus, found it reprehensible for the major prophet of individual liberty, Spencer, to defend capitalists despite the privileges they enjoyed from the state.*

. . . Mr. Spencer says that the "miseries of the poor are thought of as the miseries of the deserving poor, instead of being thought of, as in large measure they should be, as the miseries of the undeserving poor." So conservative a political economist as John Stuart Mill has admitted, nay, positively stated, that no one but a romantic dreamer could believe that in modern society the rewards are proportioned to the work, and that even those poor people, commonly called the "undeserving poor," whose condition might with perhaps a trace of justice be said to be due to their own faults, have done and do more work than those who enjoy much worldly prosperity. One would need to be a *philosopher* to appreciate the fact that poverty and misery are proportional to the laziness of the individual. The ordinary mortal, on being told that a man works a great many hours in a day, or, as they are popularly and with good reason called, "long hours," immediately jumps to the conclusion that that man's wages are small. The harder as well as the longer a man works, the smaller his wages are.

Mr. Spencer is surprised at the number of idlers that stand in the streets waiting to open cab-doors, etc., and expecting to be paid for it, and at once decides that these men are good-for-nothings, who never have worked, and who do not wish to work if they can live off some one else.

---

* October 24, 1885 (III:16, #68), pp. 7–8. Tucker's introduction: "The following are copious extracts from an essay which I wish I had room to print in full, written by Gertrude B. Kelly for the "Contemporary Review" in answer to the series of papers printed in that magazine from the pen of Herbert Spencer and since republished in a volume entitled "The Man and the State." It is needless to add that the essay was rejected by the "Contemporary."

Perhaps some of them are, and, admitting that they are, are they any worse than the titled and honorable loafers who live in the same way? But did it never occur to Mr. Spencer to question why these men are in the streets? The life in the streets is not a very enticing one, I suppose Mr. Spencer will admit; but, bad as it is, these men have discerned that it is much easier, and that a great deal more money can be made in this way than could be made by hard work continued through long, weary hours, even if that work were always to be had . . .

Admitting that the men and women found on the streets are to blame for their condition, are the men and women who work early and late eating according to their work? Let us hear Mr. Spencer himself on this subject:

> Surely the lot of the hard-handed laborer is pitiable enough without having harsh judgments passed upon him. *To be wholly sacrificed to other men's happiness,* to be made a mere human tool; to have every faculty subordinated to the sole function of work,—this, one would say, is alone a misfortune needing all sympathy for its mitigation. Consider well these endowments of his, these capacities, affections, tastes, and the vague yearnings to which they give birth. Think of him now with his caged-up desires, doomed to a daily, weekly, yearly round of painful toil, with scarcely any remission but for food and sleep. Observe how he is tantalized by the pleasures he sees his richer brethren partaking of, but from which he must forever be debarred. Note the humiliation he suffers from being looked down upon as of no account amongst men. And then remember that he has nothing to look forward to but a monotonous continuance of this till death. . . . How offensive is it to hear some pert self-approving personage, who thanks God that he is not as other men are, passing sentence on his poor, hard-worked, heavily-burdened countrymen, including them all in one sweeping condemnation because in their struggle for existence they do not maintain the same prim respectability as himself.—*Social Statics*

Mr. Spencer seems to have now joined the ranks of those "self-approving personages" . . .

In the near future men will wonder how Mr. Spencer, "*the* philosopher" of the nineteenth century, could have allowed his devotion to the *bourgeoisie* to so cloud his morality (for we cannot believe that it was his judgment that was at fault) as to cause him to say that the rich supported the poor. How do they do it? By standing by and seeing the poor work, taking away all their products, and giving back to the workers just sufficient to keep them in working order,—in many cases not even as much as that . . .

Mr. Spencer regrets very much that *laissez faire* is getting to be an exploded doctrine. Mr. Spencer evidently is not a believer in *laissez-faire*, as he comes to the assistance of the landowners and capitalists in general with all the arguments in his power, even if the views now expressed are totally opposed to those expressed before he was captured by the *bourgeoisie*. The only true advocates of *laissez faire* in modern times are the Anarchists. They are Mr. Spencer's true disciples, more true to his teachings than he is himself; they truly believe in *laissez-faire* principles, and they seek every opportunity to put them in practice. These "shareholders" to whose rescue Mr. Spencer comes in such haste are under the protection of, and are only allowed to drive their nefarious trade in flesh and blood through the intervention of, that institution Mr. Spencer pretends to abhor,—the government. But Mr. Spencer is not the first philosopher who "builded better than he knew," and the Anarchists are deeply grateful to him for the arguments he has furnished them against government in all its forms, than which there are probably none better, and his recent relapse into Philistinism does not vitiate those arguments in the least. There they stand for all time, and the "youth of America" are beginning to appreciate them.

Now, as to the "coming slavery" which Mr. Spencer so much dreads. Let me preface my remarks on this subject by telling Mr. Spencer that he dreads it no more than we Anarchists do. But does Mr. Spencer know that he and his kind, who deny the existence of the evils, and foster all the injustice, of modern society, are hastening the advent of this "slavery"? The people know, that evils exist, and that injustice exists, and, if certain people arise, and either for their own ends, or because they believe it to be the truth, tell them that State Socialism will "fix" everything, are they to be blamed if they believe it? In their work-a-day life they have not time even to work out vast problems for themselves, and, if such philosophers as Mr. Spencer tell them that their condition is all due to their own fault, their "laziness," etc., when they know very well that their life is one continuous toil, any amount of argument he can bring to bear against State Socialism will have no effect in stemming the tide in its favor. They may not be able, and probably will not try, to answer his arguments, but they know that their lot is hard, and they will follow the only persons who seem to be ready to show them a way out of their misery. It is because we fear State Socialism, fearing, nay knowing, that it would and should relapse into despotism, that we are sorry to see Mr. Spencer's arguments against it, which are excellent and incontrovertible in themselves, almost entirely nullified, at least in the minds of the mass

of the people, by his defence of the wrongs of the present state of society.
. . .

It is curious into what inconsistencies even a philosopher may be led by his desire to uphold the existing order. Mr. Spencer, in speaking of State Socialism, predicts the certain failure of the institution on account of the imperfections of human nature; "love of power, selfishness, injustice, and untruthfulness" would work against the just administration of the system; that is, as before remarked, "wherever there is an opportunity for power to exercise itself, there will power be exercised to the advantage of the holders of it." But all this is contradicted in the very next paragraph, when he comes to the aid of the railway shareholders, "who, sometimes gaining, but often losing, have made that railway system by which national prosperity has been so greatly increased," as if these men had been actuated by the highest motives of benefiting England and thereby humanity, and that the power which the State conferred on them of robbing the people had never been used. . . .

Now, the Anarchists agree with Mr. Spencer that no "Morrison's Pill" "can make an ill-working humanity into well-working institutions," and also "that benefit may result, not from a multiplication of artificial appliances to mitigate distress, but contrariwise from a diminution of them." But, more logical and more honest than Mr. Spencer, they wish to carry this diminution to the utmost, and destroy all the support which the State gives to one part of its citizens at the expense of all the others; in a word, they wish to abolish the *State*, which, according to Mr. Spencer himself, originated in aggression, and has been nurtured by aggression,— is, in fact, aggression itself. . . . Yes, the Anarchists believe in *laissez faire*, and their mission to the people is to tell them *laissez faire*; to cease sending their men into the army and navy and police; to cease supporting the government, which uses the army and navy and police (composed of their brothers) to crush them; in short, to cease to pay tribute to idlers, and to see that *he who does not work shall not eat.*

D. "Justice and Anarchism"—Victor Yarros[*]

Victor Yarros was the writer in Liberty *who took Spencer most seriously and who wrote the most often on his works.*[13] *He emphasized*

---

[*] This appeared in three parts: August 29, 1891 (VIII:12, #194), pp. 2–3; September 5, 1891 (VIII:13, #195), pp. 2–3; September 19, 1891 (VIII:15, #197), p. 2. The present excerpts are from

Spencer's scientific methods and his description of social progress. He argued that anarchists should embrace those aspects of Spencer, but that they need not accept uncritically the conclusions that Spencer drew, namely his defense of the status quo.

The present selection consists of excerpts from a long critical review of Spencer's latest book, "Justice." Yarros makes many of the same points against government as he does in his review of Salter (chapter one), but here the central question is a characteristically liberal one: "what system of appliances best protects individual rights?" Although Yarros agreed (by this time[14]) with Spencer's account of rights, he disagreed with his preferred "system of appliances," i.e., government that would coerce dissenters. Yarros argued that the very presence of dissenters undermined the government's claim to be a progressive institution. That is, government did not have even a "quasi-ethical warrant," one derived from "relative political ethics."

After reading and re-reading Mr. Spencer's "Justice," I find myself confirmed in the opinion I ventured briefly to express in the preliminary notice of the work,—namely, that whereas the basic principles common to Individualism and Anarchism have been invested with a character strictly scientific and shown to have a philosophical "authority transcending every other,"—to use Mr. Spencer's own words,—much questionable logic and lame argumentation have been resorted to in the attempt to justify certain qualifications of the principle to the various activities and interests of social life. This opinion, as well as other considerations, leads me to undertake an elaborate and detailed critical review of the book, my purpose being to afford a tolerably complete statement of the differences and parallelisms or resemblances subsisting between Spencerian individualism and Anarchism . . .

[Yarros traces Spencer's account of the evolution of justice from animal justice, to justice for gregarious species, to the development of egoism and altruism, and finally here to the law of equal freedom] The human idea of justice contains two elements. On the one hand, there is the positive element implied by each man's recognition of his claim to unimpeded activities: this element suggests inequality, since men differ in their powers and consequently must expect to find differences in the results of their activities. On the other hand, there is the negative element

---

the first two parts, with the exception of the last paragraph.

implied by the recognition of limits necessitated by the presence of others: this element involves the conception of equality, since the limits are on the average the same for all. But there is no incongruity between these two conditions. The inequality concerns the results achieved by action within the implied limits; the equality concerns the limits and the opportunities for the exercise of powers and faculties. The formula which unites the two elements and gives precise expression to the fact or necessity of limiting the liberty of each by the like liberty of all is,— "Every man is free to do that which he wills, provided he infringes not the equal freedom of any other man."

This formula has the highest warrant imaginable, and an authority transcending every other. Under one aspect it is an immediate dictum of the human consciousness after it has been subject to the discipline of prolonged social life; under another aspect it is a belief deducible from the conditions to be fulfilled, firstly for the maintenance of life at large, and secondly for the maintenance of social life. Induction agrees with deduction, since along with the growth of peaceful cooperation there has been an increasing conformity to the law of equal liberty under both its positive and negative aspects, and there has gone on simultaneously an increase of emotional regard for it and intellectual apprehension of it. History furnishes *a posteriori* supports of the belief, while *a priori* supports are furnished by biology and psychology.

I have now given a brief but accurate and fair summary of the propositions and statements of the first seven chapters of "Justice," which chapters cannot be too highly spoken of for their clearness, lucidity, profundity, and strength. There is less satisfaction in studying Mr. Spencer's application of this first principle of equal liberty, in observing his method of tracing its corollaries and drawing deductions applicable to special classes of cases. Anarchists will dissent from many of Mr. Spencer's conclusions, and regard some of his alleged applications of the first principle as singular and sad misapplications. But the fact should not be overlooked that erroneous and fallacious deductions from given principles do not invalidate the principles at all. Our logic and understanding of the facts of a given case may lead us to conclusions entirely different from those of another reasoner notwithstanding identity of our points of view and essential agreement on fundamental principles. So Anarchists may disclaim certain Spencerian applications of equal liberty

without questioning the truth and importance of his abstract principles .
. . .

How are true rights to be preserved,—defended against aggressors?
The instrumentality that most completely and economically answers the
purpose is the one to be preferred, whatever its form. No body of thinkers
will indorse all this more unreservedly or appreciate it more keenly than
the Anarchists, who, for many years, have been endeavoring to inculcate
this very lesson. But this same body of thinkers will most emphatically
dissent from Mr. Spencer's opinion as to the nature of the "system of
appliances" which *is* best adapted to the end in view. What system of
appliances does Mr. Spencer propose? . . .

Mr. Spencer's view is that the best system of appliances for the
obtainment and maintenance of equal freedom or justice, is a State, or
government, with power over the life, liberty, and property of the citizens
to the extent required by the task of maintaining the maximum of liberty
and security with which it is charged. In other words, so long as justice
is obstructed and violated by external and internal aggressors and defensive organizations are necessitated, the State, according to Mr. Spencer,
is justified in breaking the law of equal freedom in every way which tends
to make it a successful defender of its citizens. The dangers of extreme
malevolent despotism reconcile Mr. Spencer to a certain milder species
of benevolent despotism. . . . I find a respectable amount of evidence to
support the averment that Mr. Spencer's position in "Justice" is a sort of
compromise between the unqualified Anarchism of "Social Statics" and
the pronounced governmentalism of certain passages in the "Data of
Ethics" and other essays. In "Social Statics" Mr. Spencer firmly advocated Anarchism. He held that all institutions must be subordinated to the
law of equal freedom, and that no individual ought to be compelled to
belong to the political corporation and pay toward its support. He denied
that society, or the State, has any rights or claims which it may rightfully
enforce at the expense of the liberty of the individual. He believed that
what is just and proper in the relation between one individual and another
is just and proper in the relation between an individual and all his
neighbors combined in "the community." In subsequent treatises the
position taken was radically different. We were told that beyond the
question of justice between man and man there is a question of justice
between each individual and the aggregate of individuals. The right of
the individual to ignore the State was plainly denied. The State was held

to be ethically warranted in exacting such sacrifices from individuals as defensive warfare or the state of preparation for such made needful. Coercion of the individual by the State into doing things necessary for the protection of the society was declared ethically defensible. In "Justice" a position unlike either of these is chosen. State-coercion within the sphere marked by the need for defence against external and internal enemies is said to have a *quasi-ethical warrant*; in other words, it is justified under relative political ethics as a temporary necessity and as a condition of further advance. And it is of course perfectly true that evolutionists who concur in the view that the government favored by Spencer is the best instrumentality to the obtainment of true political rights must regard the infractions of justice implied in that governmental system as relatively good and as having a quasi-ethical warrant, just as we all maintain that slavery and war were at one time relatively good because they were conducive to survival of the fittest and made progress possible. But it should not be overlooked that the fact that there are men who claim to have found better appliances than those of Spencer's invention,—appliances that serve the purpose in view without entailing any of the bad consequences resulting from the others,—deprive the State and its defenders of the last excuse for coercion. If the system involving the coercive elements were the system universally regarded as best, then the coercion would be practised and no complaints would be raised against it. Historians of a later period, on looking backward, would conclude that the coercion was relatively good because serviceable to progress and congruous with the needs and sentiments of the time, though not absolutely good since contrary to the law of justice. But differences of opinion have arisen, and coercion can no longer be defended as relatively good. . . . The state in which different opinions come to be entertained upon the question of what is the best instrumentality for the obtainment of justice is the stage in which coercion by a benevolently despotic State ceases to be justifiable . . .

While, therefore, Mr. Spencer favors the system of appliances involving certain elements of coercion as the best and most congruous with present factors and agencies, he cannot consistently defend the coercion of those who deny the excellence of his system,—he cannot hold it to be the duty or the right of the State to trespass their liberty. He may advise us to unite on the individualist programme from considerations of policy, but he is not warranted in instructing the majority to secure cooperation by compulsory and aggressive means. Mr. Spencer has failed to supply an ethical or even *quasi*-ethical warrant for coercion of non-invasive individuals, and can only urge that, as individualism would be infinitely superior to the present system and would tend to merge into Anarchism, it is wise and expedient to recognize it as a proximate end. But surely liberty has nothing to gain, and a great deal to lose, from such a misrepresentation of the case as those are guilty of who encourage the people in the false belief that the State may rightfully compel inoffensive persons to sacrifice life and property at its bidding. Tyranny, if condemned and made odious, will be relinquished by those governed by the sentiment of justice as soon as they satisfy themselves as to its precise nature; but love of liberty will not be induced by apologies for tyranny. It is essential that we should clearly understand and formulate the claims of the individual as deduced from equal freedom; as to realizing and establishing these various claims,—that will necessarily be a slow process, and no sensible man will be disappointed at finding that there is no royal road or short cut to complete liberty . . .

While arguing against the ethical right of compulsory government to exist at all, Anarchists are aware that non-ethical institutions will be eliminated gradually, one by one, and one at a time. They are ready to cooperate with the individualists in any rational movement against any special abuse or evil, and only ask that no energy shall be wasted and that the most mischievous and harmful elements in the present system be selected for assault.

E.   "The Reasons Why"—Victor Yarros[*]

In 1886 and 1887, a debate over egoism raged in the pages of Liberty. Despite his later conviction that rights had evolved over the course of human progress, Yarros in 1887 held the egoist position, that individuals would associate with one another purely out of self-interest and would respect the anarchist axiom of equal liberty by calculating for themselves what actions would best serve their interests in a social context. The substantive and stylistic contrast with his essay on Spencer could hardly be more striking.

I am an Egoist.

---

[*] August 27, 1887 (V:2, #106), p. 7.

I recognize no authority save that of my own reason.

I regulate my life and my relations with the outside world in accordance with my understanding and natural instincts.

My sole object in life is to be happy,—I seek to avoid all pain and to gratify all my normal desires.

I cannot be happy unless I feel myself perfectly safe and secure in my possessions.

I can never be safe and free from fear of disturbance or injury until those around me are able to gratify all their normal desires, and they can never be completely happy without security.

Security can only be the result of perfect justice.

Justice consists in the recognition of equality and the rendering of equity.

Justice, thus defined, necessarily involves a condition of absolute liberty within its sphere.

Therefore, justice is *the* condition of my happiness as well as the happiness of all that are like me. That is to say, justice is the law of human society.

Thus I, an Egoist, recognizing no rights and no duties, become, solely and simply through prudence and a desire for security, a lover of equity, equality, and universal liberty.

But there is no credit due me for my policy. If I were strong, shrewd, and skilful enough to defy all danger; if my happiness could be achieved without the aid, cooperation, and respect of others,—I might have chosen to be a tyrant, and might have led a pleasant life, surrounded by two-legged beasts of burden. Not being superior to all creation, I involuntarily have to draw a line at men, and make terms with them.

Having wisely decided to be a modest member of society, I have by no means irrevocably surrendered my freedom. I stay in it because, all things considered, it is best for me to submit rather than rebel, but I can, at any time, reconsider my course and, risking the consequences, make war upon society. Who can say that I am under any obligation to be just? Obligation? To whom? to what?[15]

The individual, once having entered the social compact, finds himself in the presence and under the influences of new impulses, new aspirations, new yearnings. He is changed, transformed, revolutionized. Social life becomes a necessity to him, not as a condition, but as an element of happiness; not as a means, but as an appreciable and weighty constituent of the desired end. He learns to know new joys and pleasures; his wants multiply; his tastes change; and he comes to feel and realize that he would never, even if he could, isolate himself from his fellow-men or try to reduce them to slavery.

This process of adaptation, or socialization, of the individual, though largely unconscious, can, nevertheless, be theoretically and objectively conceived and analyzed. In thought man can separate his Ego from the mass of humanity and discuss the wants, interests, and advantages of his person apart from it. He may not be able to effect such a separation in reality, but the illusion is so thorough that it must be discussed as if it were real.

I *imagine* I can leave society; I *think* I am free; therefore I *am* free.[16] I feel no obligation and no duties. I act for the sake of immediate or prospective personal benefits, and obey the voice of prudence.

Am I unreliable? Quite the contrary. There would have been no confusion in our modern social relations if all men possessed these ideas, just as an isolated community of desperadoes would present an example of peaceful and harmonious relations. The whole mischief arises from the fact that so many build their castles in the air. Once plant yourself on solid ground, grasp and admit these fundamental realities, and you will logically and intelligently develop a principle of conduct which will make it possible for you to pronounce judgment on all things without tracing them back to first and bottom truths.[17]

As Danton loved peace, but not the peace of slavery, so I love justice, but not the justice of moralism and idealism.

F.   "Morality and Its Origin"—John F. Kelly[*]

The most vehement critics of egoism in Liberty *were those who, like Kelly here, felt that egoists had thrown the baby (morality) out with the bathwater (hypocrisy, religion, metaphysics). They felt that human morality could be explained on a scientific basis and that some objective account of ethics was necessary for an anarchist society to hold together. For Kelly, human evolution had resulted in the development of an organic moral sentiment, an instinct which provided the essential supplement to human rationality in the actual practice of ethics. Without this moral sentiment, rational humans would not take others' liberties into account*

---

[*] February 26, 1887 (IV:16, #94), p. 7.

and anarchy would be chaos. His foil in this article is "Tak Kak," the pseudonym of James L. Walker, one of the earliest, though not the most articulate, of the advocates of egoism.

Morals are, in the primitive sense, the manners and customs of a people, and hence, in the secondary, derivative sense, good manners and customs,—that is, such as tend to perpetuate the social life. Now, the manners that best serve towards perpetuating society cannot owe their effectivity in any wise to their being the result either of statute law or of any arbitrary convention. They owe their power to their being in accord with the inherent laws of the social organism, and any departure from them must be regarded as a societary disease. Since the earliest times in the history of the race, human groups have been coming into conflict, or at least competition, with each other, and natural selection acting on them has, on the average, preserved those which best observed the societary laws,—those which at any given time were most moral. This selection, combined with the influence of heredity, has given us in each generation people less and less inclined to infringe on the rights of their neighbors, until, at last, we have, to a great extent, become what Spencer calls organically moral. . . . Observe here that this result has been obtained by selection of groups, and also that reason has had little or nothing directly to do with it. Our forefathers were not solidary because they had calculated that it was to their advantage to be so, but those groups which acted solidarily were on that account selected for survival; and now, we, the result of this process of selection going on for ages, respect the rights of others, not because we calculate that it is to our benefit to do so, so as not to provoke retaliation, but because we suffer in sympathy with the pains of others, because our moral sense is hurt when injury is done them. It is this feeling that one should so act as not to injure others that Tak Kak attacks as superstitious, merely because most of those possessing it are unable to give any rational explanation of how they come to possess it, though from the nature of the case it is not to be expected that they should have the knowledge required. As a defender of instinct, however, he might have been willing to place the moral instinct on at least as high a plane as the others . . .

Of course the popular judgment may be in error as to what is really moral; of course priests and others claiming to be the official guardians of morality have committed great outrages in its name; but our very protests against these outrages and errors are proofs of the existence of something just and true, of some standard to which human action ought to conform. Besides, were we to throw morality overboard for such reasons, liberty would have to go too.

Now as to egoism, which Tak Kak would substitute for morality. The word has two meanings, a broad scientific, and a narrow popular one. Tak Kak has never said in which sense he used it. . . . If we regard, as we may legitimately do, all forces pushing us to action as pleasures,—and all those tending to make us abstain as pains,—deprivation of pleasure being considered a pain,—then it is evident that, however we may act, we act egoistically, since we only act because the pleasures exceed the pains. . . . Taking egoism in this broad sense, however, there can be no objection to it. It in no way excludes altruistic motives as determining human actions,—altruism simply becomes one of the forms of egoism. But it is absurd, using the term in this broad sense, to talk of the *superiority* of egoism, for, in order that egoistic action should be superior, there must be some kind of action that is not egoistic. It is fair to assume, then, that, when Tak Kak writes of the superiority of egoism, he uses the word in its popular sense, and means that purely self-regarding actions are superior to other-regarding or altruistic ones. Now, if we regard social life as a benefit,—and that we do is self-evident,—this proposition is false; for though a wrong done is always followed by evil consequences, these consequences, in fact, being the proof of the wrong, yet the units constituting the social organism are so discrete in their character that the punishment of the wrongdoing may not fall on the wrong-doer,—nay, indeed, as is familiar to readers of Spencer, the ill effects may not reach the wrong-doer's class for generations. Such being the case, egoistic motives of the narrow kind can never be sufficient to restrain men from evil-doing. Some immediate sanction is required, and this sanction is found in the feeling of sympathy with the sufferings of others and the shock to the moral sense at the sight of wrong-doing.[18] Of course these feelings of sympathy and indignation are, in the broad sense of the word, just as egoistic as is the desire to profit at the expense of another; but the real question is this: When such feelings and desires come into conflict, which ought to triumph? I admit that in any given case the stronger will do so, without any regard to its being the better; but it is in our power, when the conflict is not raging, so to cultivate either set of sentiments as to tend to give that set the preponderance in the next battle . . .

Though I believe Tak Kak has advanced in many ways beyond the founder of his school, Hobbes, yet I am compelled to look on the latter as the more logical. He believed that there is no natural morality; that there is no method of action which is in itself either right or wrong; that society, instead of being an organism obeying the laws of its own nature, is merely the result of an artificial convention, a "social contract"; and, consequently, he argued that force must be lodged with some person or persons to determine the nature of, and enforce this contract. That is, from the necessity of preserving social relations and the non-existence of natural morality he deduces despotism. . . . On the other hand, the evolutionary school, which I strive to represent, . . . holds, and thinks itself able to demonstrate, that society is an organism; that consequently, like all other organisms, it must have special methods of functional activity; that neither statute law nor private contract can alter these methods except injuriously; that they can be changed beneficially only by growth . . . Through the continued evolution of society and the development of such feelings, an *equilibrium mobile* must at last be reached, in which each individual will do of his own desire, through organic morality, just that which regard for the interests of his fellows would make him do. Then we shall have reached that state which we all desire, that state in which the greatest happiness of each coincides with the good of all. This evolutionary theory of morals calls on no one for extreme self-sacrifice; it recognizes the utility, nay, the necessity, of egoism in the narrower sense; it acknowledges that a society based on pure altruism is just as impossible as one based on pure egoism; or, to put it differently, that, just as, in the one case, the individual would be reduced to misery by the destruction of society, so, in the other, society would be destroyed by the annihilation of the individual; and it simply asks, therefore, that a due balance be maintained between the egoistic and altruistic sentiments.

G.   "The Fiction of Natural Rights"—Dyer D. Lum[*]

Dyer Lum was one of the writers driven away by the egoism controversy, though in his case several other factors were also involved. A friend of several of the Haymarket defendants, he criticized Tucker's stance on

---

[*] February 15, 1890 (VI:25, #155), p. 1. Originally appeared in "Pittsburg Truth" (probably Burnette Haskell's *Truth* of San Francisco).

*that issue and, late in 1887, the two became professional rivals as Lum
took over the editorship of the Chicago anarchist paper, the* Alarm.
Although a frequent contributor in 1885–86, Lum published nothing in
Liberty *between 1888 and this article in 1890.*[19]

*In this article, Lum articulates a "soft" evolutionary position, in which
"rights" are neither immutable deductions from some theory of justice,
nor organic instincts which have evolved over the course of human
history.*[20] *Instead, the claim of a right merely indicates that a wrong has
been perceived; it is a sign of continuing social struggle, not of the
discovery of some social principle. In short, rights are rhetorical, not
teleological.*

The very corner-stone of Anarchistic philosophy is often supposed to
be a paraphrase of Herbert Spencer's "First Principle" of equal freedom,
that "Every person has a natural right to do what he wills, provided that
in the doing thereof he infringes not the equal rights of any other person."
Yet there lurks in the expression a fallacy that correct thought must
repudiate, or we must carry with us a diagram explaining the meaning of
the words we use.

What are "*natural* rights?" In the middle ages schoolmen believed that
they had solved a problem in physics asserting that "nature abhors a
vacuum"; but a very little study sufficed to convince thinkers that "the
web of events" we group as "nature" neither abhors nor likes. With the
growth of the conception of law as a term descriptive of mode of being
rather than a fiat imposed upon events, the term "natural" has lost much
of its old teleological meaning. Still it is often used in that sense and too
often implies it.

Blackstone defined "the law of nature" as "the will of man's maker."
Mackintosh calls it "a supreme, invariable, and uncontrollable rule of
conduct to all men." Sir Henry Maine also speaks of "a determinable law
of nature" for the guidance of human conduct. Kent defines it as that
"which the creator has prescribed to man." F.Q. Stuart, in his "Natural
Rights," says expressly: "A natural right is a privilege vouchsafed by
natural law to man to exercise his faculties" . . .

The correct position is, I maintain, that what we term "natural rights"
are *evolved*, not conferred, and if so they are not fixed and unalterable.
Nature confers no more "privilege" upon us than upon dogs to exercise
our faculties or functions. In fact, to my mind, the very assumption of

"natural rights" is at war with evolution. Even if we no longer personalize nature as their giver, the term still carries with it the implication of rigidity . . . Every man is supposed to have a "natural right" to life. Is this co-eternal with man? Did it exist, though unrecognized, among our prognathous ancestors? If the savage transcended "natural right" in disposing at will of the life of a captive, where was it inscribed? . . .

Is woman's "natural right" as a "person" the same in all countries under polyandry, polygamy, and monogamy? or are those relations of the sexes, so important to "well-being and good conduct," ignored by beneficent nature? It has been conclusively shown by sociologists that human progress (and there is no other) consists in passing from the militant *regime* toward an industrial one. Yet the time was when the *lex talionis* sanctified revenge as the highest virtue. Time was when not a human being on the face of the earth differed from Aristotle's opinion of slavery as a natural condition. Where was this "privilege vouchsafed by natural law" then inscribed? The question whether society would not have been far more conducive to happiness if such right had been recognized, is as idle as whether eyes behind our heads would not have been equally so. If the "Principle" was not discoverable then, but has been now, are we to conclude that it is the final synthesis of "right reason"? or that its Incarnation is only now visible?

Having thus shown a few of the queries which arise to puzzle one who seeks for evidence of the immutability of "natural rights," let us examine closer into the nature of "rights" themselves. . . . do there exist any such inherent predicates of *human* nature as "rights?" The same theological bias which characterized "rights" as "natural" also regards their assertion as positive. On the contrary, every assertion of a right purely human, paradoxical as it may seem, is negative. The assertion of a "right" is but a protest against iniquitous conditions. Social evolution ever tends to the equalization of the exercise of our faculties. That is, social intercourse has slowly evolved the Ideal that peace, happiness, and security are best attained by equal freedom to each and all . . . Privilege finds no sanction in equity as right, because it violates the ideal of social progress— equality of opportunities.

Therefore it is that, as social relations have become more complex and integrated, the Ideal of "a more perfect form of liberty" rises in the form of a protest against what only then are discernible as socially wrong, though ostensibly as assertions, such as "rights of women," "rights of labor," "rights" of children and sailors against flogging, the right to the soil, etc. They are fierce and burning assertions just so far as they emphasize a growing protest against inequitable conditions. In this sense they are Anarchistic, inasmuch as only by the extension, in other words, the abolition of restrictions, is the wrong righted. Our specific "rights" are thus dependent upon our ability to discern wrongs, or the violation of the ever-evolving industrial ideal—equality of opportunities, and exist but as protests. Abolish vested wrongs, and there will be no vested rights, natural or otherwise.

H.   "Rights and Contract"
—Benjamin Tucker v. J. William Lloyd

If rights are not natural, or even the embodiment of an evolved moral sentiment (Kelly), but are simply rhetorical complaints against some newly-perceived wrong (Lum), then it does not seem to be going far to claim, as Tucker does here, that "rights" are purely conventional. This is the culmination of individualist anarchism's rejection of the classical liberal doctrine of natural rights. Writing against J. William Lloyd, Tucker claims that "might makes right," or rather, that "might makes might" and that practical "rights" are solely the result of contracts between egoistic individuals. For that matter, the anarchist axiom of equal liberty is itself abstract until it is put into practice by contracts, general and specific.[21] Lloyd counters that unless "rights" have more weight than that given to them by contracts, they will be routinely violated, particularly against those who are weak, whether in body or mind.[22] This selection presents extracts from their exchange.

Tucker[*]

. . . The constant difficulty that besets Mr. Lloyd in his political discussions is his inability to distinguish between that which *it is right to do*—that is, that which it is necessary to do in order to attain the end in view—and that which one *has a right to do*—that is, that which one's fellows agree to let him do in peace and undisturbed. Now, the whole matter of scientific politics is a question how far we had better give each other *a right to do* that which each may think *it is right to do*. Of course

---

[*] "Rights and Contract," December 14, 1895 (XI:16, #328), pp. 4–5.

it may be said further, and correctly, that this again is but a question of what *it is right*—that is, best or necessary—to give each other *a right to do*. But, whatever the conclusion that may be reached upon this point, it is clear that it can be put into execution only through contract, agreement, between those undertaking thus to "give each other" the right determined upon. In the absence of such a contract *the right to do* does not exist at all. It has not been called into existence. Under these non-political conditions a certain course may be *right* in the sense that it is the straight course to a certain end, but *rights* in the political sense there then are none. If a man then pursue one course or another, it is solely by virtue of the fact that he has natural and non-conventional power to pursue it. We may express this loosely, as I often do, by saying that under such conditions might is right; but the phrase is not accurate. It is more accurate, and it is sufficient, to say simply that might is might, and end it there. Rights begin only with convention. They are not the liberties that exist through natural power, but the liberties that are created by mutual guarantee.

Now, supposing ourselves assembled to establish this guarantee, to make our contract, to determine what it is right, best, necessary, to give each other a right to do, Mr. Lloyd may very properly take the floor to maintain that it is not right, best, necessary, to give any human being property in another human being, and that it is right, best, necessary, to guarantee equal liberty to all human beings. *But he must prove it.* His proposition is not an axiom; it is open to dispute. Its mere assertion does not establish it; no more is it established by spelling Natural Right with a big N and a big R. . .

So far Mr. Lloyd has backed his denial of the contract *regime* by only one argument,—that society cannot be founded upon contract because no individual is under any obligation to keep his contract, and therefore it is obligatory upon his fellows to refrain from enforcing the contract upon him. The final inference is unwarrantable. It is the contrary, rather, that follows. There is no moral obligation upon the individual either to make a contract, or to keep a contract after making it; and, similarly, there is no moral obligation upon his fellows, with whom he may have made a contract, to allow him to repudiate the contract. There is no moral obligation at all on either side. A contract is made voluntarily, for mutual advantage. For its violation penalties are fixed. If a contracting party chooses to violate, he suffers these penalties, provided the other parties have the desire and power to enforce them. And that is all there is to it. Such an arrangement is shown by experience to be practicable. Therefore a society can be founded upon it . . .

Lloyd*

Rights, I contend, should always agree with *right*, and never be confounded with *powers* or *privileges*. My right to live and be free is just the same, even though my fellows deny me the power and privilege.

Mr. Tucker says my right "can only be put into execution through contract," but I am obliged to squarely disagree here, also. If any one invades me, my right may very well be *defended* by contract, but, if men will only let me alone, I shall live and be free anyway. Nature, herself, puts my right into execution. Contract may, with perfect propriety, be the servant and soldier of right, but, when it claims to be parent and owner, the order of the universe is inverted . . .

The essentially governmental character of what Mr. Tucker calls Anarchism is stated in the baldest terms when he says that: "Rights *begin* only with convention. They are not the liberties that exist through natural power, but the liberties that are *created* by mutual guarantee"—italics mine. The logic of this is that individuals who cannot understand the guarantee, who may be excluded from its benefits, or who prefer as free individuals to remain outside, have no rights whatever.

He demands, in italics, that I shall prove "that it is right, best, necessary, to guarantee equal liberty to all human beings." (I am a little suspicious of that word "guarantee" as here used. . . . Do not make a *privilege* out of a *right*, but defend the right which exists. Old-fashioned Anarchism used to lay great stress upon "mind your own business," but the new doctrine proposes to "create" and "give" rights; and even this is not sincere, for the man who "gives" me a right may withdraw his guarantee whenever his might pleases and leave me without it) . . .

But, on the other hand, Mr. Tucker must admit, too, that, in a society fully committed to the principle that the life and liberty of all should be held inviolate, he and I would be perfectly safe and as happy as our natures would permit. That is common sense, and there is no "lingo of religion" about it. And it is equally common sense to say that we would be less safe, just in proportion as our fellows disregarded or denied this

* "Loyalty and Liberty for the Human," February 8, 1896 (XI:20, #332), pp. 6-7.

principle. If contract takes the place of principle, we are safe only within the terms of the contract, and according to the pleasure of those who have the power to make and enforce it. Under Mr. Tucker's contract the moment he or I became, by age, disease, or accident, unable to understand it, we would be outlawed and legitimate objects of exploitation.

The spirit of contract is the same as the spirit of the political and legal institutions of to-day, which are all really founded on the tacit agreement among the strong that human might creates human right. Among all civilized peoples we find the fiction that rights begin and are created by law, contract, and legislative force; and this is government, and from this society is sick and rotten, and against this there is always the rebellion of the moral and instinctive nature, the appeal to rights primitive and inherent; and for this rebellion and this appeal I stand.

I. "The Liberty of Egoism"—E. Horn[*]

With its references to Stirner, Nietzsche, and Fichte, this is one of the best evidences of the influence of German philosophy on American individualist anarchism. While Tak Kak was the first to bring Stirnerite egoism to readers of Liberty, *this selection by Horn is the most comprehensive and substantial statement of egoism applied to anarchism.*

Defining liberty as the action of a self-conscious will, Horn makes individual liberty fundamentally subjective. From this view of "I," he goes on to consider the social relations among egoists ("We the free") and between egoists and those not completely self-conscious yet. Egoists, he argues, would be unable to exploit each other and would not need to exploit non-egoists. Moreover, egoists would be "socialists" in the sense that social reform would provide the challenges necessary for acting on their wills.

1.—I.

Liberty is power, says Stirner, is might. But what is might here? Might is faculty, and faculty has its root in the *will*. That we can *will* is our liberty, that we cannot always *do* as we will is our want of liberty. A great deal has been written and said concerning free will; some deny it, some

---

[*] April 7, 1894 (IX:50, #284), pp. 6–7. From the German paper *Freie Buehne.*

affirm it. This seems to me as if one should speak, for instance, of a rocky cliff. The cliff is rock, and *the will is liberty*.

To assert the will is to act. Without deed, no will. But whether the deed succeeds is a matter for itself; it does not affect the will; that remains what it is, and renews tomorrow the effort in which it failed today. It is not necessary that it should always succeed—*if* I only act! But action requires objects and tools; the latter are my physical and mental powers. Failure is explained by the difficulty of the former and the inadequacy of the latter. Here are the barriers of my *faculty*, not of my *volition*. . . .

In these barriers there is no compulsion. This I feel only when a foreign force controls me and a *foreign* will seeks to assert itself through *my* action. Against this I revolt, and only when the foreign will has become my own by virtue of my insight, only then shall I not submit myself, but still act in liberty. To do good in consequence of free insight is true virtue, and to act independently true egoism.

Liberty is dominion, says Nietzsche. Let us admit it! Who shall govern? I. Who am I?

And what shall I govern, or rather, what *can* I govern? That which I know. First of all, I know *myself*, consequently self-consciousness directs me to self-control. But myself I know only in antithesis to another: can I govern this also? Yes, if it is not already possessed,—that is, as self-conscious as I am. Men, consequently, who are worthy of the name I cannot govern, because above all others this devolves upon each one himself. . . . Besides myself, therefore, I can govern only that which cannot govern itself,—that is, animate and inanimate nature. But every person whose self-consciousness is aroused will decline foreign government.

Liberty is consequently self-government and self-control. The former is the subjective, the latter the objective side of sovereignty . . .

Others shall not govern me. I will be my own master; for, if I am not, I come under the dominion of others. Just get drunk,—that is, relinquish your self-control; there is also an end to your self-government, and boys make sport of you. Only he can be autonomous who bridles himself.

But what do I govern in me? If I am the object, what becomes of the subject? The ego is consequently capable of analysis. I govern my body . . . I govern my instincts and passions for the sake of my self-determination; so far as they are rooted in the body, this comes under the above. My feelings,—that is, I do not allow feelings of pleasure and pain to cause me to act contrary to reason. What can still be governed in me? I am master of my conduct, however, only when I am conscious of my conduct,—that is, when I act logically. But in this I am also master of my reason, as I make use of it. Am I then superior to my thoughts? They come and go, but I seize them, I command them and put them on paper here. But in itself ideation, like feeling, is a passive state; solely active, manifesting my being, realizing myself, and asserting my existence, I am only in volition. What still remains, therefore, of the ego from which I cannot escape? *The will.* Can I also govern my will? No; for, if I posit it as the object, the subject disappears. *My will*, that *is I*. I = will = sovereignty = liberty = life.

. . . The will itself, that is the only liberty of man . . .

Am *I* still superior to my will? Can I make use of it? No, that's meaningless. I act because I am, and I am because I act. Only where I am wholly thrown back on my own resources, where I rest within myself, where I am wholly I, am I *free*; but this is the case where I *will*. My will, that is I, that is my liberty, my absoluteness . . .

My will is the expression of my existence; it becomes visible in the manifestation of being, which is identical with the struggle for existence. The question: *Must* I act? is synonymous with *Must* I live?

The will is always present—not the will to live, it is rather itself life,—that is, energy. But it requires aims, objects, in order to assert itself, to express its individuality.

I am attracted by some aim. What does that mean? What are final causes to me? My imagination anticipates the result of an action, it promises pleasure, I consider whether and how I can achieve it, then my will appears on the surface or it does not appear: accordingly I act or do not act.

Pleasure is the food of the will; for the value of every pleasure lies in this,—that it maintains and intensifies activity. But activity is will, is life. It is consequently for its own sake that the will seeks pleasure. But pleasure beckons not only at the end; it begins even with the first step and becomes keener the nearer the end, until it finally reaches its culmination. Then it breaks off, and a new aim allures me.

The will is energy, but strength grows by exercise; consequently the will grows richer by asserting itself. Richer in what? In will. It never consumes itself, but draws ever anew on itself; it is the true *perpetuum mobile*. Its manifestation is at the same time enjoyment; expenditure and income coincide; *the will is self-enjoyment, and to enjoy life is to enjoy one's self* . . .

Liberty! Do you now know what liberty is? You clamor for it. I tell you: *Be* free, for you are free! No other liberty can come to you except that which you carry *within* you. You are you, an ego, a will, wholly for yourselves, resting within yourselves; what more do you want? Is that not liberty enough? *Of what more*, then, do you want to be free?

Others shall not govern you. Well, it lies with you: govern yourselves and be sovereigns; no other will then get you in his power; you are nearest to yourselves. But so you are: as against those above you, you prate and declaim about liberty, because you think not-to-be-ruled is part of it, Anarchists that you are!—and, as against those below you, you exercise force, because you seek liberty in the dominion over others, despots that you are! But how now, if those on top will not listen to you and those below will not be governed? Then continue a slave, Anarchist! Then tremble, despot! How can you be free, if, *in order* to be free, you have *need* of others? Liberty is not outside of you; this kingdom of heaven is *within* you! . . .

If the will is my liberty, what, then, is the meaning of my want of liberty? It is the condition of liberty, and is included in the will. This sounds paradoxical, but it is not. All individuality signifies limitation; consequently also all individual volition is limited. If I always could as I would, I should not aspire to anything. The Almighty has no aspirations; to him the conception of liberty does not apply; the boundless cannot act. And the omnipotent person would die of *ennui* as well as he who is impotent.

My want of liberty, that is the object of my will. No will without deed, but no deed where there are no obstacles to be overcome. These obstacles curtail your liberty? Lazy fellow! They are the very guarantee of your life; for to live is to strive, to work. You *are* only in so far as you act; and therein precisely consists your liberty,—that you assert yourself as against these obstacles! Only *will* strongly; that is, *be* strongly what you *are*! Your manifestation of being is your struggle for existence . . .

The problem of the freedom of the human will ought not henceforth to trouble anyone. My will is not free, it is rather my whole freedom. As soon as I have recognized this, I no longer seek liberty, I shall neither beg for it nor steal it from others; for I have it. *The self-conscious is the free*
. . .

2.—WE.

Alone immediately I find myself, me, the free, the self-conscious, the particular individual and owner, as Stirner says. So resting within myself I cast about me, an aspirant as against nature and against other persons. Both are to me objects and therefore also resistances of the volition. To test my selfhood against them, to assert myself, I take to be the foundation and purpose of my life. If I *will* no longer, I *am* no longer. But, as long as I *will*, I *am*.

Nature appears to me as heterogeneous, strange, puzzling, terrible; men appear to me as homogeneous, as of the same essence. The former I seek to explore and put in the service of my will; with the latter I harmonize if they are of the same kind as I,—that is, if will meets will. . . . Are the other people of the same kind as I,—that is, free, sovereign? I make a test, and, if I find such, I recognize them as myself, and say: *We the free*.

We pride ourselves on our liberty, and this pride is our morality: we are on "yonder side of good and bad."

For morality,—what is it? Nothing surely except the mode of living together, of the intercourse of men. . . . How men have acted and do act we can learn by studying their past conduct; how they will continue to act we can infer from their—that is, our—character, which is selfishness. But who tells us, and who has a right to tell us, how we *shall* act? Is there a need of "morality" in this sense? Nietzsche justly makes of this morality itself a problem.

Slaves receive precepts of conduct; the free is his own lawgiver. . . . All "moral systems" presuppose the unfree, and because liberty is in such a plight today,—St. Manchester has betrayed and sold it,—the unbelieving world prates so much about ethics.

We the free have no need of "morality." Our mutual respect and recognition is only the result of our pride,—that is, the appreciation of our own ego,—and the principle of our conduct is selfishness. Of course, not selfishness as commonly understood, which seeks pleasure at the expense of others; rather the selfishness which aims to realize itself in positive work, or—as Hedda Gabler says—"to order life according to its idea." "Each shall do that which only he shall and only he can do, and which, if he does not do, will certainly remain undone in this standing community of individuals" (Fichte)—with this consciousness the free is imbued. The free is the good, because he is true, brave, high-minded, temperate; for lying, cowardice, baseness, extravagance do not agree with the inner liberty. The free govern themselves, because each individual is his own sovereign. This does not preclude the election by them of a *primus inter pares*, but they dispense with the guardianship of "governors" and "proprietors." Outward, politico-social liberty is only the reflection of inner, personal liberty. Inner liberty demands Anarchy. *We the free are Anarchists*, because we are sovereigns and do not require the government of others. Not overmen are we; we only do not wish to be undermen.

Not all men are free in our sense. For ages slavery has existed on the earth, and slavery produces a servile spirit which transmits itself. But all are destined for liberty. What is the relation of the free to the unfree? He does not recognize them as his equals; they are beneath him. He uses them, if he does not ignore them; for he has no need of them. . . . The more he esteems himself as the free, the more he slights those who are not what by their human form they ought to be,—the unfree, the cowardly, the base. Here meet the great contempt and the great pity.

We the free are pure egoists, such as Stirner demands. And it is precisely this egoism which unites us, paradoxical as it may sound. Our socialism is only an extended egoism: for what we concede to one another in the shape of honors and rights returns to each individual (Nietzsche, "Jenseits von Gut und Boese"). We love our neighbors really as ourselves. Is this Christian command not traceable to egoism as the *primum movens*?

But what becomes then of the task of humanity? Aye, what becomes of it? Where is it? Who sets it? What is its name? We must labor for the commonweal, we must espouse the cause of progress—who thinks so? Each labors, thinks, and creates as the spirit moves him. . . . So the free works in accordance with his nature, because he must—or what is the same thing with him—because he will. The pressure of life impels him, and the will is his life. It is possible that his thoughts and deeds work a benefit to mankind; experience teaches that this has often been the case. . . . It is neither a virtue nor a duty to work for the commonweal. Nevertheless this work will not remain undone; the common egoism of the unfree as well as the nobler egoism of the free will see to that . . .

We the free,—there is still another bond which unites us besides that inner bond of mutual respect and recognition; it is that of our common dependence on nature in respect to the struggle for existence, and our common need of it in regard to the manifestation of being.

That dependence we share with all living creatures, but the free, the proud, revolt against it, and in their displeasure consume themselves when sickness compels them to inaction. Therefore all their thinking and striving is directed toward lessening this dependence,—that is, toward exploring nature and placing it under their dominion. Science is a matter of free spirits. The food instinct compels indeed also the unfree to work upon nature, but the free do not aim merely at securing material prosperity; to them nature with all its manifestations, including human society, is rather the objective point for the realization of liberty; they work indeed also *in order* to live, but also *because* they live. Their will demands an object upon which it may spend itself. And the free *knows* what he *wants*. So it is not alone the distress of life, but also the joy of creating which unites the free spirits. *We the free* are the *true Socialists*, and we solve the social problem as far as it may be solved. Our sense of liberty, our pride, revolts at the sight of social misery and human helplessness, but our love of knowledge and our love of work search for relief. For the misery of men is the enemy of their liberty, because in the long run it leads to a paralysis of the will. But this is to be considered as on a par with death. If we combat misery, we combat the want of liberty and make men of men.

Notes

1. G.B. Shaw, "What's In a Name?" *Liberty*, April 11, 1885 (III:8, #60), p. 7. Originally appeared in a London paper, *Justice*.
2. Locke is cited favorably in *Liberty*'s reprinting of Burke's "Vindication of Natural Society," but his economic views are briefly criticized in Lysander Spooner, "A Letter to Grover Cleveland," Section XIII, November 14, 1885 (III:17, #69), p. 6; Tak Kak, "Spencer and George—II," April 22, 1893 (IX:34, #268), p. 2. In only three other instances is he mentioned at all, and that casually, rather than substantively.
3. The first two are not cited at all, and "On Liberty" is briefly criticized by Stephen Pearl Andrews in "Love, Marriage, and Divorce," January 19, 1889, (VI:11, #141), p. 2 and by G. Bernard Shaw in "A Degenerate's View of Nordau," July 27, 1895 (XI:6, #318), p. 4 and cited favorably by Vilfredo Pareto, "Letters from Italy. IV.," October 5, 1889 (VI:21, #151), p. 6.
4. See also Tucker, "Do Liberals Know Themselves?" February 4, 1882 (I:14, #14), p. 2.
5. In an early reference, Tucker put it succinctly: "Spencer . . . is as much of an anarchist, if he only knew it, as was Proudhon himself. For his theory of social

evolution from militancy to industrialism means the eventual abolition of the state."
("On Picket Duty," December 10, 1881 [I:10, #10], p. 1)

6. See, for instance, Yarross, "Intelligence and Conduct," October 5, 1889 (VI: 21, #151, p. 4). The methodological terms used here are borrowed from Comte, who was influential among some of the anarchists.

7. "An Apology," *Liberty*, November 12, 1892 (IX:11, #245), p. 1.

8. See, for example, "Extracts from the Works of Nietzsche," December 17, 1892 (IX:16, #250), pp. 1,4; "From Nietzsche's 'Morgenroethe,'" August 24, 1895 (XI:8, #320), pp. 7-8; "Nietzsche on Egoism," April 18, 1896 (XI:25, #337), pp. 7-8; "Aphorisms from Nietzsche," July 1899 (XIII:12, #362), p. 6.

9. Eunice Minette Schuster, *Native American Anarchism*, New York: Da Capo Press, 1970 (originally published in *Smith College Studies in History* 17 (1931-32); William O. Reichert, *Partisans of Freedom: A Study in American Anarchism*, Bowling Green: Bowling Green University Popular Press, 1976; Lewis Perry, *Radical Abolitionism: Anarchy and the Government of God*, Ithaca: Cornell University Press, 1973.

10. The classic statement of this view, often for sale by Tucker, was Michael Bakunin's *God and the State*. In *Liberty*, see Tucker, "The Twin Children of Tyranny," March 17, 1883 (II:8, #34), p. 3; Tucker, "Anarchy Necessarily Atheistic," January 9, 1886 (III:21, #73), p. 4; J.B. Robinson, "Is Anarchism Atheistic?" June 30, 1894 (X:4, #290), pp. 2-3. For a more sympathetic portrayal of Christianity, see Stephen T. Byington, "Anarchism and Christianity," June 16, 1894 (X:3, #289), p. 6.

11. Tucker later criticized the reissuance of Spencer's first book, *Social Statics*, without the crucial chapter "The Right to Ignore the State" ("On Picket Duty," May 21, 1892 [VIII:40, #222], p. 1).

12. These were subsequently collected in a book of essays by Spencer, *The Man Versus the State*, London: 1884.

13. Other useful articles on Spencer by Yarros include "The Basis of Individualism," July 20, 1889 (VI:18, #148), p. 4; "Man versus the State," March 8, 1890 (VI:26, #156), pp. 4-5; and "Spencer's 'Justice,'" August 8, 1891 (VIII:9, #191), p. 2 (the initial notice for the work upon which the longer series is based).

14. A few years before, Yarros had been an egoist and had denied the existence of rights (see his selection below, "The Reasons Why"), but he defended the concept now as a corollary of the law of equal freedom.

15. After Yarros had abandoned his egoism, Tucker reprinted this article under the title "Obligation? To whom? to what?" and suggested that Yarros had fallen prey to the same disease as Spencer, abandonment of youthful radicalism.

16. This essentially subjective meaning of freedom is characteristic of egoism, at least as discussed in *Liberty*. See the selection below by Horn as well as Tak Kak, "Egoism," April 9, 1887 (IV:19, #97), pp. 5-7.

17. The claim that egoism is "realistic" is again characteristic of egoism in *Liberty*. See Tak Kak, "Reply to John F. Kelly," July 2, 1887 (IV:24, #102), p. 7.

18. This is what Spencer referred to as the "sentiment" of justice, as opposed to its rational codification in an "idea" of justice (see Yarros' "Justice and Anarchism" (in *Liberty*) for discussion of this point).

19. Lum's most significant contribution was a long series entitled "Eighteen Christian Centuries: or the Evolution of the Gospel of Anarchy. An Essay on the Meaning of History," which ran from May 22, 1886 (IV:3, #81, pp. 2-3) to October 30, 1886 (#82-88).

20. Later, Lum was to move toward the second position which, like John Kelly, he called "evolutionary ethics" ("The Basis of Morals," *Monist*, July 1897, pp. 554–570).
21. See, for example, Benjamin Tucker, "Rights," March 4, 1893 (IX:27, #261).
22. The "weak" individuals that Lloyd has particularly in mind are children, for this debate evolved out of an earlier one over whether children are property (see chapter 9).

3

Libertarian Socialism

Just as Pierre-Joseph Proudhon's statement "Property is theft" is usually misunderstood, so it is easy to misunderstand Benjamin Tucker's claim that individualist anarchism was part of "socialism." Yet before Marxists monopolized the term, socialism was a broad concept, as indeed Marx's critique of the "unscientific" varieties of socialism in the *Communist Manifesto* indicated. Thus, when Tucker claimed that the individualist anarchism advocated in the pages of *Liberty* was socialist, he was not engaged in obfuscation or rhetorical bravado. He (and most of his writers and readers) understood socialism to mean a set of theories and demands that proposed to solve the "labor problem" through radical changes in the capitalist economy. Descriptions of the problem varied (e.g., poverty, exploitation, lack of opportunity), as did explanations of its causes (e.g., wage employment, monopolies, lack of access to land or credit), and, consequently, so did the proposed solutions (e.g., abolition of private property, regulation, abolition, or state ownership of monopolies, producer cooperation, etc.). Of course, this led to a variety of strategies as well: forming socialist or labor parties, fomenting revolution, building unions or cooperatives, establishing communes or colonies, etc. This dazzling variety led to considerable public confusion about socialism, and even considerable fuzziness among its advocates and promoters.

Tucker, ever the definer, tried to clarify the conceptual relationships between socialism, anarchism, communism, and the many other specters that haunted America at the end of the nineteenth century.[1] The classic attempt at this was his 1890 speech "State Socialism and Anarchism: How Far They Agree, And Wherein They Differ" (the first selection below). In this address, he states that socialism's basic demand is that "labor should be put in possession of its own" and describes the two poles of socialism, state socialism and anarchism. The differences in economic reforms between these two could be traced to the differences in their general principles: state socialism employed authority while anarchism preferred liberty. This had implications beyond economics, for state socialism would tend to extend authority into every social sphere, while anarchism would demand more liberty. Nevertheless, both were socialist, a point Tucker reaffirmed in 1892.[2] Although economic reform (putting labor "in possession of its own") was central to individualist anarchism in *Liberty*, it was not the exclusive concern, nor even a foundational one. Thus, although many of the criticisms of state socialism turn on economic principles or proposals, some are more fundamental, dealing with the implications of its authoritarian methods. While state socialists had the proper instincts and sympathies (toward labor), their logic and reasoning was confused. Liberals, on the other hand, tended to sympathize with the bourgeoisie and this clouded their logic enough so that they could not follow through on their libertarian tendencies. In *Liberty*, then, liberals and anarchists could argue together as fellow libertarians, while state socialists and anarchists could argue together as fellow socialists.

Although many of the ephemeral currents of socialism were grist for criticism in *Liberty*,[3] the two most important targets were Marxism and anarchist-communism. Because of its putative ideological similarity to individualist anarchism, the anarchist-communism of Johann Most and the anarchists of the International Working-People's Association, was subjected to some bitter criticism, particularly in the period of the latter's dramatic growth, from 1884 to 1886. Led by "X" (Henry Appleton), this attack focused on the covert and overt authoritarian tendencies and violent strategy of the anarchist-communists (see selections B, C, and D) and culminated in an expose of an arson scam in March 1886, just before the Haymarket incident.[4] Marxism received little notice in the early years of *Liberty* (the major exception being Tucker's obituary of Marx in 1883; selection E), primarily because Marxism as a political force was moribund in the early 1880s. The Socialist Labor Party had split during the 1880 presidential election over whether to support the Greenback candidate and had shrunk in membership as the revolutionary anarchist movement grew. After Haymarket, however, socialist and labor parties (including the SLP) had a resurgence and it became useful to point out individualist anarchism's differences with Marxism. Besides the economic differences, which will be dealt with more in part two, the selection below from Yarros (F) criticizes the narrowness of Marx's analysis, particularly its economic determinism, while the selection from Bouhelier (G) emphasizes the authoritarian tendencies of the Marxist movement. All in all, writers in *Liberty* followed Tucker's basic criticism of non-anarchist socialism, its reliance on authority.

Further Reading in Liberty

The most scholarly treatment of the various currents of socialism in *Liberty* was Yarros' "Unscientific Socialism" (anarchism was "scientific" to him): June 21, 1890 (VII:4, #160), pp. 6-7 (continues #161-164). Yarros surveys, in order of increasing importance: Christian Socialism, Bellamy's Nationalism, Marxism, Fabian socialism, and anarchist communism.

Tucker's "plumb-line" of liberty is further explored in an exchange between Yarros and W.D.P. Bliss over the latter's proposal for "voluntary state socialism" (Yarros, "Voluntary State Socialism," July 27, 1895 (XI:6, #318), pp. 10-11; Bliss, (#322, p. 6); Yarros (#322, pp. 2-3); Bliss (#336, pp. 6-7); Yarros [#336, pp. 2-4]). Yarros argues that, even if the state allowed private groups to compete with it in providing services, it would still hold considerable (and unjust) advantages.

A.   "State Socialism and Anarchism: How Far They Agree, And Wherein They Differ"—Benjamin Tucker[*]

Along with "The Relation of the State to the Individual," this is the most frequently anthologized and reprinted of Tucker's writings, for many of the same reasons. It exemplifies Tucker's style and his major concerns, as well as offering some general insight into his intents as a critic.

For Tucker, individualist anarchism is part of the broad socialist movement which aims to put labor "in possession of its own." More

---

[*] March 10, 1888 (V:16, #120), pp. 2-3, 6. This address was presented a number of times, for example to the Manhattan Liberal Club on January 27, 1888, to the Liberal League of Newark on January 29, 1888 to the Round Table of Boston on February 9, 1888, and to the Anarchists' Club of Boston February 12, 1888 (Tucker, "On Picket Duty," February 11, 1888 [VI:14, #118], p. 1).

specifically, it is the pole of that movement that stresses liberty, rather than authority. The authoritarian pole, state socialism, would solve the problem of monopolies by establishing one giant monopoly under state control, a project logically connected to the expansion of authority in all social realms. The libertarian pole, anarchism, would solve the same problem by abolishing the "four monopolies" (of land, money, tariffs, and patents). This would socialize the effects of capital, rather than capital itself (as state socialism would do), and thus make capital a tool, rather than the master, of labor.

Probably no agitation has ever attained the magnitude, either in the number of its recruits or the area of its influence, which has been attained by Modern Socialism, and at the same time been so little understood and so misunderstood, not only by the hostile and the indifferent, but by the friendly, and even by the great mass of its adherents themselves. This unfortunate and highly dangerous state of things is due partly to the fact that the human relationships which this movement—if anything so chaotic can be called a movement—aims to transform, involve no special class or classes, but literally all mankind; partly to the fact that these relationships are infinitely more varied and complex in their nature than those with which any special reform has ever been called upon to deal; and partly to the fact that the great molding forces of society, the channels of information and enlightenment, are well-nigh exclusively under the control of those whose immediate pecuniary interests are antagonistic to the bottom claim of Socialism that labor should be put in possession of its own . . .

For it is a curious fact that the two extremes of the vast army now under consideration, though united, as has been hinted above, by the common claim that labor shall be put in possession of its own, are more diametrically opposed to each other in their fundamental principles of social action and their methods of reaching the ends aimed at than either is to their common enemy, the existing society. They are based on two principles the history of whose conflict is almost equivalent to the history of the world since man came into it; and all intermediate parties, including that of the upholders of the existing society, are based upon a compromise between them . . .

The two principles referred to are AUTHORITY and LIBERTY, and the names of the two schools of Socialistic thought which fully and unreservedly represent one or the other of them are, respectively, State Socialism and Anarchism. Whoso knows what these two schools want and how they propose to get it understands the Socialistic movement. For, just as it has been said that there is no half-way house between Rome and Reason, so it may be said that there is no half-way house between State Socialism and Anarchism. There are, in fact, two currents steadily flowing from the centre of the Socialistic forces which are concentrating them on the left and on the right; and, if Socialism is to prevail, it is among the possibilities that, after this movement of separation has been completed and the existing order has been crushed out between the two camps, the ultimate and bitter conflict will be still to come. . . . What a final victory for the State Socialists will mean, and what a final victory for the Anarchists will mean, it is the purpose of this paper to briefly state.

To do this intelligently, however, I must first describe the ground common to both, the features that make Socialists of each of them.

The economic principles of Modern Socialism are a logical deduction from the principle laid down by Adam Smith in the early chapters of his "Wealth of Nations,"—namely, that labor is the true measure of price. But Adam Smith, after stating this principle most clearly and concisely, immediately abandoned all further consideration of it to devote himself to showing what actually does measure price, and how, therefore, wealth is at present distributed. Since his day nearly all the political economists have followed his example by confining their function to the description of society as it is, in its industrial and commercial phases. Socialism, on the contrary, extends its function to the description of society as it should be, and the discovery of the means of making it what it should be. Half a century or more after Smith enunciated the principle above stated, Socialism picked it up where he had dropped it, and, in following it to its logical conclusions, made it the basis of a new economic philosophy.

This seems to have been done independently by three different men, of three different nationalities, in three different languages: Josiah Warren, an American; Pierre J. Proudhon, a Frenchman; Karl Marx, a German Jew . . . [5] That the work of this interesting trio should have been done so nearly simultaneously would seem to indicate that Socialism was in the air, and that the time was ripe and the conditions favorable for the appearance of this new school of thought . . .

From Smith's principle that labor is the true measure of price—or, as Warren phrased it, that cost is the proper limit of price—these three men made the following deductions: that the natural wage of labor is its product; that this wage, or product, is the only just source of income (leaving out, of course, gift, inheritance, etc.); that all who derive income from any other source abstract it directly or indirectly from the natural and just wage of labor; that this abstracting process generally takes one of three forms, interest, rent, and profit; that these three constitute the trinity of usury, and are simply different methods of levying tribute for the use of capital; that, capital being simply stored-up labor which has already received its pay in full, its use ought to be gratuitous, on the principle that labor is the only basis of price; that the lender of capital is entitled to its return intact, and nothing more; that the only reason why the banker, the stockholder, the landlord, the manufacturer, and the merchant are able to exact usury from labor lies in the fact that they are backed by legal privilege, or monopoly; and that the only way to secure to labor the enjoyment of its entire product, or natural wage, is to strike down monopoly.

It must not be inferred that either Warren, Proudhon, or Marx used exactly this phraseology or followed this line of thought, but it indicates definitely enough the fundamental ground taken by all three and their substantial thought up to the limit to which they went in common . . .

It was at this point—the necessity of striking down monopoly—that came the parting of their ways. Here the road forked. They found that they must turn either to the right or to the left,—follow either the path of Authority or the path of Liberty. Marx went one way; Warren and Proudhon the other. Thus were born State Socialism and Anarchism.

First, then, State Socialism, which may be described as *the doctrine that all the affairs of men should be managed by the government, regardless of individual choice.*

Marx, its founder, concluded that the only way to abolish the class monopolies was to centralize and consolidate all industrial and commercial interests, all productive and distributive agencies, in one vast monopoly in the hands of the State. The government must become banker, manufacturer, farmer, carrier, and merchant, and in these capacities must suffer no competition. Land, tools, and instruments of production must be wrested from individual hands and made the property of the collectivity. To the individual can belong only the products to be consumed, not the means of producing them. A man may own his clothes and his food, but not the sewing-machine which makes his shirts or the

spade which digs his potatoes. Product and capital are essentially different things; the former belongs to individuals, the latter to society.[6]
Society must seize the capital which belongs to it, by the ballot if it can,
by revolution if it must. Once in possession of it, it must administer it on
the majority principle through its organ, the State, utilize it in production
and distribution, fix all prices by the amount of labor involved and
employ the whole people in its workshops, farms, stores, etc. The nation
must be transformed into a vast bureaucracy, and every individual into a
State official. Everything must be done on the cost principle, the people
having no motive to make a profit out of themselves. Individuals not
being allowed to own capital, no one can employ another, or even
himself. Every man will be a wage-receiver, and the State the only wage
payer. He who will not work for the State must starve, or, more likely,
go to prison. All freedom of trade must disappear. Competition must be
utterly wiped out. All industrial and commercial activity must be centered
in one vast, enormous, all-inclusive monopoly. The remedy for *monopolies* is MONOPOLY . . .

What other applications this principle of Authority, once adopted in
the economic sphere, will develop is very evident. It means the absolute
control by the majority of all individual conduct. The right of such control
is already admitted by the State Socialists, though they maintain that, as
a matter of fact, the individual would be allowed a much larger liberty
than he now enjoys. But he would only be allowed it; he could not claim
it as his own. There would be no more rights; only privileges. Such liberty
as might exist would exist by sufferance and could be taken away at any
moment. Constitutional guarantees would be of no avail. There would
be but one article in the constitution of a State Socialistic country: "The
right of the majority is absolute."

The claim of the State Socialists, however, that this right would not
be exercised in matters pertaining to the individual in the more intimate
and private relations of his life is not borne out by the history of
governments. It has ever been the tendency of power to add to itself, to
enlarge its sphere, to encroach beyond the limits set for it; and where the
habit of resisting such encroachment is not fostered, and the individual
is not taught to be jealous of his rights, individuality gradually disappears
and the government or State becomes the all-in-all. Control naturally
accompanies responsibility. Under the system of State Socialism, therefore, which holds the community responsible for the health, wealth, and

wisdom of the individual, it is evident that the community, through its majority expression, will insist more and more on prescribing the conditions of health, wealth, and wisdom, thus impairing and finally destroying individual independence and with it all sense of individual responsibility.

Whatever, then, the State Socialists may claim or disclaim, their system, if adopted, is doomed to end in a State religion, to the expense of which all must contribute and at the altar of which all must kneel; a State school of medicine, by whose practitioners the sick must invariably be treated; a State system of hygiene, prescribing what all must and must not eat, drink, wear, and do; a State code of morals, which will not content itself with punishing crime, but will prohibit what the majority decide to be vice; a State system of instruction, which will do away with all private schools, academies, and colleges; a State nursery, in which all children must be brought up in common at the public expense; and, finally, a State family, with an attempt at stirpiculture, or scientific breeding, in which no man and woman will be allowed to have children if the State prohibits them and no man and woman can refuse to have children if the State orders them. Thus will Authority achieve its acme and Monopoly be carried to its highest power.

Such is the ideal of the logical State Socialist, such the goal which lies at the end of the road that Karl Marx took. Let us now follow the fortunes of Warren and Proudhon, who took the other road,—the road of Liberty.

This brings us to Anarchism, which may be described as *the doctrine that all the affairs of men should be managed by individuals or voluntary associations, and that the State should be abolished.*

When Warren and Proudhon, in prosecuting their search for justice to labor, came face to face with the obstacle of class monopolies, they saw that these monopolies rested upon Authority, and concluded that the thing to be done was, not to strengthen this Authority and thus make monopoly universal, but to utterly uproot Authority and give full sway to the opposite principle, Liberty, by making competititon, the antithesis of monopoly, universal. They saw in competition the great leveller of prices to the labor cost of production. In this they agreed with the political economists. The query then naturally presented itself why all prices do not fall to labor cost; where there is any room for incomes acquired otherwise than by labor; in a word, why the usurer, the receiver of interest, rent, and profit, exists. The answer was found in the present one-sidedness of competition. It was discovered that capital had so manipulated legislation that unlimited competition is allowed in supplying productive labor, thus keeping wages down to the starvation point, or as near it as practicable; that a great deal of competition is allowed in supplying distributive labor, or the labor of the mercantile classes, thus keeping, not the prices of goods, but the merchants' actual profits on them, down to a point somewhat approximating equitable wages for the merchants' work; but that almost no competition at all is allowed in supplying capital, upon the aid of which both productive and distributive labor are dependent for their power of achievement, thus keeping the rate of interest on money, of house rent and ground-rent, and of manufacturers' profits on patent-protected and tariff-protected goods, at as high a point as the necessities of the people will bear.

On discovering this, Warren and Proudhon charged the political economists with being afraid of their own doctrine. The Manchester men were accused of being inconsistent. They believed in liberty to compete with the laborer in order to reduce his wages, but not in liberty to compete with the capitalist in order to reduce his usury. *Laissez faire* was very good sauce for the goose, labor, but very poor sauce for the gander, capital. But how to correct this inconsistency, how to serve this gander with this sauce, how to put capital at the service of business men and laborers at cost, or free of usury,—that was their problem.

Marx, as we have seen, solved it by declaring capital to be a different thing from product, and maintaining that it belonged to society and should be seized by society and employed for the benefit of all alike. Proudhon scoffed at this distinction between capital and product. He maintained that capital and product are not different kinds of wealth, but simply alternate conditions or functions of the same wealth; that all wealth undergoes an incessant transformation from capital into product and from product back into capital, the process repeating itself interminably; that capital and product are purely social terms; that what is product to one man immediately becomes capital to another, and *vice versa*; that, if there were but one person in the world, all wealth would be to him at once capital and product; that the fruit of A's toil is his product, which, when sold to B, becomes B's capital (unless B is an unproductive consumer, in which case it is merely wasted wealth, outside the view of social economy); that a steam engine is just as much product as a coat, and that a coat is just as much capital as a steam-engine; and that the same laws of equity govern the possession of the one that govern the possession of the other.

For these and other reasons Proudhon and Warren found themselves unable to sanction any such plan as the seizure of capital by society. But, though opposed to socializing the ownership of capital, they aimed nevertheless to socialize its effects by making its use beneficial to all instead of a means of impoverishing the many to enrich the few. And when the light burst in upon them, they saw that this could be done by subjecting capital to the natural law of competition, thus bringing the price of its use down to cost,—that is, to nothing beyond the expenses incidental to handling and transferring it. So they raised the banner of Absolute Free Trade; free trade at home, as well as with foreign countries; the logical carrying out of the Manchester doctrine; *laissez faire* the universal rule. Under this banner they began their fight upon monopolies, whether the all-inclusive monopoly of the State Socialists, or the various class monopolies that now prevail.

Of the latter they distinguished four of principal importance,—the money monopoly, the land monopoly, the tariff monopoly, and the patent monopoly.

First in the importance of its evil influence they considered the money monopoly, which consists of the privilege given by the government to certain individuals, or to individuals holding certain kinds of property, of issuing the circulating medium, a privilege which is now enforced in this country by a national tax of ten per cent. upon all other persons who attempt to furnish a circulating medium and by State laws making it a criminal offence to issue notes as currency. It is claimed that the holders of this privilege control the rate of interest, the rate of rent of houses and buildings, and the prices of goods,—the first directly, and the second and third indirectly. For, say Proudhon and Warren, if the business of banking were made free to all, more and more persons would enter into it until the competition should become sharp enough to reduce the price of lending money to the labor cost, which statistics show to be less than three fourths of one per cent. In that case the thousands of people who are now deterred from going into business by the ruinously high rates they must pay for capital with which to start and carry on business will find their difficulties removed. If they have property which they do not desire to convert into money by sale, a bank will take it as collateral for a loan of a certain proportion of its market value at less than one percent discount. If they have no property, but are industrious, honest, and capable, they will generally be able to get their individual notes endorsed by a sufficient number of known and solvent parties; and on such business paper they will be able to get a loan at a bank on similarly favorable terms. Thus interest will fall at a blow. The banks will really not be lending capital at all, but will be doing business on the capital of their customers, the business consisting in an exchange of the known and widely available credits of the banks for the unknown and unavailable, but equally good, credits of the customers, and a charge therefor of less than one percent, not as interest for the use of capital, but as pay for the labor of running the banks. This facility of acquiring capital will give an unheard-of impetus to business, and consequently create an unprecedented demand for labor,—a demand which will always be in excess of the supply, directly the contrary of the present condition of the labor market. Then will be seen an exemplification of the words of Richard Cobden that, when two laborers are after one employer, wages fall, but, when two employers are after one laborer, wages rise. Labor will then be in a position to dictate its wages, and will thus secure its natural wage, its entire product. Thus the same blow that strikes interest down will send wages up. But this is not all. Down will go profits also. For merchants, instead of buying at high prices on credit, will borrow money of the banks at less than one percent, buy at low prices for cash, and correspondingly reduce the prices of their goods to their customers. And with the rest will go house-rent. For no one who can borrow capital at one percent with which to build a house of his own, will consent to pay rent to a landlord at a higher rate than that. Such is the vast claim made by Proudhon and Warren as to the results of the simple abolition of the money monopoly.

Second in importance comes the land monopoly, the evil effects of which are seen principally in exclusively agricultural countries, like Ireland. This monopoly consists in the enforcement by government of land titles which do not rest upon personal occupancy and cultivation. It was obvious to Warren and Proudhon that, as soon as individuals should no longer be protected by their fellows in anything but personal occupancy and cultivation of land, ground rent would disappear, and so usury have one less leg to stand on.

Third, the tariff monopoly, which consists in fostering production at high prices and under unfavorable conditions by visiting with the penalty of taxation those who patronize production at low prices and under favorable conditions. The evil to which this monopoly gives rise might more properly be called *mis*usury than usury, because it compels labor to pay, not exactly for the use of capital, but rather for the misuse of capital. The abolition of this monopoly would result in a great reduction in the prices of all articles taxed, and this saving to the laborers who consume these articles would be another step toward securing to the laborer his natural wage, his entire product . . .

Fourth, the patent monopoly, which consists in protecting inventors and authors against competition for a period long enough to enable them to extort from the people a reward enormously in excess of the labor measure of their services,—in other words, in giving certain people a right of property for a term of years in laws and facts of Nature, and the power to exact tribute from others for the use of this natural wealth, which should be open to all. The abolition of this monopoly would fill its beneficiaries with a wholesome fear of competition which would cause them to be satisfied with pay for their services equal to that which other laborers get for theirs, and to secure it by placing their products and works on the market at the outset at prices so low that their lines of business would be no more tempting to competitors than any other lines.

The development of the economic programme which consists in the destruction of these monopolies and the substitution for them of the freest competition led its authors to a perception of the fact that all their thought rested upon a very fundamental principle, the freedom of the individual, his right of sovereignty over himself, his products, and his affairs, and of rebellion against the dictation of external authority. Just as the idea of taking capital away from individuals and giving it to the government started Marx in a path which ends in making the government everything and the individual nothing, so the idea of taking capital away from government-protected monopolies and putting it within easy reach of all individuals started Warren and Proudhon in a path which ends in making the individual everything and the government nothing. If the individual has a right to govern himself, all external government is tyranny. Hence the necessity of abolishing the State. This was the logical conclusion to which Warren and Proudhon were forced, and it became the fundamental article of their political philosophy. It is the doctrine which Proudhon named An-archism, a word derived from the Greek, and meaning, not necessarily absence of order as is generally supposed, but absence of rule. The Anarchists are simply unterrified Jeffersonian Democrats. They believe that "the best government is that which governs least," and that that which governs least is no government at all. Even the simple police function of protecting person and property they deny to governments supported by compulsory taxation. Protection they look upon as a thing to be secured, as long as it is necessary, by voluntary association and cooperation for self-defence, or as a commodity to be purchased, like any other commodity, of those who offer the best article at the lowest price. . . . Compulsory taxation is to them the life-principle of all the monopolies, and passive, but organized, resistance to the tax-collector they contemplate, when the proper time comes, as one of the most effective methods of accomplishing their purposes.

Their attitude on this is a key to their attitude on all other questions of a political or social nature. In religion they are atheistic as far as their own opinions are concerned, for they look upon divine authority and the religious sanction of morality as the chief pretexts put forward by the privileged classes for the exercise of human authority. "If God exists," said Proudhon, "he is man's enemy." And, in contrast to Voltaire's famous epigram, "If God did not exist, it would be necessary to invent him," the great Russian Nihilist, Michael Bakounine, placed this antithetical proposition: "If God existed, it would be necessary to abolish him." But although, viewing the divine hierarchy as a contradiction of Anarchy, they do not believe in it, the Anarchists none the less firmly believe in the liberty to believe in it. Any denial of religious freedom they squarely oppose.

Upholding thus the right of every indiviudal to be or select his own priest, they likewise uphold his right to be or select his own doctor. No monopoly in theology, no monopoly in medicine. Competition everywhere and always; spiritual advice and medical advice alike to stand or fall on their own merits. And not only in medicine, but in hygiene, must this principle of liberty be followed. The individual may decide for himself not only what to do to get well, but what to do to keep well. No external power must dictate to him what he must and must not eat, drink, wear, or do.[7]

Nor does the Anarchistic scheme furnish any code of morals to be imposed upon the individual. "Mind your own business" is its only moral law. Interference with another's business is a crime and the only crime, and as such may properly be resisted. In accordance with this view the Anarchists look upon attempts to arbitrarily suppress vice as in themselves crimes. They believe liberty and the resultant social well-being to be a sure cure for all the vices. But they recognize the right of the drunkard, the gambler, the rake, and the harlot to live their lives until they shall freely choose to abandon them.

In the matter of the maintenance and rearing of children the Anarchists would neither institute the communistic nursery which the State Socialists favor nor keep the communistic school system which now prevails. The nurse and the teacher, like the doctor and the preacher, must be selected voluntarily, and their services must be paid for by those who patronize them. Parental rights must not be taken away, and parental responsibilities must not be foisted upon others.

Even in so delicate a matter as that of the relations of the sexes the Anarchists do not shrink from the application of their principle. They acknowledge and defend the right of any man and woman, or any men and women, to love each other for as long or as short a time as they can, will, or may. To them legal marriage and legal divorce are equal absurdities. They look forward to a time when every individual, whether man or woman, shall be self supporting, and when each shall have an independent home of his or her own, whether it be a separate house or rooms in a house with others; when the love relations between these independent individuals shall be as varied as are individual inclinations and attractions; and when the children born of these relation shall belong exclusively to the mothers until old enough to belong to themselves.

Such are the main features of the Anarchistic social ideal. There is wide difference of opinion among those who hold it as to the best method of attaining it. Space forbids the treatment of that phase of the subject here. I will simply call attention to the fact that it is an ideal utterly inconsistent with that of those Communists who falsely call themselves Anarchists while at the same time advocating a *regime* of Archism fully as despotic as that of the State Socialists themselves. And it is an ideal that can be as little advanced by the forcible expropriation recommended by John Most and Prince Kropotkine[8] as retarded by the brooms of those Mrs. Partingtons of the bench who sentence them to prison; an ideal which the martyrs of Chicago[9] did far more to help by their glorious death upon the gallows for the common cause of Socalism than by their unfortunate advocacy during their lives, in the name of Anarchism, of force as a revolutionary agent and authority as a safeguard of the new social order. The Anarchists believe in liberty both as end and means, and are hostile to anything that antagonizes it.

B. "Anarchism, True and False"—Henry Appleton*

Henry Appleton was the most forceful critic of anarchist communism in the early 1880s, charging that it was really communism hiding behind the label of anarchism. In particular, he charged that Johann Most's followers proposed to violently destroy all existing institutions and then to build their own utopia on this scorched earth without tolerating any opposition. This violence, institution-building, and fear of competition was "false anarchism" that helped to discredit the true article.[10]

There seems to be no end of those singularly ordered minds who can conceive of no radical system of reform except something is to be torn down, ripped up, blown to pieces, or annihilated after some terrible fashion. These persons will have it that the Anarchist is a mere destructionist,—that he is bent upon levelling down all existing institutions. They see blood in his eye and dynamite in his boots as they sadly inquire: "Well, what do you propose to substitute in their place, after you have levelled down all existing institutions?"

The philosophy of Anarchism has nothing whatever to do with violence, and its central idea is the direct antipodes of levelling. It is the very levelling purpose itself projected by republican institutions against which it protests. It is opposed, root and branch, to universal suffrage, that most mischievous levelling element of republics. Its chief objection to the existing State is that it is largely communistic, and all communism rests upon an artificial attempt to level things, as against a social development resting upon untrammelled individual sovereignty. Sifted to its elements, the government of the United States is after all nothing but a mild form of State Socialism. The true Anarchist indicts it largely on this very ground. He is opposed to all manner of artificial levelling machines. How pitiful the ignorance which accuses him of wanting to level everything, when the very integral thought of Anarchism is opposed to levelling!

Unfortunately for the integrity of true Anarchistic thought, there is a class of ranting enthusiasts who falsely call themselves Anarchists, but

---

* September 6, 1884 (II:24, #50), p. 4.

who have in reality never repudiated the central idea upon which the existing State is founded. As types of these we may cite Burnette G. Haskell of the San Francisco "Truth"[11] and Johann Most of the "Freiheit." The class represented by Haskell are State Socialists who, while shouting the battle cry of "the revolution" and calling for the overthrow of existing institutions, have absolutely nothing more in their proposed machine than an enlargement of the destructive central principle which generates all that is reprehensible in the existing order. These men want more government, more centralization, more absorption of individual concerns by the central machine,—in short, in the last analysis, *more politics*. They are not Anarchists in the light of individualistic thought. They are masquerading in a livery that does not belong to them.

Herr Most occupies the still more ridiculous position of a State Communist, if indeed such a term is comprehensible. Communism is indeed levelling, and hence Anarchism is utterly and radically opposed to it. Communism being impossible in Nature, its propagandism and proposed realization can rest upon nothing short of violence. Herr Most boldly accepts the situation; hence he would destroy and confiscate property by whatever methods might seem effectual, sparing not the torch, dynamite, or any of the terrible devices of Pluto. He would assassinate rich men by the wholesale, and drive all enemies of his schemes from the earth. When the morning sun of successful revolution shall rise, he would then organize all the concerns of men into communes and level all human conditions with a vengeance. Yet Herr Most calls himself an Anarchist. I would not disturb him in whatever satisfaction he may find in that name but for the very serious reason that he is no Anarchist at all. The man who wrote "Die Eigenthums-Bestie" [The Beast of Property] expresses the very methods of remedial organization which it is the bottom purpose of Anarchism to protest against. All Communism, under whatever guise, is the natural enemy of Anarchism, and a Communist sailing under the flag of Anarchism is as false a figure as could be invented.

The Anarchist does not want to destroy all existing institutions with a crash and then inaugurate the substituting process on their ruins. He simply asks to be let alone in substituting false systems *now*, so that they may gradually fall to pieces by their own dead weight. He asks the humble privilege of being allowed to set up a free bank in peaceable competition with the government subsidized class bank on the opposite corner. He asks the privilege of establishing a private post office in fair competition with the governmentally established one. He asks to be let alone in establishing his title to the soil by free occupation, cultivation, and use rather than by a title hampered by vested rights which were designed to keep the masses landless. He asks to be allowed to set up his domestic relations on the basis of free love in peaceable competition with ecclesiastically ordered love, which is a crime against Nature and the destroyer of love, order, and harmony itself. He asks not to be taxed upon what has been robbed from him under a machine in which he has practically no voice and no choice. In short, the Anarchist asks for free land, free money, free trade, free love, and the right to free competition with the existing order at his own cost and on his own responsibility,—liberty.

Is there any violence in all this? Is there artificial levelling? Finally, is there any want of readiness to substitute something in the place of what we condemn? No, all we ask is the right to peaceably place Liberty in fair competition with privilege. Existing governments are pledged to deny this. Herein will reside the coming struggle. Who is the party of assault and violence? Is it the Anarchist, simply asking to be let alone in minding his own business, or is it the power which, aware that it cannot stand on its own merits, violently perpetuates itself by crushing all attempts to test its efficiency and pretensions through peaceable rivalry?

C.   "The Two Socialisms"—A. H. Simpson[*]

Simpson here offers an egoist critique of communism: it is not scientific, but rather religious or sentimental. Although he uses the term "communism," he means to include, indeed to target, the communist anarchists. Since Haymarket and the debate with Most, many of the individualist anarchists simply called the communist anarchists "communists," denying that they deserved the "anarchist" label. In a sense, this is an extension of Tucker's critique of state socialism to the communist anarchists.[12]

We hear of all sorts of Socialism now-a-days. There is scientific Socialism and sentimental Socialism; Christian Socialism and Bellamy Socialism; Bismarckian and Fabian; and a writer in London "Freedom"

---

[*] August 10, 1889 (VI:19, #149), p. 6.

has been endeavoring to make a distinction between Collectivist and Communist Anarchism; so that the ordinary reader must get considerably mixed in his ideas as to what Socialism really is.

Any one of these schools must necessarily be either more or less Communistic, or more or less Anarchistic, and between them there is one fundamental difference,—the difference between liberty and authority, altruism and egoism, slavery and freedom. There can be no compromise and no blending.

Anarchism is egoism; Communism is altruism. (I do not use these terms here in the sense of the evolutionary school of ethics, but in the sense of orthodox moralists.) Herein is the weak point of Communism. It is the same old superstition that has propped up all the theologies and all the tyrannies,—the "duty" of the individual to sacrifice himself to God, the State, the community, the "cause" of anything, a superstition that always makes for tyranny. This idea, whether under Theocracy or Communism, will result in the same thing—always authority. Communism, notwithstanding its pretensions to be scientific, is purely religious and sentimental. In so far as it is sentimental only it is powerless for evil, though a terrible hindrance to true development. But in so far as it is religious it is dangerous.

The difference between Communism and Anarchy is plainly observable in their methods. Abolish the State (by discrediting the idea of authority)—that bulwark of the robber system, the fortress of tyranny, says the Anarchist. Abolish private property, the source of all evil and injustice, the parent of the State, says the Communist. And he attempts to be scientific, parades the historical-development theory, and ridicules what he calls the Anarchists' folly of fighting effects rather than the cause, private property. Abolish private property by instituting compulsory Communism, and the State will go, he says; having no function to perform, it must die of itself.

Now Anarchists are not opposed to private property, except it is defined as the sum of legal privilege, but we may go on with the argument. Shall we abolish the State, or private property? The Anarchist knows very well that the present State is an historical development, that it is simply the tool of the property-owning class; he knows that primitive accumulation began through robbery bold and daring, and that the freebooters then organized the State in its present form for their own self-preservation. But how did the small property class manage to main-

tain the State against the large non-property class? The property class
never did *all* the fighting (once they did lead the fighters; now they do
not, but hire leaders); they had to have an immense army of the propertyless to do the unskilled work in the fighting. How did they get the
consent of the governed? How did they manoeuvre "the people" into
fighting for property instead of against property? Why are they fighting
for property instead of for themselves now? It is no use shutting our eyes
to the fact that they do so. Let John Most or Lum or Louise Michel[13] start
the fighting for Communism tomorrow, and who will fight against them?
The propertyless. And how has this come about? Simply by teaching the
idea that is inherent in Communism, or patriotism, or governmentalism,
or religion of any sort,—renunciation, altruism, duty, sacrifice to the
particular spook then uppermost: God, country, cause or principle. Ask
any ignorant soldier why he fights. Is it the German soldier's interest to
kill the French soldier, or *vice versa*? Is it to the personal interest of the
Jingo-drunk English volunteer to be sent to Asia or Africa to maintain
British supremacy? Does the young American citizen, who is ready to
shoulder a musket to put down Anarchism or Socialism, reason it out that
it is for his personal interest to risk being blown up with dynamite bombs?
Are any of these people self-conscious egoists? Not one. They are all
altruists, ready to self-sacrifice. The property class know well that spooks
are as necessary as the police to support the State, and that dissolving
spooks is more dangerous to them than killing policemen, and so the
preaching class, ministers and politicians, are well paid for teaching
man's duty to God and the citizen's duty to the State. "Society must be
preserved," howled Grinnell;[14] he did not say, "the property of my clients,
the Citizens' League, must be protected": that would have been too thin;
even a *bourgeois* jury is ceasing to be too scrupulous about property.
"Shall our institutions be destroyed by a horde of foreign Socialists,"
shrieked his assistant counsel, and society answered "No," and a few of
the people in a jury box, with the sanction of the community outside,
exterminated the "enemies of society." They sacrificed them for the good
of the community—at least they thought it was for the good of the
community; their mistake was one of fact. If they think it for the good of
the community to suppress Communism, they will do so. When they
become Communists, and think it for the good of the community to
suppress Anarchists, they will do so—it will be their "duty."

And so, after all, by abolishing private property, should we abolish the State? By no means. Other States existed before the present one, or rather the present State is nothing but the old machine modified to suit present economic ideas. . . . The State existed before this terrible "beast of private property" was ever conceived, and will survive as long as individual rights are ignored and the rights of the community made supreme; and under Communism the good of the community is paramount to the good of the individual.

Of course the argument applies only to aggressive Communists, like the revolutionists of the Most school, and not to the sentimental or Christian Communists who believe in teaching the brotherhood of men. Neither does it apply to the Anarchist-Communist who "hopes" that the outcome of Anarchy will be Communism, and whose hope sometimes takes the form of prophecy. If they are Anarchists first and then Communists, they are good Anarchists: whether the outcome will be Communism or vegetarianism or Dianism is a matter for speculation. My argument applies to those who make the leading idea Communism, who insist on Communism first, last, and all the time, who are willing to tag any tail to Communism, Anarchy preferred. To that school Anarchism— with no tag and no prefix—offers undivided opposition. For such Communism cannot exist without a State. Voluntary Communism can exist and, if successful, flourish under Anarchy, even if its votaries desire to have their individuality submerged in the crowd. But the Communist, like all opponents of free competition, dreads an open and fair field, where the fittest can survive. Liberty is dangerous to Communism, as it is to all present State institutions. The revolutionary Communist wants all the field, or his ideas can't have a fair chance. The principle of private property must be stamped out, and if any seedling of this idea should be overlooked and at any time shoot forth little sprouts, *they* must be crushed immediately.

D.   "Unscientific Socialism: Anarchist Communism" —Victor Yarros[*]

From his survey of major socialist currents, this excerpt finds Yarros making two points against anarchist communism. The first is charac- teristic of his Spencerian emphasis on progress: even if truly voluntary

* extract from part V, August 2, 1890 (VII:8, #164), pp. 6-7.

(not instituted or maintained by force), communism would not be likely to flourish under anarchy because it's more suited to a simple society, not to a complex, industrial one. The second suggests that communism could only be maintained by force, and thus that it could not be anarchistic.

Among those who designate themselves by this name of Anarchistic Communists, two different schools should be distinguished. There are those who hold that under a condition of perfect liberty the inherent beauty of the Communistic principle would, agreeably to the law of natural selection, speedily gain general acceptance and become the prevailing method of social organization. They would not institute a Communistic system by force, but would seek to prove theoretically and practically the supremacy of such a system, depending upon the reason of emancipated humanity. Their ideal is voluntary Communism, which they intend to reach by the Anarchistic method,—the method of trusting to individual liberty, the unmatched educator and elevator. Then there are those who plot the forcible suppression of the entire system of industrial liberty and private property; who hold that there is no way of eliminating exploitation of labor by capital save by abolishing private enterprise and organizing Communistic control and enjoyment of wealth.

It is not necessary to suggest to men of mental culture that those who predict universal Communism as the outcome of individual liberty are without any rational ground for their prediction. The evidence is all against their hypothesis. Men are becoming more and more individualized, and their modes of living more and more diversified. Variety, not uniformity, appears to be the law of development, dissimilarity, not sameness, differentiation, not simplification in combination, originality, not colorlessness. The higher the society in the scale of development, the greater its complexity, the more numerous and pronounced the distinctive differences, both of character and function, of its units. To expect or believe that Communistic methods will predominate in such an advanced society is obviously irrational, unless such a superabundance of material wealth is postulated as would do away with all care or anxiety about the proper use and distribution of it, to which case all objections to Communism are inapplicable. But it is unprofitable to dwell upon this position, since it has no bearing upon the present situation.

Referring to the Communists of the second type, attention should be directed to two considerations. In the first place, . . . it is plain that they have no case worth looking into. The process of reasoning by which they arrive at the conclusion that private property is incompatible with economic equity and that absolute Communism in the ownership of wealth alone can heal the wounds of modern society is identical with the one employed by the other Socialists. . . . But even if they could really demonstrate the truth of their doctrine, they would be far from justified in claiming to stand for voluntary or Anarchistic Communism. They have no right to assume the acquiescence of the whole society in their constructive reforms, much less to ignore the protests of those who openly oppose them. In proposing to force a system upon society they are guilty of tyrannical designs and invasive intentions. Honesty should prompt the frank confession that compulsory Communism is preferred by them to inequality in liberty, that the element of tyranny in society is less repugnant to them than the element of economic exploitation. In pretending to abhor arbitrary government and political despotism, in professing to desire individual liberty above all, these Communists manifest either incapacity or insincerity, and are much inferior to their consistent and logical opponents, who squarely espouse the principle of majority rule and reject that of individual liberty.

E.   "Karl Marx as Friend and Foe"—Benjamin Tucker[*]

Reflecting his broad definition of socialism as well as his hostility to state socialism, Tucker offers here an ambivalent obituary of Karl Marx. Though he admired Marx's critique of capitalism and his devotion to equality, he detested his authoritarian methods and proposals. Moreover, he denied that Marx was the father of socialism generally, and suggested that Proudhon was a "greater man" than Marx.[15]

By the death of Karl Marx the cause of labor has lost one of the most faithful friends it ever had. Liberty says thus much in hearty tribute to the sincerity and hearty steadfastness of the man who, perhaps to a greater extent than any other, represented, by nature and by doctrine, the principle of authority which we live to combat. Anarchism knew in him its bitterest enemy, and yet every Anarchist must hold his memory in respect.

---

* April 14, 1883 (II:9, #35), p. 2.

Strangely mingled feelings of admiration and abhorrence are simultaneously inspired in us by contemplation of this great man's career. Toward the two fundamental principles of the revolution to-day he occupied an exactly contradictory attitude. Intense as was his love of equality, no less so was his hatred of liberty. The former found expression in one of the most masterly expositions of the infamous nature and office of capital ever put into print; the latter in a sweeping scheme of State supremacy and absorption, involving a practical annihilation of the individual. The enormous service done by the one was well-nigh neutralized by the injurious effects resulting from his advocacy of the other. For Karl Marx, the *egalitaire*, we feel the profoundest respect; as for Karl Marx, the *autoritaire*, we must consider him an enemy. Liberty said as much in its first issue, and sees no reason to change its mind. He was an honest man, a strong man, a humanitarian, and the promulgator of much vitally important truth, but on the most vital question of politics and economy he was persistently and irretrievably mistaken.

We cannot, then, join in the thoughtless, indiscreet, and indiscriminate laudation of his memory indulged in so generally by the labor press and on the labor platform. Perhaps, however, we might pass it by without protest, did it not involve injustice and ingratitude to other and greater men. The extravagant claim of precedence as a radical political economist put forward for Karl Marx by his friends must not be allowed to overshadow the work of his superiors. . . . The tendency and consequences of capitalistic production were demonstrated to the world time and again during the twenty years preceding the publication of "Das Kapital," with a wealth of learning, a cogency and subtlety of reasoning, and an ardor of style to which Karl Marx could not so much as pretend. In the numerous works of P.J. Proudhon, published between 1840 and 1860, this notable truth was turned over and over and inside out until well-nigh every phase of it had been presented to the light . . .

We stand ready to give volume, chapter, and page of [Proudhon's] writings for the historical persistence of class struggles in successive manifestations, for the *bourgeoisie*'s appeal to liberty and its infidelity thereto, for the theory that labor is the source and measure of value, for the laborer's inability to repurchase his product in consequence of the privileged capitalist's practice of keeping back a part of it from his wages, and for the process of the monopolistic concentration of capital and its disastrous results. The vital difference between Proudhon and Marx is to be found in the respective remedies which they proposed. Marx would nationalize the productive and distributive forces; Proudhon would individualize and associate them. Marx would make the laborers political masters; Proudhon would abolish political mastership entirely. Marx would abolish usury by having the State lay violent hands on all industry and business and conduct it on the cost principle; Proudhon would abolish usury by disconnecting the State entirely from industry and business and forming a system of free banks which would furnish credit at cost to every industrious and deserving person and thus place the means of production within the reach of all. Marx believed in compulsory majority rule; Proudhon believed in the voluntary principle. In short, Marx was an *autoritaire*, Proudhon was a champion of Liberty.

Call Marx, then, the father of State socialism, if you will; but we dispute his paternity of the general principles of economy on which all schools of socialism agree. To be sure, it is not of the greatest consequence who was first with these doctrines. As Proudhon himself asks: "Do we eulogize the man who first perceives the dawn?" But if any discrimination is to be made, let it be a just one. There is much, very much, that can be truly said in honor of Karl Marx. Let us be satisfied with that, then, and not attempt to magnify his grandeur by denying, belittling, or ignoring the services of men greater than he.

F.   "Unscientific Socialism: Marxian Socialism"—Victor Yarros[*]

In another excerpt from his series, Yarros offers a somewhat more substantial critique of Marx than was typical in Liberty. *In the strictly economic realm, Yarros argues that Marx was too narrow in attributing the exploitation of labor solely to wage-employment by capitalists. By exploring other sources of exploitation, it would be possible to end exploitation without relinquishing competition. This narrowness extended to Marx's underlying philosophy, Yarros felt. He charged that Marx's theories of the development of ideas and social change were too simplistic because of their economic determinism.*

For those exclusively occupied with the contemplation of the labor market and with the relation between buyers and sellers of labor-power,

---

* Excerpted from parts III and IV: July 12, 1890 (VII:6, #162), pp. 6–7; July 26, 1890 (VII:7, #163), pp. 6–8.

we can easily understand that it is very natural to arrive at the simple conclusion that only expropriation of the present capitalists and the common ownership and control of the means of production will do away with the exploitation of the laborer. But this is not a scientific, but a superficial method. It is necessary to go back of the labor market, to resolve "surplus value" into the elements composing it, and to discover the laws of each of them. That Marx's analysis of the present industrial system is imperfect to a degree of worthlessness may be perceived without difficulty. The assumption that surplus value or profit wholly comes from labor is obviously false. Under the monopolies of the tariff and patents large profits may obviously be obtained from other sources than the labor-power of the workmen. Then, we find no attempt at an analysis of the law of rent and of the law of interest, without which it is impossible to have a proper insight into the present industrial order, to say nothing of constructing plans of a better social organization. Surplus value is the result of the excess of the supply over the demand in the labor market; it is obvious that if it were possible to alter this condition and either to decrease the supply or increase the demand to the point at which labor could dictate its terms to capital and insist on absorbing profits, the competitive principle might remain without the phenomenon of labor-exploitation, deemed by Marx inseparable from it, reappearing. The omission to analyze "surplus value," the treating of all forms of usury as a single category, relieved Marx from the necessity of considering the question whether the excess of the supply of labor over the demand was really a necessary consequence of industrial liberty, or whether certain forms of exploitation might be abolished and the reward of labor raised without changing the competitive system in its essentials. But such an analysis unavoidably leads to the rejection of Marxian conclusions. When it is seen that one form of exploitation, rent, is due to the monopoly in land sustained by the State in the interest of the landlord; that another form of exploitation, interest, is the result of monopoly of credit, a monopoly which limits the demand of labor and deprives capitalists and laborers of the opportunity of engaging in industrial and commercial enterprises; that profits are the result of the monopoly of industry and commerce, concentrated in fewer and fewer hands,—the conclusion is inevitable that the abolition of all these monopolies rather than the abolition of private enterprise, that the extension of freedom rather than

the suppression of the competitive system, is the remedy and the solution
. . .

But Marx's error proceeded not alone from his failure to subject our industrial order to a deeper analysis and grasp the true causes of surplus value. This one-sided view of economic development was predetermined by his general philosophy, by the view he took of men and their different affairs. His philosophy was false, and his economics unsound, but it is precisely this connection, this harmony, between the two that gave Marxian teaching a peculiar charm and appearance of solidity and profundity. When his disciples, ignorant of this consideration, attempt to paraphrase his doctrine without making the philosophy prominent, their weakness and poverty become painfully apparent.

Marx states in his preface [to Capital] that his philosophy is antithetical to Hegelianism, and that he regards the material, economic basis of society as the only real force which shapes and colors in its own image all the rest of men's interests. He held the political, social, and religious relations to be the reflex of the material, economic structure, changing with it, but contributing no independent influence of their own to the change. To expect to effect a change in the industrial relations through political or moral agencies was deemed puerile, since, from the standpoint adopted, the political arrangements, the moral laws, the religious beliefs, all appeared as the results of the economic relations. His standpoint, says Marx, "from which the evolution of the economic formation of society is viewed as a process of natural history, can less than any other make the individual responsible for relations whose creature he socially remains." He is impatient with what he styles "the very cheap sort of sentimentality" which characterizes the capitalist method of defining the value of labor-power as "brutal." For, while it is clear that "nature does not produce on the one side owners of money or commodities, and on the other men possessing nothing but their own labor-power," and that neither is the social basis of capitalism "one that is common to all historical periods," yet "it is clearly the result of a past historical development, the product of many economical revolutions, of the extinction of a whole series of older forms of social production." On the other hand, he dismissed with haughty contempt the objections against his positive plans raised by those who cultivated an attachment to the principle of personal liberty and private property. To him liberty and property were *bourgeois* terms and ideas, having no meaning or value apart from the general *bourgeois* theory and practice; and when the time comes for the downfall of the entire *bourgeois* edifice, no attention needs to be wasted on its minor ornamental appendages.

Marx, however, nowhere furnishes his own adequate explanation of the causes and factors of economic revolutions, and we do not feel called upon to cudgel our brain for the purpose of supplying this material omission. Whatever it may have been, we can unhesitatingly pronounce his philosophy of history totally absurd. With the results of the labors of the anthropologists, sociologists, and historians accessible to us, it is impossible not to know that the subordination of the social, political, and religious interests to the economic structure never existed, and that often industrial changes followed political and moral changes. At all times the actions and reactions of these distinct departments of human life have been such that it is almost impossible to say which has been the most decisive and powerful. The fatalism of Marx must be discarded in the light of the investigations of Spencer, Maine, Lubbock, Tyler, and Comte. And we find that modern progressive Socialists, like the Fabians, have discarded it and recognize the conception of a sociological science teaching men to intelligently and wisely build up a social order based on equity and justice. Nothing was farther from Marx's thoughts than such a conception. And therefore nothing is farther from the thoughts of scientific thinkers and students today than the Marxian view of social evolution. Nearly all thinkers are agreed that the problems agitating us at present—which are many, political and social as well as industrial— can only be solved by men applying themselves to a scientific study of them, by a free and full discussion, and by conscious deliberate action in accordance with truths evolved and discovered in the process of such study and discussion.

G.   "The Soul of Man Under Socialism"
—M. Saint-Georges de Bouhelier[*]

In 1907, Tucker published this critique of the goings-on at a Socialist congress, conveniently penned by a participant. It convincingly makes

[*] October 1907 (XVI:4, #400), pp. 45–49. Tucker's note: "The attractive essay to which Oscar Wilde gave the above title has done not a little mischief by encouraging people in the error that the goal, liberty, may be reached by the route of authority. For this reason I give the same title, in quotation marks, to the following portrayal (rendered in English from the French) of the effect that Socialism has had upon the soul of man so far. The picture is the more telling because painted by a

Tucker's point about Marxism's extension of authority to all realms, in this case the intellectual. Alluding to the religious character of socialist organization, it demonstrates that the intellectual mediocrity often attributed to institutionalized Marxism was not a problem of Stalinism, or even of "democratic centralism," but had roots at least as deep as the Second International.

Stuttgart is at present the seat of solemn assizes, where one may observe the method of laying the foundations of a creed. It is strange that, at the moment when Catholic discipline is falling into dissolution, another discipline is taking shape, equally minute and equally atrabilarious. For even more than at Amsterdam and at the previous Socialist congresses there is to be seen at Stuttgart a cavilling and well-nigh frantic passion for subjection. Not all who wish are welcome, and one is worthy of admission only if one is unified. Already there have been abundant exclusions from which there is no appeal, and heresy threatens everybody . . .

By taking away even the right to think they can hardly hope to please those who find their glory in thought. Their first step in expropriation is the seizure of intelligence. I doubt if, as a result, talent will gravitate in their direction. . . . It does not seem to me that any one of value will be desirous of having his inner liberty absorbed by the mass.

For there is one thing certain: here no one can ever pretend to prevail. No man has any importance if he thinks for himself; he soon finds himself completely alone; originality attracts suspicion, strips off power, annihilates. If you do not wish to act with the crowd, you will be taxed with infamy. For there is no truth save that approved by the federations or committees, national or other. Notice, moreover, that in this party the chiefs themselves are under universal control, and that they lead you less than you lead them. You, the numerous mass, the enormous anonymity, the variable and floating mystery of the wrangling-halls, you have the mastery of Jaures or Bebel, and, instead of the wise man thinking for the ignorant, the innumerable absurdity of the fanatical and illiterate multitude substitutes itself for the wise man and imposes itself upon him. Is there a more deplorable sight, one that inspires greater pain, than that of such minds in a condition of servitude? . . .

---

man whose bias is in favor of the Socialistic solution of economic problems, M. Saint-Georges de Bouhelier. It appeared in "L'Aurore" during the Stuttgart congress."

In the narrow circle of the federations no one keeps his will intact; no individual has the power to intervene according to his own conception. When he is on the point of rising to express his wish, the frightful and obscure party spirit seizes him, so to speak, by the arm, and nine times out of ten he is forced to keep his seat under the threat of heresy. The "changing infallibility" of the doctrine admits no initiative and no escape; at the present moment you must act so and so, and the sole decision to be taken is a matter of edict. Indeed, it is needless to discuss with oneself this affair or that; examine the resolutions of the last congress; there you will find your orders, and you will follow them. Accept them without any if or buts; this is the only orthodox course—until the next congress.

Next year it may be detestable or unworthy to accept them; what is taught to-day as peremptory is not absolute. What say you? That you are a patriot? And until when? As yet the party is patriotic. But let it cease, by an official vote, to be so, and no longer can you be patriotic either. . .

On points still under discussion you can follow your own tendency; but, so soon as the doctrine of the congress is formulated, you will have no right to act upon any other. However, there is nothing irremediable; as the party changes its opinion on all subjects, each one is permitted to hope that chance may effect a reconciliation. But for the moment you are to obey. Whoso bends to the regnant idea is never wrong, and one is a right-thinking man if, instead of guiding himself in his own fashion, he conforms to the party. In all matters the party substitutes itself for you. On the subject of God or country; for the daily or the extraordinary; on matters of a private nature and of domestic life; on the subject of wages, labor contracts, and affairs national or international,—on all these the party has its own ideas which it imposes upon us, and its principles alone are good. Outside the party all is wickedness and abomination. That is the general sentiment among the unified.

I know very well, however, what they say: we do not wish to enslave the individual, but, on the contrary, to free him. Meantime you take away his prime possession,—his liberty to think. The mystic, magnificent, inexhaustible treasure; that which neither persecutions or miseries or the worst misfortunes diminish; that which makes of the dirty and wretched beggar, if he is conscious of his intellectual wealth, a noble hero and the most royal king,—this you filch from everyone who joins you. And no one withdraws save at his peril. I see in this a great human danger. You have created a new authority, and, with fine phrases about healthy liberation on your lips, you organize the basest of servitudes; under pretext of liberating yourselves, you begin a course of opposition to the State, but under orders of a party more hostile to the individual than any State. In favor of our desires for freedom you labor to reestablish obscurantism. You complain of tyrannies and oppressions and religions, and, with the versatile errors of your crowds, you establish your active and mobile dogmatism. Is it from the wisdom of the great man that you derive your conceptions and your principles? No, it is from the *Consensium Omnium*. With you individuals are objects of suspicion. Among you intelligence is ill at ease; it inspires apprehension, and suffers therefrom. Be sure that real talent will less and less go toward you in sincerity. For your whole organization is hostile to it; your committees and your congresses plot its ruin; you want fanatical slaves, not frank and free thinkers.

Notes

1. See, for example, Tucker's "Two Kinds of Communism," September 3, 1881 (I:3, #3), p. 3, and "Those Three Awful Isms," November 25, 1882 (II:4, #30), pp. 2-3. See also Edgeworth, "Socialist Superstitions," April 11, 1885 (III:8, #60), p. 5.
2. Tucker, "A Denial and a Challenge," May 21, 1892 (VIII:40, #222), p. 3; "The Mistakes of Merlino," July 16, 1892 (VIII:47, #229), p. 3.
3. A good example of this was the contemptuous treatment accorded to Bellamy's "Nationalism," a fad based on his novel, *Looking Backward*. One writer said that it was dull and made him long for the bad old days of capitalism (Hubert Bland, "A State Socialist on 'Looking Backward,'" June 29, 1889 (VI:17, #147), pp. 7-8). Tucker consistently ridiculed Nationalism: "On Picket Duty," March 16, 1889 (VI:14, #144), p. 1; "On Picket Duty," June 8, 1889 (VI:16 #146), p. 1; January 25, 1890 (VI:24, #154), p. 5; April 19, 1890 (VII:1, #157), p. 8.
4. Tucker, "The Beast of Communism," March 27, 1886 (III:26, #78), pp. 1, 8. The article's title was a reference to Most's pamphlet "The Beast of Property." Although Most was not directly involved, some of his close associates were and Tucker's charges caused considerable stir among the anarchist-communists.
5. Warren (1798-1874) is generally acknowledged to have been the first significant anarchist thinker in America. Proudhon (1809-1865) was a controversial and contradictory man and the first to appropriate the term "anarchist" proudly.
6. [Tucker's note]: A friend to whom this manuscript was shown and who finds himself in general sympathy with its positions makes the criticism that the distinction between capital and product here attributed to Marx was not made by him, although it is urged by all his disciples. In my judgement it is fairly attributable to Marx himself. It is included in the very ground-work of his economic system, in his explanation of the two processes between which he draws a line,—merchandise-money-merchandise and money-merchandise-money. To avoid misunderstanding it should be noted that the claim is not put forward that Marx based this distinction upon moral grounds, but simply that he considered it a matter of economic necessity.

7. This emphasis on medicine and hygiene reflects American anarchism's legacy as part of what R. Laurence Moore has called the antebellum "sisterhood of reforms," which included many varieties of hygiene, and various practices of medicine. By the late nineteenth century, "unconventional" medical practices were coming under sustained attack by those attempting to "professionalize" medicine.

8. John (Johann) Most was a notorious German exile who arrived in the United States in 1883 and galvanized the newly organizing collectivist anarchist movement by preaching the virtues of dynamite. Peter Kropotkin (indeed a prince from an old Russian family) was the dominant figure in European anarchism and an important theoretician of communist anarchism.

9. The "martyrs of Chicago" were the four men charged, and convicted (without any direct evidence), of conspiracy in throwing a bomb that killed seven police officers at the Haymarket Square on May 4, 1886. Three of their co-defendants received prison terms, one (Louis Lingg) committed suicide in prison, and the four (Albert Parsons, August Spies, Adolph Fischer, and George Engel) were executed November 11, 1887.

10. See also his "Reform Machinists," April 25, 1885 (III:9, #61), p. 4; "Individualist Visionaries," June 20, 1885 (III:11, #63), p. 4; and Tucker, "Two Kinds of Communism," September 3, 1881 (I:3, #3), p. 3.

11. Haskell came in for particular criticism for his suggestions that the "Boston anarchists" (his term for the individualists) and the "red" anarchists like himself and Most reconcile in the name of revolutionary unity: X [Appleton], "Competition, Free and Not Free," January 3, 1885 (III:5, #57), p. 4. For Haskell's proposals, see Chester McArthur Destler, "Shall Red and Black Unite?" pp. 78–104, in *American Radicalism, 1865–1901; Essays and Documents*, New London, Conn.: Connecticut College, 1946.

12. In "Liberty and Communism" (June 27, 1896 [XII:4, #342], pp. 3–4), Tucker explicitly questions whether the anarchist communists respect liberty.

13. Most was the most prominent of the anarchist communists. Dyer Lum (see selection in chapter two) was considered to be sympathetic to the anarchist communists by many in *Liberty*. Louise Michel was a European communist anarchist who had been involved in the Paris Commune of 1871.

14. Grinnell was the prosecutor in the Haymarket case of 1886.

15. For a more detailed argument of this point, see Arthur Muelberger, "Marx versus Proudhon," April 29, 1893 (IX:35, #269), pp. 1, 2–3. Muelberger charges that Marx distorted Proudhon's "Philosophy of Poverty" in the his own "Poverty of Philosophy."

PART TWO

Economics

4

Economic Principles
of Individualist Anarchism

Liberty's affinity to both liberalism and socialism is nowhere more evident than in its economic principles. Depending upon their authors and when they were written, articles on economics in *Liberty* seem to repeat the dogmas (and mistakes) of classical economics, to echo the analyses of Marxist theory, or even to presage modern libertarians. While the overall goal of anarchism's economic reform was "socialism," in the sense that regaining the "surplus product" would put "labor in possession of its own," the means to this end was a thoroughgoing *laissez-faire*, the removal of all state intervention in the economy, including the most fundamental infrastructures (e.g., regulation of money).

An uncharitable interpreter might see all this as evidence of theoretical and practical confusion; a more charitable one might label anarchist economics as "eclectic" or "ambivalent." Another line of criticism is the Marxist one, condemning the individualist anarchists in the same terms as Marx himself critiqued their hero, Pierre-Joseph Proudhon. That is, one could explain their seeming confusion ideologically, as a petit-bourgeois reaction to industrial capitalism. Thus, despite their radical rhetoric condemning the concentration of wealth and the rise of monopolies, they remained within the orbit of classical economics by praising private property and competition. Was *Liberty*'s economic reform petit-bourgeois? It was certainly not reactionary, for the economic writers in *Liberty* did not long for a golden age of capitalism in America, whether that was situated in the 1830s or the 1780s, even though particular facets of their economic theories had substantial roots in labor reform. Nor did they offer a knee-jerk defense of the status quo against further decline. Instead, the combination of liberal and socialist influences produced a rather abstract, almost ahistorical, critique of the state's role in the economy. This was supplemented by a hope, if not always a fervent belief, that progress was tending toward greater individual liberty, not toward greater state power. There was an underlying consistency in the economic views expressed in *Liberty*, but it was not that of a petit-bourgeois reaction.

The individualist anarchists who wrote on economics in *Liberty* essentially had a liberal mind and a socialist heart. They offered an unconventional interpretation of the liberal principles in classical economics by singlemindedly criticizing the role of the state. The energy for this theoretical critique, however, came from their fundamental sympathy with the plight of workers in an industrial economy. It was precisely this combination, however, that spelled their doom as a radical labor ideology in the late nineteenth century. Swimming against the tide of labor and radical movements that increasingly turned to the state for solutions, they were more and more perceived as too liberal and not socialist enough.

In this chapter, then, we will probe the general outlines of anarchist economics in *Liberty*. Starting with an early editorial by Tucker (selection A), the "socialist heart" of individualist anarchism, as a critique of monopoly (more specifically, of the "four monopolies") and a demand for the abolition of "usury" (or, rather its reduction to "cost"), will be explored. Following this, the two main positive principles of anarchist economics, free competition and private property, are described in two lengthy excerpts (selections B and C) from a series of articles by William Bailie. Bailie details the popular misperceptions of competition and property and goes on to defend property and competition as not only consistent with equal liberty, but also essential to putting "labor in possession of its own." This radically applied liberalism shaped the individualist anarchists' analysis of popular economic reforms in the late nineteenth century. For example, producer and consumer cooperatives were a staple of American labor reform (and of Proudhonian anarchism). Because they promised the full reward of labor to the producer, and commodities at cost to the consumer, they received the enthusiastic support of Ernest Lesigne, a French writer (selection D). Francis D. Tandy (selection E), however, was much more skeptical, arguing forcefully that individual proprietorship would be more rational in economic terms. A typical outgrowth of antimonopoly rhetoric at the time was a demand for antitrust legislation, which Tucker opposed not only because it was *state* action, but also because it was radically inadequate to deal with the true extent of monopoly.

Neither cooperatives nor antitrust legislation were panaceas to the individualist anarchists, because they did not directly address the "four monopolies" (money, land, tariffs, and patents). The next three chapters cover these monopolies in detail, but the economic principles set out here allow us to sketch the outlines of the individualist anarchist argument on them. For each of them, the key was to abolish any vestige of state-created monopoly. For example, the money monopoly was basically the restriction, *by government*, of the right to issue currency, and the various regulations that surrounded this legal privilege. The abolition of such monopolies would mean "free competition," which would reduce the artificially high price of economic resources (e.g., credit, land, machines) to the actual cost of their production. This would accomplish what Josiah Warren, the antebellum anarchist, set as the goal for economic reform: "cost the limit of price." By eliminating the "middlemen," or "usurers," workers would receive the full product of their labor, and prosperity would be enhanced by ridding the economy of such parasites as bankers and landlords. Following a few general economic principles, then, the individualist anarchists hoped to achieve socialism by removing the obstacles to individual liberty in the economic realm.

From the standpoint of the late twentieth century, these theories seem again relevant. One hundred years of state solutions have produced a backlash, whether in the reforms of perestroika, the ultimate demise of communist party states, the decline of the welfare state, the rise of privatization, common markets, and free trade. Because they predicted the failure of these state solutions over and over, the individualist anarchists should by all rights be considered prophets. However, they were also advocates of socialism and critics of industrial capitalism, positions that make them less useful as ideological tools of a resurgent capitalism. Ironically, the economic ideas of the individualist anarchists, too capitalistic for many reformers in the late nineteenth century, may be too socialistic for reformers in the late twentieth century. This would be a shame, for capitalism has certainly not overcome the general problems of poverty and periodic recessions, nor have the specific issues addressed by the writers in *Liberty* become less relevant. For example, the constriction of credit, despite substantial changes in monetary policy, is still a major problem—ask the dozens of countries that have had to implement

International Monetary Fund austerity programs to obtain scarce international credit. Protectionism, antitrust, deregulation, land reform are all still being discussed, on a global scale. The nature and extent of property, the rigors and benefits of competition, are, if anything, more an issue now than when *Liberty* was published. Rather than complacency over the "defeat" of communism, then, advocates of capitalism might learn from *Liberty*'s writers to demand the full potential of capitalism and also to deal with its persistent problems.

Further Reading in Liberty

Victor Yarros discusses the "crisis" of classical political economy and argues the need for a scientific and individualistic political economy in "Individualism and Political Economy" (April 19, 1890 [VII:1, #157], pp. 4–5 and May 24, 1890 [VII:2, #158], pp. 5–6). Benjamin Tucker criticizes the antipathy of anarchist-communists to competition in "The Mistakes of Merlino" (July 16, 1892 [VIII:47, #229], p. 2.)

A.   "Who Is the Somebody?"—Benjamin Tucker[*]

In the first issue of Liberty, *Tucker sketched out the basic analysis of the problems of capitalism that would be elaborated over the next twenty-seven years. The question of the title is a socialist one, for it presumes that the worker is a victim who receives a bare subsistence and whose surplus wealth is appropriated by "somebody." The answer that Tucker gives, the "usurer," is not a Marxist one, however. The "usurer" is a broad economic category, not a social class. Moreover, the usurer is not an inevitable feature of capitalism, but rather one created by state distortions of the economy. Indeed, in another early editorial, Tucker argued that usury was not morally wrong, but rather "practically wrong."*[1]

"Somebody gets the surplus wealth that Labor produces and does not consume. Who is the Somebody?" Such is the problem recently posited in the editorial columns of the "New York Truth" . . . . A correct answer to it is unquestionably the first step in the settlement of the appalling problems of poverty, intemperance, ignorance, and crime . . .

---

[*] August 6, 1881 (I:1, #1), p. 3.

What are the ways by which men gain possession of property? Not many. Let us name them: work, gift, discovery, gaming, the various forms of illegal robbery by force or fraud, usury. Can men obtain wealth by any other than one or more of these methods? Clearly, no. Whoever the Somebody may be, then, he must accumulate his riches in one of these ways. We will find him by the process of elimination.

Is the Somebody the laborer? No; at least not as laborer; otherwise the question were absurd. Its premises exclude him. He gains a bare subsistence by his work; no more. We are searching for his surplus product. He has it not.

Is the Somebody the beggar, the invalid, the cripple, the discoverer, the gambler, the highway robber, the burglar, the defaulter, the pickpocket, or the common swindler? None of these, to any extent worth mentioning. The aggregate of wealth absorbed by these classes of our population compared with the vast mass produced is a mere drop in the ocean, unworthy of consideration in studying a fundamental problem of political economy. These people get some wealth, it is true; enough, probably, for their own purposes: but labor can spare them the whole of it, and never know the difference.

Then we have found him. Only the usurer remaining, he must be the Somebody whom we are looking for; he, and none other. But who is the usurer, and whence comes his power? There are three forms of usury: interest on money, rent of land and houses, and profit in exchange. Whoever is in receipt of any of these is a usurer. And who is not? Scarcely any one. The banker is a usurer; the merchant is a usurer; the landlord is a usurer; and the workingman who puts his savings, if he has any, out at interest, or takes rent for his house or lot, if he owns one, or exchanges his labor for more than an equivalent,—he, too, is a usurer. The sin of usury is one under which all are concluded and for which all are responsible. But all do not benefit by it. The vast majority suffer. Only the chief usurers accumulate: in agricultural and thickly-settled countries, the landlords; in industrial and commercial countries, the bankers. Those are the Somebodies who swallow up the surplus wealth.

And where do the Somebodies get their power? From monopoly. Here, as usual, the State is the chief of sinners. Usury rests on two great monopolies,—the monopoly of land and the monopoly of credit. Were it not for these, it would disappear. Ground-rent exists only because the State stands by to collect it and to protect land-titles rooted in force or fraud. Otherwise the land would be free to all, and no one could control more than he used. Interest and house-rent exist only because the State grants to a certain class of individuals and corporations the exclusive privilege of using its credit and theirs as a basis for the issuance of circulating currency. Otherwise credit would be free to all, and money, brought under the law of competition, would be issued at cost. Interest and rent gone, competition would leave little or no chance for profit in exchange except in business protected by tariff or patent laws. And there again the State has but to step aside to cause the last vestige of usury to disappear.

The usurer is the Somebody, and the State is his protector. Usury is the serpent gnawing at Labor's vitals, and only Liberty can detach and kill it. Give laborers their liberty, and they will keep their wealth; as for the Somebody, he, stripped of his power to steal, must either join their ranks or starve.

B.   "The True Function of Competition"—William Bailie[*]

In this excerpt from his series, "The Problems of Anarchism," Bailie admits that workers' perceptions of competition are very unfavorable, but argues that any problems it does have are due solely to the restrictions placed upon it. That is, what is needed is not less competition, but more. Such "free competition" would be consistent with the general principle of equal freedom and the egoistic theory of human nature.

When we remember that the most conspicuous aspect of competition is to be seen in the struggle for work and existence continually going on among the wage-workers, the supply of laborers always apparently exceeding the demand and so keeping wages down to an average that scarcely covers subsistence; and when the competition is not confined to one industry, but spreads itself without respect for persons throughout every class of workers who sell their labor, and in every country in which modern capitalism has arisen; when the immediate effects of machinery and all improvements in the methods of production are observed to intensify the competition of laborers with one another, mechanical invention itself proving an irresistible competitor; when the struggle reduces the skilled and the educated to the common level and adds to the

---

[*] June 17, 1893 (IX:42, #276), p. 1.

uncertainties and insecurity of the wage-earners' lot, increasing the burden of life by the ever-present dread of failure and starvation,—is it any wonder that competition is looked upon as a monstrous evil, held up to the working classes by social reformers as the source of all their suffering and together with the whole system of which it is a part, to be forthwith eliminated? Let us admit the fact: competition runs rampant among the toilers, and, despite the efforts of trade unions, determines the inadequate rates of wages they are compelled to accept. But before making up our minds what to do to avert these evils, we must form a clear conception of the nature of the supposed cause. What is competition, how does it arise, where is it limited, and in what manner is it confined? Is it possible to remove it if we learn its origin, or is it one of those natural forces which cannot be overcome and must therefore be reckoned with and made the best of? . . .

Competition, as it exists among the mass of workers, is, with good reason, denounced and condemned. . . . We are told that competition among the capitalists leads also to low wages, to lying, adulteration, and all manner of deception; that it is responsible for the miserable wages of sales-girls and other women-workers in our cities that throw them by thousands on the streets to eke out a living. Also it is said that competition is the parent of monopoly, that it drives the capitalists to combine, and gives us the trusts by means of which they rob the people with impunity.

But this kind of reasoning is superficial. The law of equal freedom gives every man the right to carry on his activities in any way he may choose so long as nobody else is forcibly prevented from doing likewise. His liberty to produce, to sell, and to make contracts with whomsoever among free men chooses to agree with him cannot lightly be set aside; it is the very essence of freedom's law . . . Competition cannot exist without freedom; where it is assailed today, a close analysis reveals, not the evil effect of competition, but the need of more liberty.

Any theory of society that implies the downfall of competition is in the same position as moral notions that proclaim the negation of self and seek through universal unselfishness . . . to attain social perfection. The futility of this is exemplified in the history of Christianity, which, after nineteen hundred years of experiment in reconciling the theory with individual practice, leaves the mainspring of character and conduct precisely the same as before,—that is, selfish. Egoism is demonstrably a natural, necessary, and wholly ineradicable force, which may be directed but never destroyed. Competition is simply the same force in the economic field. It is the necessary outcome of the relations of men with one another; the more pronounced it is, the freer they become. To eliminate it is neither possible nor desirable, but to direct it is within the sphere of intelligence . . .

What essential function, then, in the social economy does competition serve? Remember, it is but a means to an end, and as such alone must be judged. That end is for each individual to find his most fitting place in society. . . . The right man in the right place is a worthy ideal, and the more general the action of competition the more is this ideal fulfilled. Indeed the degree in which this function is attained is the measure of the value of competition and its only justification.

If we attempt to imagine a society without competition and the attendant phenomena of supply, demand, money, and price, we must either blot out from our minds the great complex communities of modern civilization with their unconscious interdependence, or else invent some hitherto unknown mechanism which will adequately replace and fulfill the functions performed by them in the world today. Every Utopian and Communistic scheme formulated that attempts to do without the economic competitive forces replaces them by a reactionary and insufferable hierarchy, or else, like the Communist-Anarchists, ignores the necessity for any machinery to adjust economic activities to their ends. . . . For, if they proclaim liberty and ignore the need for an economic mechanism, which competition, etc. now supplies, they exalt a chaotic and unbalanced condition to the dignity of an ideal; otherwise, they must face the issue and admit the need of economic order which arises from the action of competitive forces in a state of individual freedom. In face of this economic necessity the Communist[-Anarchists] are logically compelled to either stand with the authoritarians, accept a chaotic ideal, or admit a competitive basis as the only machinery for securing economic order in society.

I have already indicated the need of ascertaining whether the evil effects of competition arise under all the circumstances and different phases in which its working is observed, before we can proclaim it to be the real and only cause of such evils, or attempt to cure them by its overthrow. But a little thought and unbiased inquiry at once show us that only under certain conditions is competition opposed to the welfare of the laborer, and that in its widest operation it is wholly beneficent in its effects. Every modern improvement that makes life easier and raises the condition of the masses, all the methods that facilitate wealth production and distribution, the countless advantages of this over all preceding generations of men, can be traced to the breakdown of status and privilege and consequent growth, intensity, and general comprehensiveness of competition. It is the only known antidote to social stagnation, the mainspring of industrial progress, the whip that drives slothful humanity towards general well-being and happiness. What seem its shortcomings are really traceable to its restriction through various causes. The supply of labor in channels where it appears to always exceed demand will be found to be due to removable causes maintained by special interests upheld by law and authority, and only possible because of the ignorance of the victims. The demand for labor in like manner is limited, the natural channels for adjusting the activities of the producers to their needs are by custom and law choked up, the means made subservient to class interests, and thus competition is one-sided, its benefits diminished and main purpose ignored.

C. "Problems of Anarchism: Property"—William Bailie[*]

In another excerpt from the series, "Problems of Anarchism," Bailie makes an argument that parallels that on competition: in contemporary practice, private property has little charm for workers, for it is difficult for them to acquire. Nevertheless, the belief in the legitimacy of private property seems also to be growing in scope and intensity. Like competition, property is theoretically consistent with equal liberty. Bailie also connects the right to property to the right to life (albeit more in a Spencerian than in a Lockean fashion). This theoretical impregnability of the right to property was undermined by the fact that most "property" then held was illegitimately acquired (e.g., through conquest or fraud). This reflects the unfortunate fact that capitalism is "a superstructure reared upon the past."[2]

---

[*] February 18, 1893 (IX:25, #259), p. 1; February 25, 1893 (IX:26, #260), p. 1.

Life, Liberty, and Property.

If the liberty of the individual, embracing in that idea the equal liberty of all, is accepted as a standard principle, the only measure of rights, and the fulfillment of justice; then, whatever ideas are entertained upon property or any other question of principle and rights must harmonize with that leading idea. Any conception of property which traverses it and denies complete individual liberty must be rejected: it is inconsistent with its acceptance.

Talking once with an ardent Socialist, he confessed to me, with innocent candor, that the very first notion in the communistic direction had yet to be acquired by the people. "For," said he, "the idea of individual or private property lies so deep in their minds and is so securely imbedded in their habits of thought, in their very nature, that any conception of property conditions opposed to this seems almost impossible; to effect a change would require a mental revolution more gigantic than has ever been known. And yet without such a change in property ideas no communistic revolution could last a day. 'Twould be simply a dead letter."

How profoundly true!

Recalling this observation brings me to the point to be first noticed: the property idea, as we find it developed today among civilized and progressive people.

Not only is the belief in individual property general, it grows more intense, and is continually embracing a wider range of objects and ideas not previously considered as property at all . . .

The right of the individual to hold property has been allowed from the remotest times; as his power of acquiring it and need for it have grown his right has become clearer and more imperative; and private property develops with human progress. Its recognition advances with advancing civilization: experience, customs, laws, exemplify the fact.

Admitting this truth, the question for us to consider is: Does this tendency of property agree with individual liberty? Does the fact harmonize with our principle?

When an individual in the exercise of his liberty expends his energies in acquiring property without preventing others from so exercising the like liberty, he breaks not the law of individual liberty, he trespasses not on the freedom of others. So that property acquired under such conditions rightfully belongs to him who acquires it . . .

All extensions of the property idea have their justification in this principle. It is embodied in laws framed with a view to equal rights and justice. It is in accord with prevailing ideas of right and equity. Even the formula used by the Communists, "the product to the producer," entails its recognition.[3]

Though all this is true in the abstract,—which, however, does not insure that, when we come to analyze the practice in regard to the distribution of property, we shall find it so in fact,—yet it is not sufficient warrant for us to establish private property as a right and accept it as we do the right to equal liberty. If we can show the necessity for it as a condition of existence, as a part of the law of life, a biological fact which has been established by science, then no more is required of us; its justice and propriety become incontrovertible.

Continuous life is possible only when each individual receives the consequences of his own conduct, when benefits obtained are proportionate to actions performed, when he reaps the advantages of his life-maintaining powers, when the good and the evil in his nature each brings its due reward.[4]

Manifestly the possession of property, acquired without violating the liberty of others, is a direct consequence of conduct, the reward of life-sustaining energies.

To deny a man's right to the fruits of his exertions is a denial of his right to the use of his faculties, both bodily and mental, and finally of his right to life itself.

Admitting this claim as thus established, and as a necessary consequence of the sovereignty of the individual, we must recognize some truths which naturally follow. A man may acquire property—the term including all forms of wealth—by any method consistent with other men's equal liberty. He may work for it by direct labor, he may gamble for it by any kind of speculation provided nobody is coerced, he may obtain it by gift or bequest or through unrestricted exchange, and his claim is equally valid, his right equally undeniable.

But he has not just claim to it when procured through the violation of other men's rights, through the limitation or negation of their equal freedom. The same principle which establishes property rights destroys all arbitrary claims, all law-created rights. It denies all property rights due to legal privilege which is an assault upon individual liberty; to the forcible monopoly of natural resources and opportunities which establish property only through the denial of others' right to obtain it; to all arbitrarily-enforced burdens, as taxes, rent of land, mines, water, and all natural media; interest—a direct creation of unequal liberty. . .

Wherein Property is Subversive of Liberty.

I have already indicated that to demonstrate a truth in the abstract, even when it is generally accepted as such, does not imply its practical recognition and existence in fact. Nothing more plainly shows this than an inquiry into property as it exists today. For it is not one simple system based on justice that we find, but a complicated mixture of practices and ideas—the latter entailed by the former—which lead to confusion of statement and reasoning by nearly all of those who, recognizing the enormous evils of the prevailing system, criticise it or advocate its destruction. No less hopeless is the confusion of arguments used by its champions and supporters.

Violence, either direct or through law, accounts for the greater part of actual proprietary rights from the remotest past to the present time; as much in so-called free and civilized societies as in the most barbarous. The upholders of the existing order maintain the justice of current methods of obtaining wealth and the validity of present owners' titles to the possession of property, by hypocritically falling back on the true theory which declares, in the words of Adam Smith, that "the property which each man has in his own labor, as it is the original foundation of all other property, so it is the most sacred and inviolable." They defend *their* property on the assumption that it is acquired under the same conditions as the right of those who obtain it by their labor without violating others' rights . . .

And they say: "Down with the revolutionist, the robber who would deny our rights to the wealth we possess! 'Tis the poor we defend as well as the rich,—the workingman as quick as the capitalist."

And they go on building up wealth that other people produce, extracting it mercilessly from the rightful owners by means of customs, laws, and conditions that have grown up mostly in violence, wrong, and injustice, and are maintained today through force of arms and legal fraud; unmindful the while that this means of acquiring property denies completely the plain rights of others and renders private property, as conceived in the abstract and tacitly admitted by property defenders, impossible for the vast majority of its creators.

While conceding the fact that the just theory of property rights continues to gain ground both in general belief and in legal enactment, I am compelled to point out that its application is still extremely limited, and that in the industrial world under capitalistic conditions it does not obtain at all.

Modern industry and the accompanying economic conditions having arisen under the *regime* of status,—that is, under arbitrary conditions in which equal liberty had no place and law-made privileges held unbounded sway,—it is only to be expected that an equally arbitrary and unjust system of property should prevail.

On one side a dependent industrial class of wage-workers and on the other a privileged class of wealth-monopolizers, each becoming more and more distinct from the other as capitalism advances, has resulted in a grouping and consolidation of wealth which grows apace by attracting all property, no matter by whom produced, into the hands of the privileged, and hence property becomes a social power, an economic force destructive of rights, a fertile source of injustice, a means of enslaving the dispossessed.

Under this system equal liberty cannot obtain.

The law of life, that each should receive the benefits of his own conduct, that nobody should obtain, without equivalent benefits given, the results of another's life-sustaining actions, that every individual should reap the reward of his energies, the fruits of his labor,—this law, in conformity to which only can the race develop and any society of human beings continue to evolve, is not fulfilled. Industrialism, while growing up under the adverse circumstances just pointed out, has nevertheless developed the need and desire of complete individual freedom and consequently the demand for more equitable property conditions. So that, while private property in its true sense can hardly be said to exist, and certainly is outside the conception of modern capitalism, the abstract belief in it, showing the conscious need, has steadily grown.

History affords many examples of a growing belief, due to the realization of some pressing need and generally going along with a desire for enlargement of individual liberty, preceding the change which ends by making the belief an actuality. All true reforms are of this character. It is safe therefore to predict that the next step in the evolution of property, if it be not in the nature of a reaction,—a circumstance not impossible,— will be toward a fuller recognition of the right of private property.

D.   "Cooperation a Panacea?"—Ernest Lesigne[*]

Many of the individualist anarchists believed that consumer and producer cooperatives could help to insure that workers would receive the full product of their labor. Yet this was not an essential belief in Liberty. *It would only happen if free competition were first established and even then, cooperation was simply consistent with equal freedom, not necessary in order to establish (or maintain) it.[5] In this selection, the French anarchist Lesigne describes the Proudhonian ideal of coopera- tion, a linked system of producer and consumer cooperatives, as preferable to the "Rochdale" ideal, which would operate consumer cooperatives as a normal business, returning any profits to members in the form of dividends.*

Cooperation a panacea?

Sharpers have said so, greenhorns have believed them. In reality, cooperation might be, and, if it is desired, will be, a potent peaceful agent of social transformation.

But on this condition,—that the greenhorns shall not let the sharpers put the tool in their pocket . . .

To fall into the beaten path of political economy would be the height of confusion for cooperation. Never again would they get out of that rut. Danger! cooperating friends.

Do you remember the early days when the roll-call of cooperation was beaten and you grouped yourselves in enthusiastic choruses, singing the captivating hymn of solidarity?

You were to replace from top to bottom the old, heavy, burdensome commercial edifice, to renew the worn-out, rusty, dirty tools of exchange which returned scarcely twenty-five percent of the force expended and rendered useless millions of intelligent heads, excellent hearts, and skilful hands, occupied in the parasitic labor of a decrepit commerce . .
.

---

[*] February 11, 1888 (V:14, #118), p. 7 (originally appeared in *Le Radical.* Original title in *Liberty:* "Socialistic Letters").

This could not last, and the following reform was proposed.

The consumers should form groups. They know almost surely that they will want boots and shoes, overcoats, food. They should combine to the number of one hundred, two hundred, five hundred, and assure houses established for the purpose that they will regularly buy food, shoes, and coats of them.

On the other hand, these houses should turn to the laboring people in the different productive regions and say to them:

What need is there of a mass of middle-men, monopolists, devourers, adulterators, who thrust themselves between you, creators of products, and us, final distributors of products? Group yourselves, then, for cooperative production, as those who need to consume group themselves to cooperate in consumption; and we, the houses of distribution, will guarantee to purchase of you as we are guaranteed a sale by our consumer-customers. You, producers, will receive the value of your product, of your effort, without having to deal with a mass of hucksters and exploiters, who profit by your crises, by your accidents, and who hold the knife at your throats in order to pay no more for your sweat than they would for clear water. You, consumers, will find on our shelves every thing that you need, at cost, cost of sale included, without having to pour your hard-earned money into the hands of the multitude of middlemen allowed by the present system of exchanging products.

And again, all the activities uselessly devoted to operating the disastrous machinery of exchange would be restored to useful labor, and such labor would never be lacking.

Thus understood, cooperation is a solution of the great problem of social economy,—the delivery of products to the consumer at cost.[6]

Now, this hope from cooperation would be destroyed and cooperation would be compromised, if the vote passed by the Lyons Congress in 1886 should be persisted in. That Congress, in fact, adopted the following principle as one of its formal objects:

To sell at retail prices and capitalize the profits.

The ambush was prepared. The economistic serpent, to tempt the cooperators and make them abandon their promised land, has said to them, not "Ye shall be as gods," which is stale, but "Ye shall be capitalists!"

"What! buy at cost! A vulgar instinct, showing lack of foresight. And then, would you not grievously annoy the parasite next you, who, added to the parasites who supply him with merchandise, succeeds in extracting from your pocket a fourth or a third of its contents? Leave this commonplace of gross immediate gain; do not annoy parasitism; do not restore to useful labor those who are wearing themselves out in the absurd gearing of the commercial machine; renounce all ideas of emancipation; and follow simply the movement of the day, make profits."

? ? ?

"Yes, make profits. You shall establish a cooperative store. When you need a pound of candles, you will go to your store, which will have received this pound of candles with all charges paid and all risks covered, and you will lay down fifteen sous. If you profess Socialistic doctrines, you will give your store the fifteen sous and take away your candles. But that is an inferior way of doing things, and if you are imbued with the healthy doctrines of political economy, you will hasten to pay the price fixed by the old-time parasitism; you will give twenty-five sous. Then you can say that you have made a profit,—that you have gained the ten sous paid by you in excess."

! ! !

"Why yes! since at the parasite's you never would have seen them again, while by cooperation thus practised you have chances of getting them once more."

"But would it not be better to keep my ten sous paid in excess and use them in buying shoes for my baby, who just now needs a pair!"

"What low instincts you have! Is it not a virtue to become a capitalist? When you have pinched the bellies of your entire family for a whole year by paying too high prices for everything, for a virtuous object and not to annoy those who sell everything for twice as much as it is worth, you will be in control of a small capital."

"And this capital?"

"Ah! be careful not to touch it; leave it religiously in the treasury. It will be invested in bonds paying a handsome income, which you will receive later if you are not dead, or else in real estate the rents from which you will likewise receive in the future provided you are alive."

This is how the cooperative idea can be turned from its path. If the famous pioneers of Rochdale had understood cooperation in consumption to mean the supply of products at actual cost, perhaps English commerce would have been revolutionized. They applied, on the contrary, this principle: *Sale of goods at city retail prices and accumulation of the profits as savings*, and thus they have simply ended by having a large sum of money in the society's coffers, by means of which they have increased by several thousands the number of individuals who, by lending money at the highest possible interest, withdraw from other laborers a part of the product of their labor without any effort of their own.

E. "Voluntary Cooperation"—Francis D. Tandy[*]

The "cooperation" here criticized is the Rochdale system also criticized by Lesigne. Rather than offering the Proudhonian alternative, however, Tandy offers a more capitalistic one, individual proprietorship. Such individually held concerns would be more rational than coopera-tives because they would take advantage of the division of labor. Thus, even in an anarchist economy, characterized by the abolition of rent, interest, and profit, the criteria of "political economy" (as Lesigne would deride it) are relevant. This raises the question of whether such anarchist economics is socialist in anything other than its goal, putting labor in possession of its own. Can an economy in which even cooperation is considered optional be "socialist" in any meaningful sense?

. . . Under free conditions there would, in most cases, be no necessity for cooperation as usually understood. In fact, such an arrangement would often prove to be more of a curse than a blessing. To make this clear, let us take an example. Suppose several men, realizing that goods can be bought cheaper in large quantities, agree to buy their groceries together and divide them among themselves. They will find that they effect a saving by this arrangement. But they have really performed so much extra labor, and the pay for that labor is all they have saved. They have performed the services of one middleman and so save his profit. As they go into the business more extensively, this becomes apparent. They will soon find that a great amount of time and labor is requisite, if they would keep informed of the state of the market,—the price and the quality of the various commodities. So great will this soon become that it will more than counterbalance any saving they may effect. It is absurd to suppose that several men, engaged in other callings, can perform the functions of the retailer in any line as well as men who devote their whole

---

[*] January 11, 1896 (XI:18, #330), p. 3.

time to that business. To obviate this difficulty, the cooperators must either give up their scheme, or else employ a competent manager to take care of the business. That it will pay them to employ the most efficient manager they can obtain is obvious. But such a man will demand the highest wages he can get. In the absence of rent and interest, his wages will necessarily be just what he could get by conducting such a business for himself. So, after paying the salary of the manager, the goods will cost the consumers as much as if they had bought from a retailer in the first place. In addition to this, they will have all the trouble of looking after the manager for nothing. The ordinary retailer's wages depend upon the success with which he conducts his business, but the salary of the manager of a cooperative concern is not dependent upon the results of his efforts in anything like the same degree.

. . . When a man does a little carpenter-work for himself, he thinks he saves the amount he would otherwise have paid a carpenter. In reality he has merely earned the carpenter's wages. But, as he is probably a poor carpenter, it will take him longer to do the work than it would a good mechanic. So he will be earning lower wages. It would be better for him to devote the same amount of time and labor to his ordinary occupation and, out of the money so earned, pay a carpenter to do the work for him. The same is true in regard to the retailer.

These considerations, however, may be modified by circumstances. It may be a pleasure, for example, for a bookkeeper to do a little wood-work in the evening. Or it may be that the conditions of a man's business are such that the time spent in this kind of work could not be profitably employed at his usual occupation. But these factors in no way invalidate the tenor of my argument. They apply only in isolated cases, and disappear as soon as the cooperative associations are organized.

In the present day, of course, the retailer collects rent and interest in addition to his wages. So there is a direct saving in such cooperation when conducted on a small scale. But, as soon as a regular business is established, the rent and interest have to be paid in one form or another, and so the benefits are neutralized as soon as they promise to become of any importance.

To conduct such enterprises, it is necessary that all the cooperators form an agreement. Such an agreement will often prove a hindrance to the individual members, if they should wish to act at variance with the policy of the association. No matter how liberal the contract might be, it would necessarily curtail the liberty of the members more than if no such organization existed, and each were free to purchase his goods when, where, and how he liked, without reference to the wishes of any of the rest of the community. We have already seen that there would be no economic advantages to offset this restriction of liberty; so such associations would be a positive detriment to those concerned.

Some few instances might be found where, from the nature of some special business, it could be conducted more economically upon such a cooperative plan.

But such instances are very few. I apprehend that even Mutual Banks and Protective Associations will, in the end, be conducted by individuals, who will cater to the wants of their customers and make what wages they can out of the business, rather than by communistic associations of the customers.

F.   "The Attitude of Anarchism
Toward Industrial Combinations"—Benjamin R. Tucker*

If, as Tandy suggested, consumer cooperatives seemed to make little sense in an industrial capitalist economy, producer cooperatives, at least in the form of trusts, certainly did. Responding to the enthusiasm in labor circles for antitrust measures, Tucker analyzed the question in theoretical terms. In the abstract, such cooperation was completely legitimate, even if it restricted competition, so long as the restrictions it imposed were not by arbitrary decree, force, or fraud, but were rather the result of the superior competitiveness of cooperating companies. In practice, of course, the formation of trusts was not so benign or legitimate, for they owed their power to government backing. Trusts, Tucker argued, were not the result of too much competition, but of too little, namely the restrictions in competition enforced by the "four monopolies," briefly described at the end. Tucker's address was evidently well received, although the famous labor economist John R. Commons declared it impractical and "too logical."[7]

---

* December 1902, (XIV:4, #366), pp. 2-4. Tucker's note: An address delivered by Benj. R. Tucker in Central Music Hall, on September 14, 1899 before the Conference on Trusts held under the auspices of the Civic Federation. [NB: the gap between the address and its publication in *Liberty* reflects a break in publishing the newspaper between December 1900 and December 1902].

Having to deal very briefly with the problem with which the so-called trusts confront us, I go at once to the heart of the subject, taking my stand on these propositions: That the right to co-operate is as unquestionable as the right to compete; that the right to compete involves the right to refrain from competition; that cooperation is often a method of competition, and that competition is always, in the larger view, a method of cooperation; that each is a legitimate, orderly, non-invasive exercise of the individual will under the social law of equal liberty; and that any man or institution attempting to prohibit or restrict either, by legislative enactment or by any form of invasive force, is, in so far as such man or institution may fairly be judged by such attempt, an enemy of liberty, an enemy of progress, an enemy of society, and an enemy of the human race.

Viewed in the light of these irrefutable propositions, the trust, then, like every other industrial combination endeavoring to do collectively nothing but what each member of the combination rightfully may endeavor to do individually, is *per se*, an unimpeachable institution. To assail or control or deny this form of cooperation on the ground that it is itself a denial of competition is an absurdity. It is an absurdity, because it proves too much. The trust is a denial of competition in no other sense than that in which competition itself is a denial of competition. The trust denies competition only by producing and selling more cheaply than those outside of the trust can produce and sell; but in that sense every successful individual competitor also denies competition. And if the trust is to be suppressed for such denial of competition, then the very competition in the name of which the trust is to be suppressed must itself be suppressed also. I repeat: the argument proves too much. The fact is that there is one denial of competition which is the right of all, and that there is another denial of competition which is the right of none. All of us, whether out of a trust or in it, have a right to deny competition by competing, but none of us, whether in a trust or out of it, have a right to deny competition by arbitrary decree, by interference with voluntary effort, by forcible suppression of initiative.

Again: To claim that the trust should be abolished or controlled because the great resources and consequent power of endurance which it acquires by combination give it an undue advantage, and thereby enable it to crush competition, is equally an argument that proves too much. If John D. Rockefeller were to start a grocery store in his individual capacity, we should not think of suppressing or restricting or hampering his enterprise simply because, with his five hundred millions, he could afford to sell groceries at less than cost until the day when the accumulated ruins of all other grocery stores should afford him a sure foundation for a profitable business. But, if Rockefeller's possession of five hundred millions is not a good ground for the suppression of his grocery store, no better ground is the control of still greater wealth for the suppression of his oil trust. It is true that these vast accumulations under one control are abnormal and dangerous, but the reasons for them lie outside of and behind and beneath all trusts and industrial combinations,—reasons which I shall come to presently,—reasons which are all, in some form or other, an arbitrary denial of liberty; and, but for these reasons, but for these denials of liberty, John D. Rockefeller never could have acquired five hundred millions, nor would any combination of men be able to control an aggregation of wealth that could not be easily and successfully met by some other combination of men.

Again: There is no warrant in reason for deriving a right to control trusts from the State grant of corporate privileges under which they are organized. In the first place, it being pure usurpation to presume to endow any body of men with rights and exemptions that are not theirs already under the social law of equal liberty, corporate privileges are in themselves a wrong; and one wrong is not to be undone by attempting to offset it with another. But, even admitting the justice of corporation charters, the avowed purpose in granting them is to encourage cooperation, and thus stimulate industrial and commercial development for the benefit of the community. Now, to make this encouragement an excuse for its own nullification by a proportionate restriction of cooperation would be to add one more to those interminable imitations of the task of Sisyphus for which that stupid institution which we call the State has ever been notorious . . .

At this point in the hunt for the solution of the trust problem, the discerning student may begin to realize that he is hot on the trail. The thought arises that the trusts, instead of growing out of competition, as is so generally supposed, have been made possible only by the absence of competition, only by the difficulty of competition, only by the obstacles placed in the way of competition. . . . And it is with this thought that Anarchism, the doctrine that in all matters there should be the greatest amount of individual liberty compatible with equality of liberty, approaches the case in hand, and offers its diagnosis and its remedy.

The first and great fact to be noted in the case, I have already hinted at. It is the fact that the trusts owe their power to vast accumulation and concentration of wealth, unmatched, and, under present conditions, unmatchable, by any equal accumulation of wealth, and that this accumulation of wealth has been effected by the combination of several accumulations only less vast and in themselves already gigantic, each of which owed its existence to one or more of the only means by which large fortunes can be rolled up,—interest, rent, and monopolistic profit. But for interest, rent, and monopolistic profit, therefore, trusts would be impossible. Now, what causes interest, rent, and monopolistic profit? For all there is but one cause,—the denial of liberty, the suppression or restriction of competition, the legal creation of monopolies.

This single cause, however, takes various shapes.

Monopolistic profit is due to that denial of liberty which takes the shape of patent, copyright, and tariff legislation, patent and copyright laws directly forbidding competition, and tariff laws placing competition at a fatal disadvantage.

Rent is due to that denial of liberty which takes the shape of land monopoly, vesting titles to land in individuals and associations which do not use it, and thereby compelling the non-owning users to pay tribute to the non-using owners as a condition of admission to the competitive market.

Interest is due to that denial of liberty which takes the shape of money monopoly, depriving all individuals and associations, save such as hold a certain kind of property, of the right to issue promissory notes as currency, and thereby compelling all holders of property other than the kind thus privileged, as well as all non-proprietors, to pay tribute to the holders of the privileged property for the use of a circulating medium and instrument of credit which, in the complex stage that industry and commerce have now reached, has become the chief essential of a competitive market.

Now, Anarchism, which, as I have said, is the doctrine that in all matters there should be the greatest amount of individual liberty compatible with equality of liberty, finds that none of these denials of liberty are necessary to the maintenance of equality of liberty, but that each and every one of them, on the contrary, is destructive of equality of liberty, Therefore it declares them unnecessary, arbitrary, oppressive, and unjust, and demands their immediate cessation . . .

It clearly follows that the adequate solution of the problem with which the trusts confront us is to be found only in abolition of these monopolies and the consequent guarantee of perfectly free competition.

Notes

1. Benjamin Tucker, "The Philosophy of Right and Wrong," October 29, 1881 (I:7, #7), pp. 2–3.
2. William Bailie, "Problems of Anarchism—Property: Part 6," March 18, 1893 (IX:29, #263), pp. 1, 4.
3. Marxists would of course object that this is a *socialist* formula, the ultimate communist formula being "to each according to his needs" (not to his individual contribution to production).
4. Bailie seems to be paraphrasing Herbert Spencer's "law of consequences" here.
5. Tucker said that "Without unrestricted competition there can be no true coopera- tion." ("On Picket Duty," December 10, 1881 [I:10, #10], p. 1). See also Tucker, "The Mistakes of Merlino," July 16, 1892 (VIII:47, #229), p. 2 and John S. Crosby, "Corporations and Co-operation," December 1907 (XVI:6, #402), p. 30.
6. This Proudhonian formulation neatly parallels Josiah Warren's ideal, "cost the limit of price."
7. Tucker published a number of excerpts of press accounts of this conference, including Commons' remarks from the *Chicago Tribune*: "Anarchism at the Trust Conference," September 1899 (XIV:1, #363), p. 5, continued November 1899 (XIV:2, #364), p. 5.

5

Interest, the Money Monopoly, and Mutual Banking

Monetary reform was an obsession that *Liberty* shared with much of the American labor and radical movement, an obsession whose intensity roughly corresponded to downturns in the business cycle. The first significant wave of anarchist monetary reform occurred around the time of the monetary panic of 1837. In the late 1820s, Josiah Warren was experimenting with "labor notes," a currency denominated in hours of labor time which could be exchanged among members of a community in lieu of scarce legal tender.[1] Such labor notes had several significant problems, so most of the anarchists associated with *Liberty* advocated some version of the monetary reform that William B. Greene had worked out in the late 1840s, the "mutual bank." Greene's views on money paralleled those of Pierre-Joseph Proudhon, who had tried to implement a similar scheme of mutual banking during the Revolution of 1848.[2]

Despite their debt to anarchist money reformers, the complaints writers in *Liberty* raised about money that were not so different from those of many Americans (farmers, workers, etc.) in times of economic depression: there was not enough money, credit was tight, and interest was high. Periodic waves of dissatisfaction with monetary policy had led to several significant reform movements, most notably the Greenbackers in the late 1870s and the free-silver forces in the early 1890s. What united all these "money faddists" (so called by the "hard money men," advocates of the gold standard) was a belief that economic downturns were due, in large part, to arbitrary restriction of money and credit and that prosperity could be encouraged in the short and long term by monetary and credit expansion. In addition, most believed that such restriction gave considerable economic power to those who controlled the supply and

133

amount of money in circulation, as exemplified by their ability to compel interest on the loan of money. The differences between the faddists had to do with how much more money was necessary, whether it should be explicitly inflationary, and what would be the basis of money (gold, silver, government debt, government fiat, etc.). While most of the reformers suggested government action to resolve the problem (e.g., recognizing the "greenbacks" issued during the Civil War as permanent currency, or allowing currency to be redeemable in silver as well as gold), the anarchists argued that government intervention in monetary supply had to be abolished altogether. Their analysis was radical because they suggested that the problem was not too little legal-tender currency, but legal-tender currency itself. For the government to establish only one permissible currency was to establish a "money monopoly." This monopoly might issue *more* currency if, as reformers suggested, it would base money on government debt (greenbacks, or twentieth-century Federal Reserve notes) or on silver as well as gold (bimetallism), but it would still be a monopoly.

The individualist anarchist answer to the money monopoly was, at least in theory, "free banking," in which any individual could issue her own notes as currency, typically backing them up with some promise that they could be redeemed in real property. In practice, however, this myriad of currencies (or rather, IOUs) would be too cumbersome, so the expedient of "mutual banking" would tend to be established. In a "mutual bank," a group of individuals would pool pledges to their property and issue notes as a bank. To the extent that this bank became known as secure and its notes actually circulated as currency, it would effect the aim of mutual banking: expanding the money supply by basing money on property other than precious metals or on government fiat. Put another way, the mutual banks "monetized" credit, making it easier for people to transform their private "good credit" (based on their actual property or reliability) into public, circulating credit. This, most felt, would also reduce the rate of interest to the cost of running the mutual bank, somewhat under one percent.

Because of the general consensus among the anarchists in *Liberty* on mutual banking, there were very few general explanations of the money monopoly, of interest, or of mutual banking. Typically, Greene's seminal work, *Mutual Banking*, was cited to any newcomers that needed an introduction to the topic. When the individualist anarchists discussed monetary reform (and they did, at considerable length) it was usually a very detailed discussion of the finer points of their theories and of monetary theory generally. They were consumed with such questions as "Is money capital or simply a means of exchange?" "Is capital productive in itself and thus deserving of some return?" "Is money simply an instrument of exchange, or must it also be a standard and basis of value?" This concern with detail makes it quite difficult to select coherent, much less concise, debates on money from the pages of *Liberty*. Luckily, in 1897 John Beverley Robinson wrote an article that summarized the major themes of interest, the money monopoly, and mutual banking. Although fairly long, it has the virtue of comprehensiveness and is thus the only selection in this chapter (it is supplemented by extensive endnotes to other articles in *Liberty*).

Monetary reform was considered by Benjamin Tucker to be *the* central reform of the economy, but it is hard to escape the feeling that monetary reform deserves the obscurity it has, not only for the radical notions of the anarchists, but even the more mainstream demands of Greenbackers and free-silver advocates. In retrospect, particularly, the demands for more money and more credit seem to have been met. The gold standard has been abandoned, the Federal Reserve explicitly aims to manipulate the money supply for macroeconomic ends, and credit is freely (perhaps too freely) offered by banks, department stores, and so on. Would the anarchists have anything to complain about now? Doesn't the combination of public and private actions to expand money and credit obviate their notion of a money monopoly? Perhaps, but their discussions of monetary reform are still relevant. Monetary theory is still little understood and subject to centralized decision-making (the Fed, Bundesbank, IMF, etc.). Money and credit are still essential, though usually discussed at the national level, e.g., third-world development, establishing convertible currencies in the former communist party-states of Eastern Europe. That is, there still seems to be money monopoly, or perhaps oligopoly (on the world scale), even if there isn't a monetary orthodoxy any more (the hard money men have been replaced by Keynesians and monetarists). Moreover, there are currently advocates of free banking, making much the same recommendations as the anarchists, though usually without the "socialist" overlay.[3] This leads to the central paradox, which J. Greevz Fisher insistently pointed out over and over in *Liberty*. Fisher contended that free banking would lead to greater stability and would stimulate commerce, but would not end the exploitation of labor. History seems to have borne out his analysis, for credit is much expanded now, the basis of money has been broadened, and institutions like credit unions perform functions similar to mutual banks (extending credit, rather than currency directly). What does not seem to have happened is for workers to have been enabled by this to gain control of production; they have simply been enabled to consume more. But, perhaps this mass affluence would have satisfied Tucker, if individual liberty went along with it.

Further Reading in Liberty

The earliest substantial discussion of monetary reform in *Liberty* was a dialogue between "Basis" and Tucker: "Apex or Basis," December 10, 1881 (I:10, #10), pp. 2-4. Tucker was also involved in a lengthy set of exchanges with Joshua K. Ingalls, the land reformer: Ingalls, "Unescapable Interest," December 15, 1894 (X:16, #302), pp. 4-5 with Tucker's comment "Narrowing the Issue," #302, p. 2; continues January 26, 1895 (X:19, #305), pp. 4-5; March 9, 1895 (X:22, #308), p. 4; May 4, 1895 (X:26, #312), pp. 6-7, 4.

The Englishman J. Greevz Fisher favored mutual banking, but did not think that it would have all the benefits that Tucker and others claimed for it. He disputed with Tucker directly on mutual banking: "Free Trade in Banking," July 11, 1891 (VIII:6, #188), pp. 3-4; "The Equalization of Wage and Product," August 22, 1891 (VIII:11, #193), pp. 2-3. With Hugo Bilgram, he argued over whether interest was just (he took the affirmative): Bilgram, "Interest is Unjust," March 10, 1894 (IX:48, #282), p. 11; Fisher, "Interest is Just," May 19, 1894 (X:1, #287), p. 8 (with Bilgram's rejoinder); continues July 28, 1894 (X:6, #292), pp. 8-9; November 17, 1894 (X:14, #300), pp. 4-5; January 12, 1895 (X:18, #304), pp. 4-5; March 9, 1895 (X:22, #308), pp. 4-5. In 1896, he denied John Badcock, Jr.'s argument that there was a shortage of money: Badcock, "The Money Famine," July 11, 1896 (XII:5, #343), pp. 6-8; Fisher, "The (Alleged) Money Famine, October 1896 (XII:8, #346), p. 6 (with Badcock's response, pp. 6-7; continues January 1897 (XII:11, #349), pp. 4-5; April 1897 (XIII:2, #352), p. 7. Most of the above are cited as endnotes to Robinson's selection.

"Interest"—John Beverley Robinson*

In this lengthy introduction to the questions of interest, the money monopoly, and mutual banking, Robinson tried to make monetary reform understandable and urgent. Insisting that reform, and consequently knowledge, of money was essential for general prosperity and for a more egalitarian distribution of wealth, Robinson touched on most of the themes that had already provoked detailed debates in the pages of Liberty. *The extensive endnotes to this selection refer the reader to points of controversy and to representative articles that discussed these points.*

Interest is what is paid for the use of money.[4] Undoubtedly interest is paid for the use of other things than money, as when a house or a piano is rented; but other things command a price for the use of them only because restrictions upon the issue and loan of money make it impossible, except by paying a price for its use, to borrow money with which these other things might be bought.

So it is that the question of interest hangs upon the money question; and whoever would understand how it is that a large part of the products of labor is taken from the producers by those who do not labor must have some idea of money and finance.

Money and finance! Oh, horrible! exclaims the reader; I never could understand anything about finance!

Nevertheless, it is a matter of life and death. We are in misery now, because we don't understand finance; we shall be destroyed, unless we set about understanding it. The people that grasps clear ideas on the money question will be the people best adapted to its environment, and will survive; should no people prove capable, as a people, of grasping clear ideas on the question, there can be no doubt that the whole of the nineteenth-century civilization, such as it is, will perish.

We have reached a point in social development where the social assimilation of correct ideas about money is imperative. The astonishing state of affairs with which we now find ourselves unexpectedly confronted in these last days of the century is wholly a problem of distribution. Things enough, in all conscience, we have, and we have unlimited power of making more things,—enough for everybody to have plenty; but, strange to say, for some hitherto unperceived cause, the people who

---

* May 1897 (XIII:3, #353), pp. 5–7.

want to go to work to make things cannot, and the people who want things cannot get them, and everything is in an economic muddle.

As I said, it is a problem of more skillfully dividing up what we have produced, or what we can produce,—a problem of distribution; and a problem of distribution is a money problem, because money, after all, is but a tool to accomplish distribution.

In trying to get light on this paramount question, begin by discarding everything that is usually read or said about it.

On general principles, when we are looking for a solution of a social problem, we must expect to reach conclusions quite opposed to the usual opinions on the subject; otherwise it would be no problem. We must expect to have to attack, not what is commonly regarded as objectionable, but what is commonly regarded as entirely proper and normal.

Therefore, begin by disbelieving all the usual talk, and all that is printed in newspapers and the regular run of books upon money. A good deal of what they say is true, but it is so mixed with what is false that, until you have your fundamental ideas straightened out, by which to discriminate for yourself, you will be as much misled by what is true as by what is false.

As for incomprehensibility, don't for a moment imagine that these money and finance questions are as complicated as the people who write about them make them out to be. For the most part, these writers do not in the least understand the matters they write about, and they inevitably jumble the mere accidents of the practical workings with the essential principles of the theory.

In the concrete money is complicated enough; in the abstract it is simplicity itself. Let me try to give you some clear idea of the simple bottom principle.

In the first place they will tell you, with a profound air of wisdom, that the only really real money is gold and silver. Money-metals they call them, in their supercilious, round-eyed superiority, as if there could be any inward unweighable virtue in gold and silver, rather than in any other metal, or even than in any other substance, which must forever make them the only possible money! That is the first falsity that you will have to deny to yourself in your own mind, irrespective of my denial of it here.

For in these matters each must think for himself. Believe nothing on the authority of others. Weigh and understand and decide for yourself.

True enough it is that gold and silver have been much used for money, have in their time served a good purpose; but it is also true that these gold and silver coins are but a sort of merchandise themselves, and to exchange other merchandise for them is, after all, nothing but a kind of barter.[5]

Besides this, it is long since gold and silver were the only money. For many years now paper documents of various kinds have been used as money,—have been paid out and received for goods and services in final settlement. So that gold and silver are evidently not the only money.[6] Paper promises, we see with our eyes, are just as good as gold and silver themselves as a machine for exchanging the real things, the bread and meat and clothes and houses, which are what we really want. Better, in fact, because, if we could use paper documents only, we might use the gold and silver coins and bricks for far better purposes than jingling them in pockets and passing them from hand to hand, from purse to till and from till to purse, until they are worn to dust again. Sheer waste, that is, of good gold and silver, useful as they might be in their incorrodibility above tin and copper for sauce-pans, fly-screens, and many other purposes.

If paper will do, why not, in common sense, use paper?

Yet here our wiseacres will step forward, put on their spectacles, and solemnly announce that, as long as there is gold and silver to pay off the paper promises with, the paper promises are all right, but—and so on.

True enough, in a sense, too, this is, and once upon a time it was thought necessary for the man who paid out paper promises to have an equal amount of coin-money in his strong-boxes to redeem his paper promises. But now there is not enough coin in the world to redeem more than a small part of the paper promises that are used every day.

The truth is that, as the exchanges of the world increased, and the time came when there was not enough gold and silver to effect these exchanges, so that people had to resort to paper promises, with gold and silver as security, the exchanges of the world increased so vastly that now there is not enough gold and silver in the world even for security for the paper promises that are required as a machine to exchange things.

Consequently the paper money of today, in spite of the demonstrations of the wiseacres, is not secure. There is three or four or eight or ten times as much paper as there is coin which the paper promises to pay, so that the time must come, and does come every little while, when there is more coin wanted than can be had for redeeming the promises, and one of the financial crises, or panics, ensues,—one of these panics that are becoming so ominously frequent and fatal.

Still, up to the panic point, we see for ourselves that paper promises serve sufficiently well. Were it not that they promise to do what it is well known to be impossible to do, they might serve even better. But, notwithstanding this drawback, paper it is nowadays, and paper of some sort apparently it must be.

Let us drop, then, this word money, along with the old conception of gold as the only money. What we want to do is to trade, to exchange, by the easiest means. Paper so far is the easiest means. Call it no longer money; call it currency, simply for convenience of nomenclature. Paper currency we know is possible; it seems to be inevitable; as a fact, it is almost the only currency used.

Consider now the fact that a certain quantity of this paper or other currency is needed to carry on the horse trades and innumerable other trades in these wide-spread United States, in this wider-spread globe surface. As things are at present, what currency we have is restricted in quantity in two ways. The first of these restrictions is the surviving belief that gold or silver is the only possible commodity that can redeem paper currency. Although it is absurd to suppose that a currency is safe when there is enough gold and silver to redeem a part of the currency, yet the superstition survives that a certain proportion must be maintained, and that, although we may require normally thrice as much paper as gold, yet it would not be "safe" to have more than twice as much.

The second restriction is the method by which alone more currency can be obtained when it is needed.

Think of currency, all the time, as simply paper documents, destitute of value in themselves, but necessary to keep the running accounts straight between men. Statisticians will point out that by far the greater part of the business of the world is done by checks and drafts and such commercial devices, and will urge that currency is really a trivial matter, almost a superfluity.[7]

Anybody who has passed through the financial crisis of the year 1893 will know how essential this matter of currency is. During the height of the panic no currency could be obtained. The consequence was that business was almost stopped.

Other devices were used as far as possible, especially credit; people kept on buying groceries and the necessaries of life; what few factories kept at work had to put off the payment of wages for week after week. In every way people tried to get along without currency. Nevertheless it was only demonstrated how indispensable currency is. Checks and mercantile paper are really founded upon currency, being all of them promises to pay currency; credit does well enough for a while, in the expectation of currency to settle balances, but neither commercial paper or credit can take the place of the organized credit that we call currency.[8]

This currency, these documents that pass from hand to hand, without endorsement and in final settlement, must be had, and must be had every year in greater quantities as the trade of the world grows.

Now, in order to get these instruments of exchange, what do we do? Manufacture them or buy them? By no means. We have to borrow them, borrow them from the banks. We do not realize it, most of us plain people, because we so seldom come in contact with banks and banking devices. Most of us do our work and get our wages at the end of the week, pay our grocer's and butcher's bills, and think little of where the bills come from or go to. Where they go is plain enough; the butcher or grocer deposits them in some banks; but where they come from is not so plain.

Where does the bank get them?

The bank gets them from a set of politicians at Washington, who are in the service of the banks and bankers.

They have these bills printed, and lend them to the banks at a charge of one percent, which is called a tax, but is the same as one percent interest.[9]

The banks lend them for as high a rate of interest as they can get, and the scarcer currency is, the more they can get for it.[10]

Remember, too, that the banks do not lend without taking security from the borrower. He who would borrow from a bank must either deposit with the bank some tangible security, or he must give his personal note for it, which is the same as pledging his stock, whatever it may be. The bank lends him no wealth, because he must have wealth himself to pledge, to the amount he wishes to borrow. All the bank does is lend its name to certify to his solvency.[11] And, for this insurance of his credit, so to speak, the bank can make him pay at least six percent, lending the bills that it receives for one percent, for six, or even more, in proportion to the stress, up to one or two percent, not yearly, but monthly, on a certain class of loans.

By the necessity that people are under of depositing their currency with a bank in order to do business, and by the equal necessity they are under of borrowing from the bank at times, the banks are enabled to tax us all, on every transaction, six percent and upwards.

Nor is the payment of this forced tax the greatest wrong. Indeed, we might pay all they demand, and still be happy, were it not for a far greater ill that is involved. This ill is the intolerable restriction on the amount of work that can be done, on the amount of wealth and comfort that can be produced,—a restriction that is caused by the arbitrary limitation of the currency supply.

We see at the present moment thousands, yes, hundreds of thousands, of men throughout the country anxious to go to work to produce each the things that the others want to buy. They are longing, all of them, to exchange the products of their labor. The coal-miners dying because they are not allowed to dig coal to warm the shoemakers, and going without shoes which the shoemakers may make, but are forbidden to exchange with the coal miners. And so it is throughout the industrial world; one cannot produce, because another cannot produce.[12] Yet the bankers will tell you—and probably it is true—that there is a vast hoard of currency which they would be only too glad to lend. Yes, no doubt, but at rates of interest higher than anybody can pay for it; or, if at lower rates, then under conditions regarding time of repayment that make it useless to borrow. On loans for a definite period not less than five percent—for the most part six—will satisfy their demand. In other kinds of business, when they cannot make a sale, they know the price is too high, and put it down. The banks do not put the price down, and will not. Why? Because the banks have a monopoly.

How is that? you ask. Cannot anybody start a bank? Yes, in a way; in another way, decidedly not. In the first place, there are laws which absolutely forbid the issue of any more bank currency, except by the deposit, not of any good security, but of government bonds which practically cannot be had.

In the second place, there is about as much paper currency already in existence as the gold and silver in existence will warrant, and, as long as gold and silver are the only legal security for currency, there cannot be much more currency.[13]

But why not, you will ask, leave other things for security, beside gold and silver, if there is not enough of these?

Here is precisely the trouble. There is a United States law heavily taxing any such issue of currency and there are separate State laws making it a criminal offence to issue or pass any other currency than that authorized by the government.

So that the monopoly of the banks, although not a formal monopoly, is maintained by so many legal restrictions that it is just as close a monopoly really as if it were formally so constituted.

Were it not so, in crises like the present business concerns of high standing would pay off their employees in small due-tickets, which the employees in turn could pay to the coal-dealers and hatters, who would receive them on the credit of the standing of the issuing concern. Shortly institutions would spring up of even wider connections, to make a business of handling such wage-tickets, issuing their own in place of them, and a currency system would grow up, undefended by law, dependent on its merits for its existence, and furnishing a method of exchange without any interest charge at all.

This is what is meant by free banking. The old State banks were not free at all, but subject to as many restrictions as banks now are, with the same result of making their services expensive and inefficient, or even detrimental.

Really free currency means, in the first place, no legal-tender laws.

Why? Because a really sound currency people will receive on its merits. Only an unsound currency needs a legal-tender law to compel people to take it. Our present currency needs it because it is necessarily unsound; there is supposed to be enough gold to redeem it, but everybody knows that there is not; consequently it requires law to compel people to receive it. Take away the law, and the fact that a currency commands confidence is assurance of the sufficiency of its security.[14]

Really free currency means, in the second place, no legal requirement of any particular kind of wealth to redeem it,—not gold or silver or anything else,—leaving that to the judgment of those who are to receive it, but who cannot be compelled to receive it, in the absence of compulsory legal tender laws, if they do not like the security.[15]

Really free currency means, in the third, fourth, fifth, and nth places, the removal of all other taxes, inspections, certifications, and restrictions of every kind.

In the absence of such restrictions, imagine the rapid growth of wealth, and the equity in its distribution, that would result. Thus, for a supposition, a group of men would pledge their possessions, houses, workshops, goods, and chattels to a sufficient amount.

They would print notes of certain small amounts,—one dollar, two dollars, and so on,—and scrip of even smaller denominations. A farmer needs to stock his farm. Now he must mortgage for six, eight, ten percent. Then he would go to the free bank and pledge his farm, and receive the use of its notes, a handful of them, to the amount of half the value of his farm, for which he would pay not six, or four, or even two percent. Three-quarters of one or one percent would be all he would have to pay.[16]

Why? Because there would be other free banks competing with this bank, so that the price of currency would shortly come down to the mere cost of running the bank, paying the clerks, and printing the notes.[17]

Although starting as local concerns, and at first commanding only local confidence, it would be but a short time before a system of currency would be developed that would extend over the world, as even now bankers' letters of credit are international, while most government notes are only national.

Enough. If you have not yet caught the idea, keep thinking about it, and you will eventually seize it.

In doing away with interest for the use of money, we do away, at one blow, with interest of all kinds, whether called interest, or under the name of house-rent, dividends, or share of profits; the trifling amount that would be paid for the use of currency would not, properly speaking, be interest at all, but wages, paid for their labor to the people who made it their business to provide currency.

All that is produced, it must be borne in mind, naturally belongs to the producer. It is only by the artificial legal restrictions that we have permitted to exist that a large part of the product is taken from the producer and handed to the idler in the forms of rent and interest.

By abolishing these we permit the producer to retain his whole product, to the advantage of all concerned; for every one knows and no one better than the idlers themselves, that man's greatest happiness is in congenial and productive labor.

But a far greater advantage will accompany the abolition of interest. Not only does interest now take a large slice of the proceeds without giving any equivalent, but it actually prevents people from producing anything like what they could produce otherwise.

To go to work at all, land is essential; to work to any advantage, exchange is essential. No machinery ever invented has the wealth-producing power of division of labor and exchange of products.

Yet we have so arranged it that, before anybody can go to work, he must pay a tax to somebody who owns the land, and before anybody can trade, he must pay a tax to somebody who owns the tools of exchange.

Remove these bonds, and the volume of production would more than suffice for all human wants.

In doing away with interest, the cause of inequality in material circumstances will be done away with; the frightful scene of overfed luxury and of helpless destitution that now shocks us will disappear.

For ages the dream of mankind has been equality; for ages the achievement of equality has eluded our efforts.

Even now men's minds are filled with devices which are expected to at least bring equality nearer,—devices such as the taxation of inheritances and the taxation of large incomes; all bungling attempts to remedy by legislation the ills which are the outcome of previous legislation . . .

When we learn that the only work that is work at all, economically speaking, is productive work, and that the well-to-do are well-to-do in proportion as they do less productive work, and depend more upon other people's earnings; when we find that they have, as it is called, an independent income, which, clever or stupid, industrious or lazy, honorable or scoundrel, they continue to receive, we begin to doubt the correctness of the opinion which so loudly announces that men have only what they merit.

Yet even when we have reached this point of questioning the validity of interest, we are still at a loss. It seems so reasonable, it is undoubtedly so just, that one should receive for lending what another is willing to pay that we are quite baffled in our inquiries. The old-fashioned indignation against the money-lender seems so misplaced, for we perceive quite clearly that the money-lender is doing only what the borrower is anxious that he should do.[18]

Still another contradiction comes when we reflect that this interest, which seems so natural, is, from another point of view, quite absurd and impossible.

We all know the astonishing stories of the accumulating power of compound interest,—how a dollar, set to grow in the year one, would now outvalue several worlds,—and we can figure for ourselves that these statements are substantially true. When we consider, moreover, that a good deal of all interest is compound interest, because many people who receive interest do not spend it all, but invest some of it to draw more interest, we see that it is impossible; that at a certain point the rate of increase is greater than the whole product of the globe could pay.

It is only when we begin to understand that the borrower does not really pay freely,—that he is compelled by a monopoly, backed by rifles, to pay what he must,—that we begin to see the cause of inequality, and to understand the remedy . . .

Notes

1. James J. Martin, *Men against the State: The Expositors of Individualist Anarchism in America, 1827-1908* (Colorado Springs: Ralph Myles, 1970), pp. 14-24; Bowman N. Hall, "The Economic Ideas of Josiah Warren, First American Anarchist," *History of Political Economy*, 6:1 (1974), pp. 95-108.

2. Martin, *Men against the State*, pp. 125-138; Bowman N. Hall, "William Greene and His System of 'Mutual Banking,'" *History of Political Economy*, 8:2 (1976), pp. 279-296.

3. Lawrence H. White, *Free Banking in Britain: Theory, Experience, and Debate, 1800-1845*, Cambridge: Cambridge University Press, 1984, especially chapter two.

4. There was considerable debate on whether interest was paid for the use of *money* or for the use of *capital* (commodities actually used in the production process, e.g., machines): Hugo Bilgram, "Is Interest Just?" April 22, 1893 (IX:34, #268), pp. 1, 3; J. K. Ingalls, "Interest Just and Unjust," June 10, 1893 (IX:41, #275), p. 1; J. Greevz Fisher, "The Value and Volume of Money," April 1897 (XIII:2, #352), p. 7.

5. Substantially the same argument is made by Hugo Bilgram ("Is Interest Just?" #268, pp. 1, 3) and J. Greevz Fisher ("Interest is Just," November 17, 1894 [X:14, #300], pp. 4-5; "The Value of Money and Its Volume," January 1897 [XII:11, #349], pp. 4-5; "The Value and Volume of Money," April 1897 [XIII:2, #352], p. 7).

6. Fisher makes this as a point *against* the urgent need for mutual banks: "The Power of Government over Values," June 27, 1891 (VIII:5, #187), p. 3.

7. Fisher insisted that this practical "monetization" of credit obviated the need for mutual money: "Interest is Just," July 28, 1894 (X:6, #292), p. 8.

8. That is, as Tucker insisted contrary to Fisher, credit must be *effectively* "monetized": response to Fisher, "The Equalization of Wage and Product," August 22, 1891 (VIII:11, #193), pp. 2-3.

9. This, along with the "reserve ratio" of specie held to currency in circulation, was acknowledged by Fisher to be a genuine, albeit trivial, restriction placed by government on the money supply: "The Power of Government over Values," #187, p. 3.

10. Fisher again dissented, attributing the interest rate to the amount of *capital* available, not to the amount of money: "Free Trade in Banking," July 11, 1891 (VIII:6, #188), p. 3; "Interest is Just," November 17, 1894 (X:14, #300), pp. 4–5.
11. Bilgram describes this as an exchange of promissory notes, in which the bank has the advantage because *its* notes are government-backed, i.e. money: "Is Interest Just?" April 22, 1893 (IX:34, #268), pp. 1, 3.
12. John Badcock, Jr. also complained of this "money famine," insisting that monetary reform was essential to an industrial economy, because of the centrality of indirect exchanges: "The Money Famine," July 11, 1896 (XII:5, #343), pp. 6–8.
13. Tucker complained that the problem with money is "limiting by law the security for these promises to pay to a special kind of property, limited in quantity and easily monopolizable." (response to J. K. Ingalls, "Free Money," December 13, 1884 [III:4, #56], p. 4) This led, he felt, to inflation in the value of gold: "the present value of gold is a monopoly value sustained by the exclusive monetary privilege given it by government." (response to J. Greevz Fisher, "The Power of Government over Values," June 27, 1891 [VIII:5, #187], pp. 3–4) See also Tucker's response to Fisher, "The Equalization of Wage and Product," August 22, 1891 (VIII:11, #193), pp. 2–3.
14. That is, people should be free to issue their own currency and, in the context of free competition, only secure currencies will be readily circulated. See Tucker, "On Picket Duty," July 30, 1887 (IV:26, #104), p. 1; Tucker, "An Unwarranted Question," October 18, 1890 (VII:13, #169), p. 4; John Badcock, Jr., "The Money Famine," July 11, 1896 (XII:5, #343), pp. 6–8.
15. This was a central premise of free (and mutual) banking: Tucker, "Apex or Basis," December 10, 1881 (I:10, #10), pp. 2–4; Tucker's response to Fisher, "The Equalization of Wage and Product," August 22, 1891 (VIII:11, #193), pp. 2–3. A Proudhonian had argued that what was needed was that "merchandise, products, social wealth must be enabled to exchange . . . without the aid of *specie*." ("How to Establish Credit," December 31, 1892 [IX:18, #252], p. 1).
16. The figure for the ultimate rate of interest varied, but was usually below one percent: Tucker, "Apex or Basis," #10, pp. 2–4; Tucker, "Narrowing the Issue," December 15, 1894 (X:16, #302), p. 2.
17. That is, it would approach Josiah Warren's ideal, "cost the limit of price": Tucker, "Narrowing the Issue," #302, p. 2. Fisher dened this, suggesting that lenders would always have the incentive to lend at higher rates: J. Greevz Fisher, "The (Alleged) Money Famine," October 1896 (XII:8, #346), p. 6.
18. This is implicit in the argument that interest is due the borrower because she has "sacrificed" the use of her money for some period of time, an argument made by Fisher ("The Equalization of Wage and Product," August 22, 1891 [VIII:11, #193], pp. 2–3; "Interest is Just," July 28, 1894 [X:6, #292], p. 8), but challenged by Tucker ("Apex or Basis" #10, pp. 2–4), Henry Appleton ("Professor Sumner on Interest," March 27, 1886 [III:26, #78], p. 4), and Hugo Bilgram ("Is Interest Just?" #268, pp. 1, 3; Bilgram's rejoinder to Fisher, "Interest is Just," November 17, 1894 [X:14, #300], p. 5).

6

Rent and the Land Monopoly

Land reform, like monetary reform, was a perennial in the garden of American radicalism. Nowhere else among the industrialized countries was the hold of agrarianism so strong and so linked to individualist premises. America's promise of wide open spaces, the Jeffersonian emphasis on the yeoman farmer, and the actual spread of individual land proprietorship across the country made any changes in land ownership seem especially threatening. By the 1880s, those threats were mounting: huge government land grants to railroads, the limited distribution of land under the Homestead acts, the "closing" of the frontier, and the constant debt problems of farmers. Land reform received further impetus from the massive emigration of landless Irish to America. In 1880, Henry George published his bestseller, *Progress and Poverty*, which argued that rent was not earned by the landowner, but was rather a reflection of the increased value of land in settled and developed communities. Because rent was thus a social product, George proposed a tax to confiscate rent for society's benefit. This "single tax" would be more than sufficient to meet the fiscal needs of government and, moreover, would not infringe on any individual's right to use land, merely attacking the landlord's unjust extraction of rent. It was with such governmental land reforms, as well as with lingering justifications of the status quo in land, that the individualist anarchists had to contend in *Liberty*.[1]

Their analysis of land and rent paralleled in many ways that of money and interest. Like interest, rent was considered by most of the individualist anarchists to be the artificial creation of a government-backed monopoly. In this case, the government provided legal titles to land and protected the exclusive property rights of such titled owners. Because landowners controlled an essential factor of production, they were enabled to extract a portion of the labor product, demanding rent as the price for using their land. The key, then, was to break the land monopoly, to open up access to land. While the money supply could be increased by allowing commodities other than precious metals to serve as the basis of value, there was no substitute for land: its quantity was fixed. Thus, in order to break up land monopolies, there had to be some redistribution; the amount of land that any person could control had somehow to be limited. How could this be accomplished within an anarchist society? Governments could certainly set and enforce some arbitrary limits, or even "rational" ones, but anarchists had to find some method consistent with their emphasis on individual liberty. The concept of "equal liberty" came to the rescue: an individual's freedom to use land had to be limited by the equal freedom of others to use land. For the individualist anarchists, the principle of "occupancy and use" of land would ensure this relative equality of land use. According to this principle, an individual could claim exclusive rights to a plot of land only as large as she could personally occupy and use, and for only as long as it was still being occupied and used. Of course, defining occupancy and (especially) use could be quite tricky, especially without the expedient of a legal code, but the anarchists felt that it would be possible.

The selections below from *Liberty* reflect the historical context and theoretical problems of their proposal for land reform. Selection A comes from the preeminent anarchist land reformer, Joshua King Ingalls, and contrasts the approach of Henry George with the land limitation scheme of George Henry Evans in the antebellum period. Selection B finds Benjamin Tucker debating with Stephen T. Byington, an advocate of George's "single tax," over the nature of rent. Finally, Tucker addresses the complaints of Auberon Herbert (selection C) and the questions of Bolton Hall (selection D) about the concept of "occupancy and use."

Further Readings in Liberty

John Beverley Robinson wrote an article called "Rent" (December 1896 [XII:10, #348], pp. 6-8) that was very similar in form and intent to his article "Interest." Victor Yarros wrote several articles on land, paying particular attention to the views of Herbert Spencer, criticizing both his early argument against individual land ownership and his later support of existing individual ownership: "Private Property and Freedom,"

November 15, 1890 (VII:15, #171), pp. 4–5; "Justice and Anarchism—III," September 19, 1891 (VIII:15, #197), p. 2.

Henry George was the target of at least two lengthy articles in *Liberty*: J.K. Ingalls, "Henry George Examined. Should Land Be Nationalized or Individualized," supplement to October 14, 1882 (II:1, #27); Tak Kak [James Walker], "Spencer and George," April 1, 1893 (IX:31, #265), p. 2 (continues #268, p. 2; #272, p. 2; #275, p. 2).

A.   "Land Reform in 1848 and 1888"—J. K. Ingalls[*]

Ingalls, a veteran of land reform, had long published articles in the Irish World, from which Tucker recruited several writers on reform. Like most of the individualist anarchists, he was an advocate of limiting land holdings in order to preserve access to land. This ran counter to the most famous land reform of the 1880s, Henry George's "single tax," which would preserve present land ownership, but tax away rent. Here, Ingalls contrasts George's reform (the 1888 of the title) with the land limitation scheme of the American reformer George Henry Evans (1848).[2]

I do not propose to discuss the respective claims of [Henry] George and [George Henry] Evans as authorities on the land question, nor, at any length, the nature of their peculiar plans or schemes; but will state the "measure" of the one, and the "remedy" of the other, briefly, leaving you to judge between them as reason or prejudice may determine. So far as a statement of the pernicious influence of land monopoly is concerned, Mr. George has simply reiterated the arguments and statements of the early reformers, and, if in more attractive phrase, it does not necessarily follow that the influence of his utterances will be more enduring. So far the two men and their eras present no important differences. Only in respect to: "What is to be done?" do they differ. They represent in this not only different eras, but quite different systems of philosophy, social and political. It is true they agree that reform must come through the ballot and through legislation. But Mr. Evans belonged to the school that believes government to be a necessary evil, and that we are to have as little to do with it as possible. That nature is to be relied on mainly, and that to correct the evils of already existing legislation is the great aim to

---

[*] June 9, 1888 (V:22, #126), p. 5. Excerpted from two articles published under this title in *Truth Seeker*.

be sought by the reformer. Thus far he is an optimist. The line of Mr. George's thought is decidedly pessimistic. He accepts the theories of Malthus and Ricardo that rent, that synonym of all subjection and the oppression men suffer from it, is a result of natural law, which can only be eliminated through Statecraft and the rule of force, and that the onward march of progress, with its natural adjunct, poverty, can only thus be stayed . . .

The plan of Mr. Evans was this: By political agitation and control of the legislature to place a limit to the ownership of land. This principle had already been applied to religious and other corporate institutions, and to the patenting of the public lands "only to actual settlers in limited quantities." The maximum had been fixed at one hundred and sixty acres. Mr. Evans suggested this as a limit to private ownership, not as a fixed quantity, but to obtain a recognition of the right of government to so limit it, to be modified as wisdom should direct in the future. He contemplated a peaceful attainment of this object, by wise gradations, invading no "vested rights," yet effectually preventing any further accumulation of landed estates beyond the legal limit, whether by purchase, gift, or inheritance. All of these matters are held to be subjects properly regulative by statute law. The advocates of land nationalization propose to have the State resume the title to the land it has once already sold to private parties; to be rented back to those who want and are able to hire. Mr. George simplifies this process by treating land values as simply the amount of rent the land will yield, and taxing it back entire without any disturbance to owners or to occupiers. This may be termed "a short method" of "land nationalization." It means "confiscation of rent."

You have here substantially the means proposed by the two men, representing different schools and distinct periods, for the reform of a universally admitted evil, the monopolized control of the only passive factor in production,—the home and standing-place and work-room of the whole human family. They are in accord fully as to the nature of the evil to be remedied, and, indeed, as to the necessity of securing political supremacy to accomplish the reform. The great object, as both agree, is justice to labor, the abolition of poverty, and the promotion of the public good. But the measures for which such political power is to be wielded in order to accomplish those ends are wholly incompatible with each other. The one sought equality through limitation of power and restriction of privilege, mutually operative as to all citizens of a State. The other seeks the annihilation of a class, allodial owners, embracing those whose ownership promotes social prosperity as well as those which endanger it, and the making of every occupant of the land a tenant of the State, but offers no guarantee whatever against the unlimited control of the land through lease-hold, or the extension of legal privilege to the lordly rule of capital, such leases would give.

Now, limitation of powers is involved in, and is, indeed, the professed burden of, all forms of legislation whatever. Limitation to private owner-ship of an essential, natural element, indispensable to the life and to the well-being of the individual, is a logical and constitutional means of redress, under any view of law which ever prevailed. It accords with our system of tenure, which assumes that the right of occupancy is in every one of the whole people. "Confiscation of rent," on the other hand, would require an entire subversion of our system of occupancy and of well-es-tablished principles of property; it is inconsistent with our Constitution, if we have one; and, being revolutionary in its character, should only be resorted to in the last extremity, even were it in itself wise and feasible. This remedy is, doubtless, compatible with the fictions of English law and of monarchy by "divine right"; but not by any theory of democracy or principles of equity with which I am acquainted. But I think the time for promoting any positive reform of the land system through political ascendancy, and by legislative preponderance of an honest purpose to effect a public good, has long since passed away, through either Mr. George's or Mr. Evans's schemes. For it is quite apparent now to clear-headed people that the land question, and all other questions of human interest, will take care of themselves, if governments will let them alone, withdraw their bailiffs, tax-gatherers, detective police, and bandit, mercenary soldiery . . .

B.   "Economic Rent"
—Stephen T. Byington vs. Benjamin Tucker[*]

In this selection, Byington, a tenacious advocate of the single-tax within Liberty, *asks how anarchism will do away with economic rent, that is, the benefit that landholders derive from the natural superiority of one plot of land over another. Tucker responds that, even though such economic rent is really an "extra and usurious reward," it will not*

* November 5, 1892 (IX:10, #244), pp. 2-3.

directly be abolished by the principle of occupancy and use in land. Thus, the single-taxers proposal to confiscate this rent through taxation is a violation of property designed to promote an arbitrary scheme of equalization. Tucker's closing comments on the nature of equal liberty led to a continuation of the debate for several more issues, but the central arguments occur here.[3]

To the Editor of Liberty:
    I have often seen it claimed that under the Anarchistic organization of society economic rent would disappear, or be reduced to an insignificant amount. But I have never yet been satisfied with any explanation of the way in which this is to be brought about.
    Some speak as if the abolition of rent were to be an immediate result of the abolition of interest, apparently taking the ground that rent is a product of the selling price of land and the interest of money. But according to the accepted theory of economists (the only one that I have learned to understand), rent is the independent factor, and the selling price is the product of rent and interest . . .
    As to the freeing of vacant land, I do not remember to have heard that this would destroy any but "speculative" rent. There might perhaps be a greater relief at first, while the vacant land was being taken. But certainly within a short time—within a year, I should say—all land which had any special advantage over ordinary farming land would be occupied, and these special advantages would be in the hands of the occupiers.
    On the other hand, it must be remembered that, if any economic rent is left, every advance in prosperity will naturally tend to increase this rent. And liberty is to cause an advance in prosperity . . .
    How, then, is economic rent to be got out of the way?
                                                                                Stephen T. Byington

    Liberty has never stood with those who profess to show on strictly economic grounds that economic rent must disappear or even decrease as a result of the application of the Anarchistic principle. It sees no chance for that factor in the human constitution which makes competition such a powerful influence—namely, the disposition to buy in the cheapest market—to act directly upon *economic* rent in a way to reduce it. This disposition to buy cheap, which in a free market is fatal to all other forms of usury, is on the contrary the mainstay of economic rent, whether the market be free or restricted. . . . The occupant of land who is enabled, by its superiority, to undersell his neighbor and at the same time to reap, through his greater volume of business, more profit than his neighbor, enjoys this economic rent precisely because of his opportunity to exploit the consumer's disposition to buy cheap . . .

There are other grounds, however, some of them indirectly economic, some of them purely sentimental, which justify the belief of the Anarchist that a condition of freedom will gradually modify to a very appreciable extent the advantage enjoyed by the occupant of superior land. Take first one that is indirectly economic. . . . When the laborer, in consequence of his increased wages and greater welfare resulting from the abolition of interest, shall enjoy a larger freedom of locomotion, shall be tied down less firmly to a particular employment, and shall be able to remove to the country with greater facility and in possession of more capital than he can now command, and when the country, partly because of the advances of science, shall continually offer a nearer approach to the undoubted privileges of city life, the representatives of commercial and other interests in the great cities will be able to hold their patrons about them only by lowering their prices and contenting themselves with smaller gains. In other words, economic rent will lessen. Here the disposition to buy cheap, not any special commodity, but an easy life, does exert an indirect and general influence upon economic rent . . .

Upon the sentimental grounds for believing in the evanescence of economic rent it is perhaps not worth while to dwell. I have an aversion to definite speculations based on hypothetical transformations in human nature. Yet I cannot doubt that the disappearance of interest will result in an attitude of hostility to usury, in any form, which will ultimately cause any person who charges more than cost for any product to be regarded very much as we now regard a pickpocket. In this way too economic rent will suffer diminution.

I think my correspondent fails to understand what is meant by the freeing of vacant land. It does not mean simply the freeing of unoccupied land. It means the freeing of all land not occupied *by the owner*. In other words, it means land ownership limited by occupancy and use. This would destroy not only speculative, but monopolistic rent, leaving no rent except the economic form, which will be received, while it lasts, not as a sum paid by occupant to owner, but as an extra and usurious reward for labor performed under special advantages.

But even if economic rent had to be considered a permanency; if the considerations which I have urged should prove of no avail against it,—it would be useless, tyrannical, and productive of further tyranny, to confiscate it. In the first place, if I have a right to a share of the advantages that accrue from the possession of superior land, then that share is mine; it is my property; it is like any other property of mine; no man, no body of men, is entitled to decide how this property shall be used; and any man or body of men attempting so to decide deprives me of my property just as truly as the owner of the superior land deprives me of it if allowed to retain the economic rent. In fact, still assuming that this property is mine, I prefer, if I must be robbed of it, to be robbed by the landowner, who is likely to spend it in some useful way, rather than by an institution called government, which probably will spend it for fireworks or something else which I equally disapprove. If the property is mine, I claim it, to do as I please with; if it is not mine, it is impertinent, dishonest, and tyrannical for any body to forcibly take it from the land-occupant on the pretense that it is mine and to spend it in my name. It is precisely this, however, that the Single-Taxers propose, and it is this that makes the Single Tax a State Socialistic measure. There was never anything more absurd than the supposition of some Single-Taxers that this tax can be harmonized with Anarchism . . . [4]

There are two ways, and only two, of effecting the distribution of wealth. One is to let it distribute itself in a free market in accordance with the natural operation of economic law; the other is to distribute it arbitrarily in accordance with statute law. One is Anarchism; the other is State Socialism. The latter, in its worst and most probable form, is the exploitation of labor by officialdom, and at its best is a *regime* of spiritless equality secured at the expense of liberty and progress; the former is a *regime* of liberty and progress, with as close an approximation to equality as is compatible therewith. And this is all the equality that we ought to have. A greater equality than is compatible with liberty is undesirable. The moment we invade liberty to secure equality we enter upon a road which knows no stopping-place short of the annihilation of all that is best in the human race. If absolute equality is the ideal; if no man must have the slightest advantage over another,—then the man who achieves greater results through superiority of muscle or skill or brain must not be allowed to enjoy them. All that he produces in excess of that which the weakest and stupidest produce must be taken from him and distributed among his fellows. The economic rent, not of land only, but of strength and skill and intellect and superiority of every kind, must be confiscated. And a beautiful world it would be when absolute equality had been thus achieved! Who would live in it? Certainly no freeman.

Liberty will abolish interest; it will abolish profit; it will abolish monopolistic rent; it will abolish taxation; it will abolish the exploitation of labor; it will abolish all means whereby any laborer can be deprived of any of his product; but it will not abolish the limited inequality between one laborer's product and another's. Now, because it has not this power last named, there are people who say: We will have no liberty, for we must have absolute equality. I am not of them. If I can go through life free and rich, I shall not cry because my neighbor, equally free, is richer. Liberty will ultimately make all men rich; it will not make all men equally rich. Authority may (and may not) make all men equally rich in purse; it certainly will make them equally poor in all that makes life best worth living.

C.   "Property under Anarchism"
—Albert Tarn, Auberon Herbert, Benj. Tucker[*]

Responding to Tarn's defense of the "occupancy and use" principle, Herbert, an English near-anarchist, complains that anarchism would lead either to "hard crystalline customs" in land tenure or to a "perpetual scramble." The best alternative to this, he felt, was the free market in land, in which titles would be based on purchase and sale, not use (which would limit, if not eliminate, the market in land).[5] Tucker dissents, claiming that what "scramble" there would be could easily be managed, and that titles based on occupancy and use would be no more rigid than those based on purchase and sale.

The current objection to Anarchism that it would throw property titles and especially land titles into hopeless confusion has originated an interesting discussion in "The Free Life" between Auberon Herbert, the editor, and Albert Tarn, an Anarchistic correspondent. Mr. Tarn is substantially right in the position that he takes; his weakness lies in confining himself to assertion,—a weakness of which Mr. Herbert promptly takes advantage.

---

[*] July 12, 1890 (VII:6, #162), p. 5.

Mr. Tarn's letter is as follows:

To the Editor of The Free Life:

Sir,—In your article on "The Great Question of Property" in last week's "Free Life" you speak of the weakness of the Anarchist position as involving either "hard crystalline customs very difficult to alter," or "some perpetually recurring form of scramble."

It seems strange that you can attribute to Anarchy just the very weaknesses that characterize our present property system. Why, it is now that we have "hard crystalline customs very difficult to alter," and a "perpetually-recurring"—nay, a never-ceasing—"form of scramble."

Anarchists, above all, though in favor of free competition, are averse to the eternal scramble which is now going on for the privileges which legal money and legal property confer, of living at ease at the expense of the masses . . .

Yours faithfully,
Albert Tarn

In Mr. Herbert's rejoinder the case against Anarchism is exceptionally well put, and for this reason among others I give it in full:

It is not enough for our correspondent, Mr. Tarn, to say that Anarchy does away with scramble; we want to know "the how" and "the why." Our contention is that under the law of the free market everybody knows, first, who owns a particular piece of property, and, secondly, the conditions under which property can be acquired. All is clear and definite, and that clearness and definiteness are worth far more to the human race in the long run than any temporary advantage to be gained by forcible interferings with distribution. On the other hand, we say that under Anarchy nobody would know to whom a piece of property belonged, and nobody would understand how it was to be transferred from A to B. Take any instance you like. Anarchists generally define property by use and possession; that is, whoever uses and possesses is to be considered owner. John Robins possesses a plot of three acres, and manages to feed two cows on it. John Smith possesses neither land nor cow. He comes to John Robins and says: "You are not really using and possessing these three acres, I shall take half of them." Who on earth is to judge between these men? Who is to say whether John Robins is really possessing or not? Who is going to say to John Smith that he shall not get a bit of land by "scramble" from John Robins, seeing that under the Anarchist system

that was the very way in which John Robins himself got his three acres
from the big landowner, who, as he said at the time, was not truly owning,
because he was not possessing.

Mr. Tarn finds fault with us for saying that Anarchy, or no fixed
standard of acquiring or owning, must lead either to rigid crystalline
custom or to scramble. But is that not almost absolutely certain? At first
it must be scramble. Everybody, who could, would take or keep on the
plea of possession. We presume even a weekly tenant would claim under
the same plea. But even when the first great scramble was over, the
smaller scrambles would continue,—the innumerable adjustments between John Robins and John Smith having to be perpetually made. But
after a certain time the race would tire of scramble, as it always has done,
and then what would happen? Why, necessarily, that a community would
silently frame for itself some law or custom that would decide all these
disputed cases. They would say that no man should hold more than two
acres; or that no man should be disturbed after so many years' possession;
or they would fix some other standard which would tend to become rigid
and crystalline, and be very difficult to alter just because there was no
machinery for altering it.

We say that our friends the Anarchists—with whom, when they are
not on the side of violence, we have much in common—must make their
position clear and definite about property. They are as much opposed as
we are to State-regulated property; they are as much in favor of individualistic property as we are; but they will not pay the price that has
to be paid for individualistic property, and which alone can make it
possible. When once you are away from the open market, there are only
two alternatives,—State-regulation (or law), and scramble. Every form
of property-holding, apart from the open market, will be found to be some
modification of one of these two forms.

. . . Mr Herbert, as I understand him, believes in voluntary association,
voluntarily supported, for the defense of person and property. Very well;
let us suppose that he has won his battle, and that such a state of things
exists. Suppose that all municipalities have adopted the voluntary principle, and that compulsory taxation has been abolished. Now after this
let us suppose further that the Anarchistic view that occupancy and use
should condition and limit landholding becomes the prevailing view.
Evidently then these municipalities will proceed to formulate and enforce
this view. What the formula will be no one can foresee. But continuing

with our suppositions, we will say that they decide to protect no one in the possession of more than ten acres. In execution of this decision, they, on October 1, notify all holders of more than ten acres within their limits that on and after the following January 1 they will cease to protect them in the possession of more than ten acres, and that, as a condition of receiving even that protection, each must make formal declaration on or before December 1 of the specific ten-acre plot within his present holding which he proposes to personally occupy and use after January 1. These declarations having been made, the municipalities publish them and at the same time notify landless persons that out of the land thus set free each may secure protection in the possession of any amount up to ten acres after January 1 by appearing on December 15 at a certain hour and making declaration of his choice and intention of occupancy. Now, says Mr. Herbert, the scramble will begin. Well, perhaps it will. But what of it? When a theatre advertises to sell seats for a star performance at a certain hour, there is a scramble to secure tickets. When a prosperous city announces that on a given day it will accept loans from individuals up to a certain aggregate on attractive terms, there is a scramble to secure the bonds. As far as I know, nobody complains of these scrambles as unfair. The scramble begins, and the scramble ends, and the matter is settled. Some inequality still remains, but it has been reduced to a minimum, and everybody has had an equal chance with the rest. So it will be with this land scramble. It may be conducted as peacefully as any other scramble, and those who are frightened by the word are simply the victims of a huge bugbear.

And the terror of rigidity is equally groundless. This rule of ten-acre possession, or any similar one that may be adopted, is no more a rigid crystalline custom than is Mr. Herbert's own rule of protecting titles transferred by purchase and sale. Any rule is rigid less by the rigidity of its terms than by the rigidity of its enforcement. Now it is precisely in the tempering of the rigidity of enforcement that one of the chief excellences of Anarchism consists. Mr. Herbert must remember that under Anarchism all rules and laws will be little more than suggestions for the guidance of juries, and that all disputes, whether about land or anything else, will be submitted to juries which will judge not only the facts but the law, the justice of the law, its applicability to the given circumstances, and the penalty or damage to be inflicted because of its infraction.[6] What better safeguard against rigidity could there be than this? "Machinery for altering" the law, indeed! Why, under Anarchism the law will be so flexible that it will shape itself to every emergency and need no alteration. And it will then be regarded as *just* in proportion to its flexibility, instead of as now in proportion to its rigidity.

D.   "Pertinent Questions"—Bolton Hall and Benj. Tucker[*]

Tucker was evidently in a good mood when he got Hall's letter, for he sometimes dismissed such questions about the details of the anarchist future as impertinent.[7] In this case, he provides some practical examples of how the general principle of occupancy and use might be applied. Tucker's point by point response here is typical of many of his replies to correspondents.

Hall:

First: I assume that Anarchic associations will protect me in the "use and occupation" of an acre around my house, stocked as a chicken-yard. Is that correct? (a) And, if so, will they protect me if the acre be on the corner of Wall St.? (b) Or in the use and occupation of one hundred thousand acres used and stocked as a deer-park, which would otherwise be waste-land? (c)

Second: will they protect me in the "use and occupation" of a home site, although I let out one room to a lodger? (a) If so, will they protect me in the "use and occupation" of the Mills building? (b)

Third: if a girl finds it more profitable to work for me tending those chickens than to work for herself, will I still be protected in the use and occupation of my chicken-yard? (a) If so, will I be protected in the use and occupation of a coal-mine as long as (by my power of organization, for example), I pay the miners more than they could earn working for themselves? (b) Will I be protected in its use and occupation if I do not work it up to its full capacity? (c) Or if another could get more out of it?

. . .

---

* June 1, 1895 (XI:3, #314), pp. 4–5.

Tucker:

First: (a) yes, provided you do actually so occupy and use it. (b) Yes. (c) No; for the hypothesis, "otherwise waste-land," excludes the need of protection.[8]

Second: (a) yes, but they would not collect your rent, and might not even evict your tenant. (b) If you personally occupied and used the land on which the Mills Building stands, that is, we will say, the basement and ground floor,—you would be allowed to add as many more stories as you chose to add and to make your own arrangements with tenants. But your tenants would not be forced to pay you rent, nor would you be allowed to seize their property. The Anarchic associations would look upon your tenants very much as they would look upon your guests.

Third: (a) yes, provided there was no obvious intent on your part to occupy more land than you could personally use for the given purpose, and provided it was not clearly impossible for one person to occupy and use so much land. Your own limitation of the area to one acre meets these provisions; so the answer in the given case is unqualifiedly in the affirmative. (b) . . . I can make only the general answer that Anarchic associations would recognize the right of individual occupants to combine their holdings and work them under any system they might agree upon, the arrangement being always terminable at will, with reversion to original rights. (c) If you did not occupy your coal-mine as your sole residence; and if you limited your working of it to the taking-out of one bucketful of coal per day; and if you continued this practice until it became reasonably sure that your method of procedure was not a temporary matter, due to illness or some other incidental cause,—I fancy that, some fine morning, after you had taken out your bucketful and gone away, the Anarchic association would proclaim your mine abandoned . .

Notes

1. Tucker in particular was opposed to the "single tax": "The Single Tax is a Communistic dogma, and the Individualists who uphold it are scandalously inconsistent." ("On Picket Duty," May 19, 1894 [X:1, #287], p. 1)
2. For more on Evans' role, see Kenneth R. Gregg, "George Henry Evans and The Origins of American Individualist-Anarchism," in Michael E. Coughlin, et al, eds., *Benjamin R. Tucker and the Champions of Liberty: A Centenary Anthology*, St. Paul: Michael E. Coughlin and Mark Sullivan, [1986], pp. 106–115.

3. Byington, "Liberty and Property," December 31, 1892 (IX:18, #252), pp. 1, 3; "The Meaning of Equal Liberty," February 18, 1893 (IX:25, #259), p. 2; "Try Freedom First," April 15, 1893 (IX:33, #267), pp. 2-3; "The Occupancy and Use Theory," June 3, 1893 (IX:40, #274), pp. 2-3.

4. Tucker made a similar point several years earlier: "I oppose the land-tax scheme because it would not make land free, but would simply make a change of landlords, and because it would enormously increase the power of a worse foe to labor than the landlord—namely the State." (Labor's Friend, "Bound to Go Slow, Even If He Goes Backward," November 5, 1887 [V:7, #111], p. 6)

5. Tucker acknowledges, but downplays, the difficulty of selling land under "occupancy and use" in a response to Byington ("Occupancy AND Use," January 25, 1896 [XI:19, #331], p. 4). Victor Yarros was much more sympathetic to Herbert's reliance on the free market: "Solutions of the Land Problem," August 10, 1889 (VI:19, #149), p. 5.

6. This is an allusion to a common belief among the individualist anarchists, first articulated by Lysander Spooner, that the role of juries had been very substantial in the English common-law tradition and that they had been gradually emasculated by government. Because of their specific functions, limited terms, and popular composition, juries would be a useful (and legitimate) organ of anarchist adjudication. Spooner's major argument for radically expanding the power of juries was *An Essay on the Trial by Jury* (1852). It is summarized in Martin, *Men against the State*, pp. 185-191 and is abridged by Victor Yarros in "Free Political Institutions: Their Nature, Essence, and Maintenance. An Abridgement and Rearrangement of Lysander Spooner's "Trial by Jury," *Liberty*, June 8, 1889 (VI:16, #146), pp. 2-3; continues #147, pp. 3, 6; #148, p. 3; #149, p. 2; #150, pp. 2-3; #151, pp. 2-3; #152, p. 3; #153, p. 3. See also Michael E. Coughlin, "The Jury: Defender or Oppressor," in Coughlin, et al., eds., *Benjamin R. Tucker and the Champions of Liberty*, pp. 44-64.

7. See, for example, his exasperation with Byington in "Occupancy AND Use," January 25, 1896 (XI:19, #331), p. 4. Byington suggested that Tucker's hesitancy was understandable, for when pressed he often gave absurd answers: "The Difficulties of Occupancy and Use," February 1897 (XII:12, #350), pp. 6-7.

8. Earlier, Tucker had acknowledged that hunters would be unlikely to be able to claim a very large tract of land as a hunting preserve: "On Picket Duty," February 9, 1895 (X:20, #306), p. 1.

7

Tariffs, Patents, and Copyright

Although the money and land monopolies were clearly the two most important of the "four monopolies," Tucker, if not all the writers in *Liberty*, insisted on attacking the last two monopolies: tariffs (a monopoly on foreign trade), and patents and copyrights (monopolies on ideas). Unlike money and land, tariffs, patents, and copyrights were not traditional targets of labor reformers. Indeed, labor reformers often demanded protectionist tariffs, while patents and copyrights seemed peripheral to the concerns of most workers. Tucker included them as sources of the exploitation of labor because they were obvious and unnatural creatures of government intervention. Protecting titles to land and providing money seemed to be impartial actions of a liberal government, because they simply provided an economic infrastructure. Erecting tariffs and issuing patents and copyrights, however, were clearly examples of positive state action, and not so obviously infrastructural. Consequently, even though there was no pressing demand among anarchists or workers for the abolition of tariffs, patents, and copyrights, this was seen, by Tucker at least, as essential in clearing the way for free competition.

The tariff issue pitted the individualist anarchists in another dispute with individualists, those who hadn't quite gone the distance to anarchism. While Tucker and others agreed wholeheartedly with the arguments put forward by individualists for free trade, they called on them to extend their logic and to focus on the more important evil of the money and land monopolies. As Tucker put it bluntly: "For a just cause, that of the anti-custom-house reformer is the pettiest that I know of in proportion to the importance that is claimed for it."[1] Like taxation generally, the tariff was clearly an evil of government, but (at least in Tucker's day) its economic impact was limited: "The amount abstracted from labor's pockets by the protective tariff and by all other methods of getting governmental revenue is simply one of the smaller drains on industry."[2] The vehemence with which the free traders attacked the tariff suggested that they were less interested in a libertarian critique of the modern industrial economy than in a defense of the interests of plutocrats.[3] For these reasons, then, there was relatively little extended discussion of tariffs in *Liberty*, and only one selection (A) is offered, Tucker's attack on William Graham Sumner.

Patents and copyrights, especially the latter, were much more controversial among the individualist anarchists.[4] The anti-copyright position, headed by Tucker, argued that the right to deny copying of an author's work was simply a monopoly and could not be justified on theoretical or practical grounds. The basic point of contention was whether an author's works could be considered property, that is, whether there was "property in ideas." Tucker made two related points against such "property," implicitly reverting back to the labor theory of property. The natural reward of productive labor, according to this theory, was property in the objects produced by that labor. The problem was that authors (or inventors, for that matter) produced *ideas*. These ideas were abstract, not concrete. Moreover, Tucker argued, they did not even *produce* these ideas, but really only *discovered* them. Without a concrete product corresponding to an author's "discovery," there was no grounds for property, and hence no right to deny copying. Of course, there was a concrete product, the book, but that was the result, not of the author's labor, but of the publisher's and printer's labor. Those individuals had property rights in the book produced by their labor, but under free competition, they could not prevent other publishers and printers from putting out identical books through their own labor. The defenders of copyright, such as Henry George (selection B), argued that, while the discovery of an idea could not create property, the specific expression of that idea was an act of production and thus created property. That is, anyone could write a similar book about the same ideas, but no one could steal an author's product, her particular expression of the ideas in a specific, concrete book. Along with a host of corollary issues (e.g., whether copyright should have a limited term or whether in the absence of copyright there would be sufficient incentive to write and publish books), this drove one of the most interesting and relevant of the debates in *Liberty*. Here, the debate is represented by critical views from Victor

Yarros (selection C) and Hugo Bilgram (selection D), as well as by Tucker's later attack on the concept of property in ideas (selection E).

Further Reading in Liberty

Two of *Liberty's* most prolific contributors, J. William Lloyd and Tak Kak, weighed in on Tucker's side in this dispute: Lloyd, "Copyright," February 7, 1891 (VII:21, #177), pp. 6–7; Tak Kak, "The Question of Copyright," February 21, 1891 (VII:22, #178), p. 5, continues #179, pp. 5–6, #180, pp. 4–5, #185, pp. 3–4.

Victor Yarros engaged in a heated dispute with Tucker over copyright, basically defending Spencer's justification, although insisting on a perpetual, rather than a limited copyright: Yarros, "More on Copyright," December 27, 1890 (VII:18, #174), pp. 4–5; "The 'General Principle' and Copyright," January 24, 1891 (VII:20, #176), pp. 5–6; "Property in Ideas and Equal Liberty," February 7, 1891 (VII:21, #177), pp. 4–6 (excerpted below); "The Right to Authorship," February 21, 1891 (VII:22, #178), pp. 4–5.

A. "Will Professor Sumner Choose?"—Benjamin Tucker[*]

This selection is characteristic not only of Liberty's *take on free trade but also on one of the latter's most prominent advocates, William Graham Sumner. Just as free trade was a necessary, but narrow reform, so Sumner spoke the truth, but not the whole truth. Here, Tucker calls on Sumner, much as he and others had called on Spencer, to follow out the logic of his position.*

Professor Sumner, who occupies the chair of political economy at Yale, addressed last Sunday the New Haven Equal Rights Debating Club, before which Henry Appleton recently spoke.[5] He told the State Socialists and Communists of that city much wholesome truth. But, as far as I can learn from the newspaper reports, which may of course have left out, as usual, the most important things that the speaker said, he made no discrimination in his criticisms. He appears to have entirely ignored the fact that the Anarchistic Socialists are the most unflinching champions in existence of his own pet principle of *laissez faire*. He branded

---

[*] November 14, 1885 (III:17, #69), p. 4.

Socialism as the summit of absurdity, utterly failing to note that one great school of Socialism says "Amen" whenever he scolds government for invading the individual, and only regrets that he doesn't scold it oftener and more uniformly . . .

I fancy that, if I should ask you what the great evil in our taxation is, you would answer that it is the protective tariff. Now, the protective tariff is an evil certainly, and an outrage, but so far as it affects the power of the laborer to accumulate capital it is a comparatively small one. In fact, its abolition, unaccompanied by the abolition of the banking monopoly, would take away from very large classes of laborers, not only what little chance they now have of getting capital, but also their power of sustaining the lives of themselves and their families. The amount abstracted from labor's pockets by the protective tariff and by all other methods of getting governmental revenue is simply one of the smaller drains on industry. The amount of capital which it is thus prevented from getting will hardly be worth considering until the larger drains are stopped. As far as taxation goes, the great evils involved in it are to be found, not in the material damage done to labor by a loss of earnings, but in the assumption of the right to take men's property without their consent, and in the use of this property to pay the salaries of the officials through whom, and the expenses of the machine through which, labor is oppressed and ground down. Are you heroic enough, Professor Sumner, to adopt this application of *laissez faire*? I summon you to it under penalty of conviction of an infidelity to logic which ought to oust you from your position as a teacher of youth. . .

The battle between free trade and protection is simply one phase of the battle between Anarchism and State Socialism. To be a consistent free trader is to be an Anarchist; to be a consistent protectionist is to be a State Socialist. You are assailing that form of State Socialism known as protection with a vigor equalled by no other man, but you are rendering your blows of little effect by maintaining, or encouraging the belief that you maintain, those forms of State Socialism known as compulsory taxation and the banking monopoly. You assail Marx and Most mercilessly, but fail to protest against the most dangerous manifestations of their philosophy. Why pursue this confusing course? In reason's name, be one thing or the other! Cease your indiscriminate railing at Socialism, for to be consistent you must be Socialist yourself, either of the Anarchistic or the governmental sort; either be a State Socialist, and denounce liberty everywhere and always, or be an Anarchist and denounce authority everywhere and always; else you must consent to be taken for what you will appear to be,—an impotent hybrid.

B. "Ergo and Presto!"—Benjamin Tucker[*]

Quite consistently with his position on copyright, Tucker copies a long passage from Henry George in this article, finding in George's words a concise and convincing explanation of his own view. He particularly admires George's distinction between discovery and production as a basic argument against property in ideas. However, he dissents from George's conclusion that while ideas are discovered, the means by which authors express them is a matter of production.

Tucker's attack on George, and the specific way in which he phrases it, is not attributable solely to George's slipperiness on this issue, nor even to his prominence as a labor reformer by virtue of his book, Progress and Poverty. *The grudge here was much more personal, for George did not condemn the Illinois Supreme Court's upholding of the Haymarket verdict, an act of "betrayal" for which Tucker never forgave him.*[6]

In Henry George may be seen a pronounced type of the not uncommon combination of philosopher and juggler. He possesses in a marked degree the faculty of luminous exposition of a fundamental principle, but this faculty he supplements with another no less developed,—that of so obscuring the connection between his fundamental principle and the false applications thereof which he attempts that only a mind accustomed to analysis can detect the flaw and the fraud. We see this in the numerous instances in which he has made a magnificent defence of the principle of individual liberty in theory, only to straightway deny it in practice, while at the same time palming off his denial upon an admiring following as a practical affirmation . . .

One of the latest and craftiest of his offences in this direction was committed in the "Standard" of June 23 in a discussion of the copyright problem. A correspondent having raised the question of property in ideas, Mr. George discusses it elaborately. Taking his stand upon the principle that productive labor is the true basis of the right of property, he argues through three columns, with all the consummate ability for which credit it given him above, to the triumphant vindication of the position that there can rightfully be no such thing as the exclusive ownership of an idea.

No man, he says, "can justly claim ownership in natural laws, nor in any of the relations which may be perceived by the human mind, nor in any of the potentialities which nature holds for it. . . . Ownership comes from production. It cannot come from discovery. Discovery can give no right of ownership. . . . No man can discover anything which, so to speak, was not put there to be discovered, and which some one else might not in time have discovered. If he finds it, it was not lost. It, or its potentiality, existed before he came. It was there to be found. . . . In the production of any material thing—a machine, for instance—there are two separable parts,—the abstract idea or principle, which may be usually expressed by drawing, by writing, or by word of mouth; and the concrete form of the particular machine itself, which is produced by bringing together in certain relation certain quantities of matter, such as wood, steel, brass, brick, rubber, cloth, etc. There are two modes in which labor goes to the making of the machine,—the one in ascertaining the principle on which such machines can be made to work; the other in obtaining from their natural reservoirs and bringing together and fashioning into shape the quantities and qualities of matter which in their combination constitute the concrete machine. In the first mode labor is expended in discovery. In the second mode it is expended in production. The work of discovery may be done once for all, as in the case of the discovery in prehistoric time of the principle or idea of the wheelbarrow. But the work of production is required afresh in the case of each particular thing. No matter how many thousand millions of wheelbarrows have been produced, it requires fresh labor of production to make another one. . . . The natural reward of labor expended in discovery is in the use that can be made of the discovery without interference with the right of any one else to use it. But to this natural reward our patent laws endeavor to add an artificial reward. Although the effect of giving to the discoverers of useful devices or processes an absolute right to their exclusive use would be to burden all industry with most grievous monopolies, and to greatly retard, if not put a stop to, further inventions, yet the theory of our patent laws is that we can stimulate discoveries by giving a modified right of ownership in their use for a term of years. In this we seek by special laws to give a special reward to labor expended in discovery, which does not belong to it of natural right, and is of the nature of a bounty. But as for labor expended in the second of these modes,—in the production of the machine by the bringing together in certain relations of certain quantities and qualities of matter,—we need no special laws to reward that. Absolute ownership attaches to the results of such labor, not by special law, but by common law. And if all human laws were abolished, men would still hold that, whether it were a wheelbarrow or a phonograph, the concrete thing belonged to the man who produced it. And this, not for a term of years, but in perpetuity. It would pass at his death to his heirs or to those to whom he devised it."

The whole of the preceding paragraph is quoted from Mr. George's article. I regard it as conclusive, unanswerable. It proceeds, it will be noticed, entirely by the method of *ergo*. But it is time for the philosopher to disappear. He has done his part of the work, which was the demolition of patents. Now it is the prestidigitator's turn. It remains for him to justify copyright,—that is, property, not in the ideas set forth in a book, but in the manner of expressing them. So juggler George steps upon the scene. *Presto*! he exclaims: "Over and above any 'labor of discovery' expended in thinking out *what* to say, is the 'labor of production' expended on *how* to say it." Observe how cunningly it is taken for granted here that the task of giving literary expression to an idea is labor of production rather than labor of discovery. But is it so? Right here come comes in the juggler's trick: we will subject it to the philosopher's test. The latter has already been quoted: "*The work of discovery may be done once for all . . . but the work of production is required afresh in the case of each particular thing.*" Can anything be plainer than that he who does the work of combining words for the expression of an idea saves just that amount of labor to all who thereafter choose to use the same words in the same order to express the same idea, and that this work, not being required afresh in each particular case, is not work of production, and that, not being work of production, it gives no right of property? In quoting Mr. George above I did not have to expend any labor on "how to say" what he had already said. He had saved me that trouble. I simply had to write and print the words on fresh sheets of paper. These sheets of paper belong to me, just as the sheets on which he wrote and printed belong to him. But the particular combination of words belongs to neither of us. He discovered it, it is true, but that fact gives him no right to it. Why not? Because, to use his own phrases, this combination of words "existed potentially before he came"; "it was there to be found"; and if he had not found it, some one else would or might have done so. The work of copying or printing books is analogous to the production of wheelbarrows, but the original work of the author, whether in thinking or composing, is analogous to the *invention* of the wheelbarrow; and the same argument that demolishes the right of the inventor demolishes the right of the author. The method of expressing an idea is itself an idea and therefore not appropriable . . .

C. "Property in Ideas and Equal Liberty"—Victor Yarros [*]

By early 1891, a full-fledged debate over copyright had broken out. The defenders of copyright in Liberty *pointed to flaws in Tucker's argument, such as his position that even the expression of ideas was not "production," but rather "discovery."[7] Yarros did not accept Tucker's position that even the expression of ideas (in books or inventions) was a matter of discovery. Thus, there could be property in ideas. The question then was whether such property could be consistent with the "general principle": equal liberty. He argued that it was, because no one was prevented from writing a similar book expressing the same ideas, just from writing an identical one, i.e., copying it. Indeed, Yarros argued that Spencer's argument for a limited-term copyright was too timid, for if property in ideas existed at all, it implied a permanent copyright.*

. . . The argument that "ideas are there to be found" is, as I have said, too silly to need refutation. The only question to decide is whether property in ideas is negatived by the principle of equal liberty. "From the moment a patent or copyright is granted," says Mr. Tucker, "no man is free to acquire the same facts—to elaborate from them, if he can, the same new ideas—and in a similar manner employ these new ideas for his private advantage." Whether this is true or not depends on the sort of patent or copyright the man is granted. . . . Suppose that, in accordance with the law of justice, we recognize a man's absolute right of property in his invention or literary production, while warning him that no infringement on the equal right of others to discover or elaborate and exploit a similar thing will be allowed. As long as no competitor appears, the man, if he sells copies of his book, violates nobody's right. . . . The fact that Spencer has published his works does not justify me in

---

* February 7, 1891 (VII:21, #177), pp. 4–6.

republishing them. Can Mr. Tucker show that a denial of his or my right to republish Spencer's works is a denial of our equal liberty to acquire the facts, elaborate the ideas, and publish *our own works*? Of course not. Then, I repeat, as long as no competitor appears, Spencer's right of absolute property in his works may be recognized without a denial of the principle of equal liberty. . . . Now, suppose another man appears with a book in many or all respects identical with one of Spencer's. The question arises: is this man a thief, or has he really written this book and stolen nothing from Spencer? This question must be decided before a jury of experts, or before an ordinary jury on the testimony of experts.[8] If the man is proved a thief, he is punished, and the right to sell the book is denied him. If juries disagree, or the man is proved honest and the real author of the book, he is permitted to compete with Spencer. Again justice is satisfied, and still, as before, no third man has a right to publish and sell either of the books.

So far, then, as the "general principle" is concerned, property in ideas has the same sanction as property in material things. In no case does the author or inventor who has the monopoly of the use or sale of *his* invention or discovery infringe on the equal right of others. Other men, provided they can prove to the satisfaction of a jury that the things they claim as the products of their own labor are really such, have the right to use *their* ideas or things for their private advantage, secretly or publicly. Only those are debarred from using the ideas who either make no claim to authorship at all or who, having made the claim, are convicted of falsehood and robbery by juries.

But the reason why Spencer, without being "absurd" or "contradictory," introduces his limitation of the right to property in ideas is that in many cases it is impossible to *prove* the claim of originality. The "general principle" is clear, but its application is found to be difficult. It is deemed expedient, therefore, to qualify an inventor's right of property, and allow him a temporary instead of a perpetual monopoly. When absolute justice cannot be had, relative justice is sought to be obtained. Spencer does not hold that property in ideas abridges others' liberty of action; he merely admits that it is often impossible for honest men to prove their titles to their own property, and considers it advisable to remedy the injustice that the claimants would suffer if the protectors of the first inventor's title insisted on convincing evidence, by abridging the first inventor's right. Should it become possible to decide the claims of all competitors in all cases, Spencer would withdraw his qualification and adhere to the principle of absolute property in ideas.

Here it becomes clear that, holding as I do that there is no tendency for any form of literary expression to be reproduced by independent writers and that the practical difficulties that embarrass us in the case of inventors are conspicuously absent in the case of authors, I cannot follow Spencer in his attempt to abridge the right of authors to their literary works. I see no reason for violating the "general principle" in this case. Here, I say, absolute justice, not merely relative justice, may be had. To be sure, Mr. Tucker denies the logical impossibility of two men being sufficiently alike to write substantially the same book. He himself, he tells us, has known men closely resembling each other in physical, mental, and moral traits and qualities. But this, instead of damaging my position, powerfully tells against Mr. Tucker himself. For, if two such men should appear before a jury, and the jury should conclude that it is more reasonable to suppose them capable of producing books substantially alike than books widely different, the right of the second claimant would be recognized and justice secured. While I still maintain that no jury would ever be called to decide such a case, and deny Mr. Tucker's "confident" statement that "substantial similarity" has not infrequently occurred, I am willing to assume that he is right and appeal to intelligent readers to say whether it would be difficult for a jury to distinguish between truth and imposture in such a case. I am confident that it would not be difficult, but very easy.

I think I have succeeded in showing that the "general principle" is on my side, that property in ideas is logically deduced by Spencer from the principle of equal liberty, and that only certain practical difficulties in the way of the application of the principle render it inexpedient to abridge this right in certain cases.

D.   "The Reward of Authors"—Hugo Bilgram[*]

A much more practical criticism was offered by Bilgram: wouldn't the absence of copyright remove a powerful incentive for authors and publishers? Tucker offers an interesting answer: as an expert (i.e., as a book publisher), he can testify that this would not be the case and gives a hypothetical case to illustrate why not. Underlying this "practical"

---

[*] January 10, 1891 (VII:19, #175), pp. 5–6.

critique, however, is the specter of "communism," for Bilgram's focus on incentive is one of the most common critiques that private property advocates (such as Tucker himself) level against communists. In the next selection, Tucker offers a more theoretical argument for why the conditions that necessitate private property do not apply when it comes to ideas.

Bilgram:

... Were it considered proper for any publisher to copy any new work without the author's consent, the authorized publisher should be obliged to compete with the copying publisher, and could therefore in no way afford to remunerate the author for his labor. And, authors having no earthly chance of being financially remunerated by any other means, they would simply not write, and we should be without a literature. (A) It cannot avail to say that some would write notwithstanding, feeling fully remunerated by one sentiment or another. It might as well be said that the hatter, even if the hats he produces are confiscated for the general good, will work for the fame of making superior hats, or the shoemaker, for the honor of producing the best-fitting shoes, or that all workmen will emulate their superiors in the endeavor to excel them. (B)

Tucker:

... (A) I deny that, in the absence of copyright and in the presence of competition, authors would have "no earthly chance of being financially remunerated." In what I shall say under this head, I shall speak as a book publisher and an expert, and I claim for my statements as much authority as may rightfully be awarded to expert testimony. It is a rule, to which exceptions are very rare, that, even in the absence of copyright, competing editions are not published except of books the demand for which has already been large enough to more than reasonably reward both author and publisher for their labor. Take, for instance, a paper novel that retails at fifty cents. We will suppose that for this book there is a demand of ten thousand copies. These copies cost the publisher to make and market, say, seventeen cents each. He pays the author five cents for each copy sold,—that is, the customary royalty of ten percent of the retail price. The total cost to the publisher, then, is twenty-two cents per copy. He sells these books to the jobbers at twenty-five cents each, leaving himself a profit of three cents a copy. He probably has orders from the book-trade for three to six thousand copies before publication. If the final demand is not to exceed the edition of ten thousand copies, the sale of the balance will drag along slowly and more slowly, through several years. During this time the author will receive as his royalty five hundred dollars in payment for a book which he was probably less than sixty days in writing. I maintain that he is more than reasonably paid. No rival edition of his book has sprung up (we are supposing an absence of copyright) for the reason that the demand did not prove large enough to induce a second publisher to risk the expense of making a set of plates. But now let us suppose that on publication so brisk a demand had immediately arisen as to show that the sale would be twenty thousand instead of ten thousand. The publisher, as before, would have sold three to six thousand in advance, and the balance of the first ten thousand would have disappeared before any rival publisher could have made plates and put an edition on the market. As before, then, both author and publisher would have been more than adequately paid. But at this point steps in the rival. Having to pay no author and to do no advertising, he can produce the book at say fourteen cents a copy, and perhaps will sell it to the trade at twenty cents. It now becomes optional with the author and first publisher to maintain the old price and sell perhaps one thousand of the second ten thousand, or to reduce, the one his royalty and the other his profit, sell the book to the trade almost as low as the rival, and control nearly half of the subsequent market. In either case, both author and publisher are sure to get still further pay for services that have already been more than reasonably rewarded, and the public meanwhile benefits by the reduction in price. Why has no competing edition of "The Rag-Picker of Paris"[9] been published during the six months that it has been on the market? Simply because, though a more than ordinarily successful novel, it did not develop a sufficient demand to tempt another publisher. Yet it has paid me more than equitably. Why, on the other hand, did two competing editions of "The Kreutzer Sonata"[10] appear on the market before mine had had the field two months? Simply because the money was pouring into my pocket with a rapidity that nearly took my breath away. *And after my rivals took the field, it poured in faster than ever*, until I was paid fifty times over for my work. I long to find another book that will tempt somebody to compete with me. Competition in the book business is not to be shunned, but to be courted. How ridiculous, then, to claim that, when there is competition, authors will not be rewarded! But why, it will be asked, do authors and publishers clamor for copyright? I'll tell you why, Mr. Bilgram; because they are hogs and want the earth. I am sorry that you are so anxious to give it to them. As G. Bernard Shaw has well said, the cry for copyright is the cry of men who are not satisfied with being paid for their work once, but insist upon being paid twice, thrice, and a dozen times over.

(B) Even though authors, without copyright, could not get their reward, I think it would still avail a good deal to say that they would write notwithstanding. It does not follow that, because a hatter will not make hats for pleasure, an author will not write books for pleasure. . . . There is something in art and literature that compels their devotees into their service. And I am of the opinion that it would be much better for both and for the world if they could be entirely divorced from commerce.

E.   "The Attitude of Anarchism toward Industrial Combinations"—Tucker[*]

In his 1899 talk at the Chicago Conference on Trusts (see chapter four), Tucker made a long digression on the question of copyright. He had evidently abandoned the argument that even the expression of ideas was a matter of discovery, for he opposes property in ideas here on somewhat different grounds. Finding the practical justification for private property in the fact that concrete objects cannot be used simultaneously by different people in different locations (that is, in the language of economic theory, they're "excludable"), he argues that ideas, because they are abstract, are not subject to such limitations. Because they can be used simultaneously without affecting any of the users adversely (or excluding any who currently are non-users), there is simply no need to establish private property in ideas. Such an argument clearly indicates the distance that Tucker had travelled from classical economics and natural-rights justifications of property.

. . . Of these four monopolies—the banking monopoly, the land monopoly, the tariff monopoly, and the patent and copyright monopoly—the injustice of all but the last-named is manifest even to a child. . .

---

[*] December 1902 (XIV:4, #366), pp. 2–4.

For the fourth of these monopolies, however, . . . a more plausible case can be presented, for the question of property in ideas is a very subtle one. The defenders of such property set up an analogy between the production of material things and the production of abstractions, and on the strength of it declare that the manufacturer of mental products, no less than the manufacturer of material products, is a laborer worthy of his hire. So far, so good. But, to make out their case, they are obliged to go further, and to claim, in violation of their own analogy, that the laborer who creates mental products, unlike the laborer who creates material products, is entitled to exemption from competition . . .

Convincing as the argument for property in ideas may seem at first hearing, if you think about it long enough, you will begin to be suspicious. The first thing, perhaps, to arouse your suspicion will be the fact that none of the champions of such property propose the punishment of those who violate it, contenting themselves with subjecting the offenders to the risk of damage suits, and that nearly all of them are willing that even the risk of suit shall disappear when the proprietor has enjoyed his right for a certain number of years. Now, if, as the French writer, Alphonse Karr, remarked, property in ideas is a property like any other property, then its violation, like the violation of any other property, deserves criminal punishment, and its life, like that of any other property, should be secure in right against the lapse of time. And, this not being claimed by the upholders of property in ideas, the suspicion arises that such a lack of the courage of their convictions may be due to an instinctive feeling that they are wrong.

The necessity of being brief prevents me from examining this phase of my subject in detail. Therefore I must content myself with developing a single consideration, which, I hope, will prove suggestive.

I take it that, if it were possible, and if it had always been possible, for an unlimited number of individuals to use to an unlimited extent and in an unlimited number of places the same concrete things at the same time, there never would have been any such thing as the institution of property. Under those circumstances the idea of property would never have entered the human mind, or, at any rate, if it had, would have been summarily dismissed as too gross an absurdity to be seriously entertained for a moment. Had it been possible for the concrete creation or adaptation resulting from the efforts of a single individual to be used contemporaneously by all individuals, including the creator or adapter, the realization, or impending realization, of this possibility, far from being seized upon as an excuse for a law to prevent the use of this concrete thing without the consent of its creator or adapter, and far from being guarded against as an injury to one, would have been welcomed as a blessing to all,—in short, would have been viewed as a most fortunate element in the nature of things. The *raison d'etre* of property is found in the very fact that there is no such possibility,—in the fact that it is impossible in the nature of things for concrete objects to be used in different places at the same time. This fact existing, no person can remove from another's possession and take to his own use another's concrete creation without thereby depriving that other of all opportunity to use that which he created, and for this reason it became socially necessary, since successful society rests on individual initiative, to protect the individual creator in the use of his concrete creations by forbidding others to use them without his consent. In other words, it became necessary to institute property in concrete things.

But all this happened so long ago that we of today have entirely forgotten why it happened. In fact, it is very doubtful whether, at the time of the institution of property, those who effected it thoroughly realized and understood the motive of their course. Men sometimes do by instinct and without analysis that which conforms to right reason. The institutors of property may have been governed by circumstances inhering in the nature of things, without realizing that, had the nature of things been the opposite, they would not have instituted property. But, be that as it may, even supposing that they thoroughly understood their course, we, at any rate, have pretty nearly forgotten their understanding. And so it has come about that we have made of property a fetich; that we consider it a sacred thing; that we have set up the god of property on an altar as an object of idol-worship; and that most of us are not only doing what we can to strengthen and perpetuate his reign within the proper and original limits of his sovereignty, but also are mistakenly endeavoring to extend his dominion over things and under circumstances which, in their pivotal characteristic, are precisely the opposite of those out of which his power developed.

All of which is to say, in briefer compass, that from the justice and social necessity of property in concrete things we have erroneously assumed the justice and social necessity of property in abstract things,— that is, of property in ideas,—with the result of nullifying to a large and lamentable extent that fortunate element in the nature of things, in this case not hypothetical, but real,—namely, the immeasurably fruitful possibility of the use of abstract things by any number of individuals in any number of places at precisely the same time, without in the slightest degree impairing the use thereof by any single individual. Thus we have hastily and stupidly jumped to the conclusion that property in concrete things logically implies property in abstract things, whereas, if we had had the care and the keenness to accurately analyze, we should have found that the very reason which dictates the advisability of property in concrete things denies the advisability of property in abstract things. We see here a curious instance of that frequent mental phenomenon,—the precise inversion of the truth by a superficial view . . .

Notes

1. Tucker, "On Picket Duty," November 22, 1884 (III:3, #55), p. 1.
2. Tucker, "Will Professor Sumner Choose?" November 14, 1885 (III:17, #69), p. 4 (excerpted below as first selection).
3. Tucker, "On Picket Duty," June 29, 1895 (XI:4, #316), p. 1.
4. See Wendy McElroy, "The Non-Economic Debates in *Liberty*," in Michael E. Couglin, et al, eds., *Benjamin R. Tucker and the Champions of Liberty. A Centenary Anthology*, St. Paul: Michael E. Coughlin and Mark Sullivan, n.d. [1986], pp. 139–145.
5. This club offered a forum for several of *Liberty*'s writers, including Henry Appleton, who wrote under the pseudonyms Honorius and X.
6. Tucker, "On Picket Duty," October 8, 1887 (V:5, #109), p. 1; "On Picket Duty," September 29, 1888 (VI:4, #134), p. 1; "On Picket Duty," January 5, 1889 (VI:10, #140), p. 1. By 1894, Tucker described his attitude toward George as "a contempt that is well-nigh unspeakable" ("On Picket Duty," November 17, 1894 [X:14, #300], and in 1896, capped this grudge by publishing "Henry George, Traitor" (November 1896 [XII:9, #347], pp. 3–5.). See also Martin, *Men against the State*, pp. 229–231 and Jack Schwartzmann, "Henry George and Benjamin R. Tucker: A Dialogue," in Coughlin, ed., *Benjamin R. Tucker and the Champions of Liberty*, pp. 175–180.
7. Victor Yarros, "The 'General Principle' and Copyright," January 24, 1891 (VII:20, #176), pp. 5–6; A.H. Simpson, "Property in Ideas," #176, p. 6.
8. Again, as with disputes over land possession under the anarchist principle of occupancy and use, disputes would be handled by a jury.
9. Written by Felix Pyat, it was serialized in *Liberty* between March 10, 1888 (V:16, #120) and March 8, 1890 (VI:26, #156) and offered for sale as a book by Tucker for about four years thereafter.
10. This book by Leo Tolstoi, described by Tucker in advertisements as "the boldest work yet written by the famous Russian author," figured in some of the controversy over sexual relations in the pages of *Liberty* (see next chapter). Tucker began selling it in May 1890.

PART THREE

Social Controversies

8

Free Love and Women's Freedom

Reform in sexual relations, like reform in the economy, had been one of the major themes of antebellum anarchism and, because of the prominence of Emma Goldman, was strongly identified with American anarchism after the turn of the century.[1] Free love, with its critique of conventional marriage, its demands for birth control, and its insistence on regaining women's control in consensual sexual relations, fits well with anarchism's general demands for freedom from state interference, from the constraints of traditional morality, and even the barriers to freedom posed by economic inequality. Yet sexual reform was not one of *Liberty*'s major concerns. This is due partly to the existence of two contemporary "free love" papers with strong anarchist leanings: Ezra Heywood's *Word* (with which Tucker had been active in the 1870s) and Moses Harman's *Lucifer, the Light Bearer*.[2] However, *Liberty*'s reticence on sexual reform is mostly attributable to Benjamin Tucker's editorial preferences. Tucker was certainly not opposed to free love, having been introduced to the subject in all its political and personal aspects by a notorious free-love advocate, Victoria Woodhull. Nor was the subject completely ignored; it just occupied much less space than many other topics in *Liberty*, and was virtually ignored by Tucker himself. Ironically, this may have contributed to the quality of what was written, for the purely agitational articles and excruciatingly detailed debates that characterized such topics as monetary reform were generally absent, replaced instead by fairly sophisticated considerations of the interrelated issues of love reform.

What, then, were the concerns of *Liberty*'s writers on sexual relations? Some of the contemporary concerns of the women's movement were clearly not on the agenda, in particular women's suffrage. Others received a distinctive slant from anarchist principles. For example, prostitution was generally not considered a moral or a gender issue, but rather an economic one. Prostitution, it was argued, was symptomatic of the low wages women received and its fundamental solution was to increase women's economic power, both relative to men in the present economy, and absolutely as workers in an oppressive industrial economy. That is, as the article from Gertrude Kelly (selection A) shows, socialist feminism was anticipated. However, the Marxist distinction between productive and reproductive labor, perhaps particularly appropriate here, was usually not made, many considering marriage and prostitution to be simply two forms of the same exchange. Both were based on the premise, put bluntly by Florence Finch Kelly, that "a woman's sexual favors are rightfully a matter of commerce" and that "prostitution gets better pay than marriage"[3] (see selection B).

In both its sexual and economic aspects, then, as well as in the interpersonal relations it entailed, marriage was the central point of debate among *Liberty*'s writers on "free love." Virtually all were agreed that "conventional" marriage was irredeemably flawed, but the question was which flaws were the fundamental ones. Was it the economic inequality of husbands and wives? Was it the sexual subordination of women to their husbands, enshrined in traditional morality and religion and still enforced to some extent by law? Was it the fact that conventional marriage was a "monopoly," an *exclusive* contract between men and women for sex? Was it that truly free individuals could not reasonably expect to stay with one person for a lifetime? The roles of money, sex, morality, and personality were interwoven in the critiques of conventional marriage and the ideals of "free love" discussed in *Liberty*. John Beverley Robinson's critique of marriage (selection C) is a good discussion of these themes. Given reform, many believed that monogamy, or a "free-love home," was still possible and that promiscuity was not the necessary result of attacking conventional marriage. The essay by Victor (selection D) exemplifies this belief, expressed cogently by J. William Lloyd: "The sexual relations will be the test of citizenship, and the free-love home will be the foundation and fountain of free society, just as marriage and the communistic home are now the school and source of government."[4] Such a conclusion gained considerable force from the most common attack on critics of marriage: "What about the children?" Some kind of stable partnership seemed essential to deal with the challenges of child-rearing. Others, however, were more skeptical of the possibility (and desirability) of long-term monogamy and advocated innovative solutions to the problem of child-rearing. The final selection (E), from "Zelm," the pseudonym of Sarah Holmes, echoes the accomodation reached many years before between an early English anarchist, William Godwin, and his mate, the feminist Mary Wollstonecraft: separate households. The debate between Victor and Zelm, then, is pivotal in defining "free love," because the two writers were substantially in agreement on eliminating economic inequality and traditional moral constraints from sexual relations and in seeing sex as a natural, and unobjectionable, basis of attraction. The question they addressed was "Can men and women 'make a home' and still be free?"

Further Reading in Liberty

Two general articles worth looking at are a vignette portraying marital conflict (Miriam Daniell, "Conjugal Bliss," September 24, 1892 [IX:4, #238], p. 3) and John Beverley Robinson's vision of free love: "The Marriage of the Future," May 19, 1894 (X:1, #287), pp. 2-4.

The question of whether sex itself posed a substantial barrier to equitable relations between men and women was raised in *Liberty* by reviews of Tolstoi's "The Kreutzer Sonata": J. William Lloyd, "The Kreutzer Sonata," September 27, 1890 (VII:12, #168), pp. 5-6; Victor Yarros, "The Filthy Horror of Sexual Passion," ibid, pp. 6-7; A.H. Simpson, "Love and Sex," October 18, 1890 (VII:13, #169), pp. 2-3. Another sticky subject, handled at more length in *Lucifer, the Light Bearer,* was "age-of-consent" laws. Tucker probably expressed the majority opinion when he held that the "age-of-consent" (not in law, of course) ought to be puberty ("Anarchy and [Statutory] Rape," March 10, 1888 [V:16, #120], p. 4), a position discussed more substantially by Lillian Harman: "An 'Age-of-Consent' Symposium," February 9, 1895 (X:20, #306), pp. 2-5.

A.   "The Root of Prostitution"—Gertrude B. Kelly[*]

In this extract from a typical heavily documented article, Kelly expresses the most common analysis of prostitution, that its "sole cause" is

_____
[*] September 12, 1885 (III:14, #66), p. 5.

poor wages. This is a socialist, not a liberal, analysis, for Kelly demands not merely relative equality in wages between men and women, but an absolute improvement in the wages of all workers, male and female.

Do the working-people realize that it is their daughters, and theirs only, that are being sacrificed by the thousand every year to the money lords in the manner that has been recently exposed by the "Pall Mall Gazette"? Do they realize that the capitalistic system, after extorting the last cent from the working-women, forces them into the street to re-earn by prostitution a part of the wages that have been stolen from them? Do they realize that both directly and indirectly the present unjust distribution of the products of labor is the *sole* cause of prostitution? Some may assert that the viciousness of men is the cause, or, at least, a cause. To these we make answer that, if the people did not furnish to these men the time and means to support their viciousness, it could not exist. Of all the societies, White Cross, Social Purity, etc., which have arisen to combat the "social evil" not one has struck a single blow at its root. No society that we have ever heard of, no government, has ever proposed to pay women sufficiently well for their work, so that they would not be forced to eke out by prostitution their miserable wages. In the published governmental and society reports we often find admissions that destitution is the chief cause of prostitution, but, when we come to examine the remedies proposed, we find not a word on the subject of paying women, not justly (this we could scarcely expect), but even of making their wages equal to those of a man for the same work. We find all sorts of schemes for making men moral and women religious, but no scheme which proposes to give woman the fruits of her labor . . .

B.   "The Economic Freedom of Women"—Florence Finch Kelly[*]

Florence Finch Kelly also distinguishes between the relative economic freedom of what would be called today "equal pay for equal work" and the absolute freedom that would only come about with an anarchist economy. She portrays the former not only as an economic reform, but also as one that will whittle away at the long habits of tyranny men have become used to. This echo of Abigail Adams also anticipates Zelm's demand for the "separate individual existence of the man and woman (see selection E below).

[*] February 25, 1888 (V:15, #119), p. 4.

I cannot see that much advance toward individualism in the relations between men and women is possible until the economic freedom of women shall have become an established fact. Nor do I use economical freedom in its large and true sense, but simply with a relative meaning. I use it in the sense of the same economical plane that the other sex is on. That they should be on that same plane, wherever or whatever it may be, seems to me a thing so desirable that it is to be ranked alongside of free banks. Though the latter, I imagine, will be realized many decades before the former. It is not solely for the sake of its benefit to woman that this condition of relative economical freedom is desirable. It will have a wholesome effect upon man as well. For man is still a little bit tyrannical. Even the best of men and those most imbued with a desire for justice and equity and the best able to apply individualist ideas to actual life,—even these still have something of the tyrant left in their feeling toward and their treatment of women. They are not to blame for it, I suppose, any more than they are for the fact that hair grows on their heads instead of on their feet. For so many, many ages man has been superior to woman, has been accustomed to have her clinging dependently to his fingers and begging to be taken care of, that it has become a part of his nature for him not only to feel, but also to use, his superiority. Vestiges of it still cling to him. Not until woman becomes a self-supporting independent creature who has ceased to beg alms of him and who can and does support herself as easily and with as much comfort as he does, will he respect her as his equal and lose the last remnants of that old spirit of tyranny which made him get everything under his thumb that he could. He will become a freer being by this one step in woman's emancipation.

For woman herself this condition would bring unnumbered goods. It is the only escape for her from the bondage of conventional marriage, which, according to the confessions of women themselves, is a condition which could have given Dante points for the Inferno. Until at least relative economical freedom for women is realized, the separate individual existence of the man and the woman is an impossibility. But I am afraid it will not be realized for many a long year . . .

C. "The Abolition of Marriage"—John Beverley Robinson[*]

Although this appeared after the debate between Victor and Zelm, logically it is prior, for Robinson's critique of conventional marriage sets the stage for the other two to consider the anarchist alternatives. Actually, Robinson does offer a vague alternative, on which most anarchists could agree, sexual relationships based on consent rather than compulsion. However, he also argues that this ideal was not designed to break up marriages nor to increase promiscuity, for relationships already based on consent and friendship could only be strengthened by removing the aspect of compulsion. In this sense, Robinson's critique of existing marriage strongly parallels the critique of economic monopoly, and his ideal seems to be "free competition" for love and companionship.

What is marriage?

Is it the happy association of a man and a woman, suited to each other in body and in mind, in tastes and in sentiments, by harmony or by contrast, rejoicing each in the mere presence of the other, moved each by the mere sound of the voice of the other; with children, to whom they rather acknowledge themselves under obligations, for the softening and expanding influence of childhood (in babyhood, charming toys, the bringers of hope in childhood, in maturity companions) than assert harsh authority upon the ground of obligations conferred upon them, is this marriage?

By no means. This is not marriage. This is love. No marriage is necessary for such sweet involvements.

Marriage is not the happy and voluntary living together of men and women.

Marriage is a club. Now I have got you; if you try to get away, I will club you. That is what marriage is. And anyone can see its endearing influence.

Marriage is the privilege conferred by law, which is in the end by force, by which one person holds the person or the property of another against their will.

Theoretically each partner by marriage is endowed with claims upon both the person and property of the other. In practice usually it is the person of the wife that the man is after, and the property of the husband that the woman is after. When they get married, the woman exchanges her right to dispose of her body as she pleases for the substantial benefit of cash, either as support or otherwise. (By otherwise I mean, for instance, alimony).

---

* July 20, 1889 (VI:18, #148), pp. 6–7. Originally a lecture read before the Manhattan Liberal Club.

. . . When I denounce marriage, I have no objection to anybody living happily together. I only say that the possession of a club is not conducive to happiness.

If my wife wants to leave me, the only possible right that I have to retain her is the right of love. I absolutely deny that I have any right to shoot her or to shoot the man that she prefers to me, or to imprison her or in any way coerce her.

More than that; I really should not care to coerce her. The companionship of one we love is worthless when it is forced. Who would think of inviting a friend to go a-fishing, and threaten him with imprisonment if he should change his mind? Would the fishing excursion be much fun if one went under compulsion?

The result of the abolition of compulsion in marriage would soon be that only happy unions could exist. If a man were cruel (and many men are cruel without throwing dishes at their wives), the woman could simply leave him without asking permission of anybody.

It is not possible, if people ever loved each other, that they would leave each other lightly. The flavor of friendship grows with age like wine. And if marriage now is not based on friendship, under liberty it could not be based upon anything else. Now a girl usually catches a man by his passion, and there could be no more uncertain and fleeting foundation for a permanent union. When a marriage is happy now-a-days it is because friendship has grown after marriage.

But if a woman had no power to compel her husband to support her, she would be very sure first that his love for her was a deep affection. The rapidly growing equality of the sexes will make intimate friendship more and more possible. In the future the marriage of hearts will come first rather than afterwards, or not at all, as now . . .

It is commonly felt that all who urge the abolition of marriage particularly wish to be free themselves to lead a reckless life sexually. In my opinion it is chiefly those who are happily married who have reason to desire the abolition of marriage. I say this because anybody who wants to lead a loose life can easily do so. They must be a little careful, cultivate their powers of deceit and hypocrisy, and loudly condemn anybody who suggests that marriage is not all it is supposed to be.

While for those who love, the fact of possessing any power of coercion continually comes up as a little drop of bitterness. She only married me to get taken care of. He only married me from passion. Such feelings at moments arise. Without marriage they could not arise. Each would know that, however love might seem to be lacking, it could but exist; doubt would be impossible; for, with the departure of love (and by love I do not mean merely sexual desire) association would not be maintained . .

If I were to speak merely of the abolition of marriage as a desirable thing only, it need have little weight with anybody. What I really feel, and what I really urge, and what must have weight with everybody, is that the abolition of marriage (not the happy living together, but the ceremony, the legalization) is really inevitable . . .

Notice how many women are being forced to depend upon themselves for support. For each woman thus forced to support herself the wages of men are in proportion reduced.

The tendency is toward an equalization of men's and women's wages, making it more and more difficult for a man to support a woman, and for a woman to find a man who can support her. . . . When men and women shall be equal financially, is it probable that marriage will survive? With no need on the part of the woman for support, will she give any man power to control her? Will she vow life-long obedience to any man? Would it be especially virtuous that she could vow life-long obedience to any man? . . .

It will not be long before we shall all of us see the absurdity of demanding that she should place her body for life in the power of any man. We shall see the absurdity of the feeling that any ceremony can add sanctity to the holiness of nature. We shall see the absurdity of the prejudice that a pledge of temporary association and aid for mutual pleasure in begetting and rearing children is necessarily morally abominable, while a permanent pledge to the same effect is necessarily laudable.

We shall see too that one person's taste does not constitute a rule for all men. That, if I admire monogamy, it is no reason why I should abhor those who prefer polygamy or polyandry. We shall see that good faith and honor and uprightness are quite as possible where men exercise no compulsion upon each other in sexual matters as where they do; that, in fact, as for the absolute slave faith and honor are impossible, so it is only for the entirely free that perfect faith and perfect honor and perfect virtue are possible.

D. "The Woman Question"—Victor*

Although Victor claims to be presenting "conservative" views on the question, he starts off liberal enough, accepting the need for equal opportunity and rejecting chivalry. However, he goes on to insist that women's particular problems will be resolved by the general strategies of fighting for an anarchist economy and increasing "intelligence." As has so often been the case, he asks women to cooperate first with their male comrades in combatting mutual enemies and afterwards the "woman question" will be dealt with.

Victor's major objection, however, is to the demand of "the most extreme radicals in our ranks" for separate households for men and women. This he finds utopian, because it does not consider the practical disadvantages in which maternity inevitably places women. Since women, even when economic liberty prevails and intelligence is widespread, are likely to be rendered dependent if they become mothers, why should they not be able to choose to "make a home" with their mate, he asks? Victor indeed ends by offering a "conservative" view on the "woman question."

Possibly at the expense of my reputation as a radical, but certainly to the entertainment and interest of Liberty's readers, I intend to express in this article some conservative thoughts on the so-called Woman Question. This I will do, not so much because of my desire to present my own views, but because it appears to me a good way of eliciting elaborate statement and clear explanation from those with whom I shall take issue. The discussion (if such it may be called) of the Woman Question has so far been confined to platitudes and trivial points, while it has been deemed one of the absolute requisites of an advanced, progressive, and liberal thinker to believe in equality of the sexes and to indulge in cheap talk about economic emancipation, equal rights, etc., of the "weaker sex." Declining to repeat this talk in a parrot-like fashion, I ask to be offered some solid arguments in support of the position which I now, with all my willingness, cannot consider well-grounded.

But let me state at the outset that I have not a word to say against the demand—which, alas! is not very loud and determined—on the part of women for a "free field and no favors." I fully believe in liberty for man,

* May 12, 1888 (V:20, #124), pp. 6–7. This is probably Victor Yarros.

woman, and child. . . . [I am not] jealous of the privileges and special homage accorded by the *bourgeois* world to women, and do not in the least share the sentiments of E. Belfort Bax, who declaims against an alleged tyranny exercised by women over men. Not denying that such "tyranny" exists, I assert that Mr. Bax entirely misunderstands its real nature. Man's condescension he mistakes for submission; marks of woman's degradation and slavery his obliquity of vision transforms into properties of sovereignty. Tchernychewsky[5] takes the correct view upon this matter when he makes Vera Pavlovna say: "Men should not kiss women's hands, since that ought to be offensive to women, for it means that men do not consider them as human beings like themselves, but believe that they can in now way lower their dignity before a woman, so inferior to them is she, and that no marks of affected respect for her can lessen their superiority." What to Mr. Bax appears to be servility on the part of men is really but insult added to injury.

Recognizing, then, this fact of injury and insult which woman complains about, I sympathize with her in the aspiration for self-control and in the demand to be allowed freedom and opportunities for development. And if this desire to work out her own salvation were the whole sum and substance of the "woman question," that would have been to me a question solved.

Women, in the first place, are the slaves of capital. In this their cause is man's cause, though the yoke of capitalism falls upon them with more crushing effect. This slavery would not outlive the State and legality for a single day, for it has no other root to depend upon for continued existence.

In addition to this burden of economic servitude women are subjected to the misery of being the property, tool, and plaything of man, and have neither power to protest against the use, nor remedies against the abuse, of their persons by their male masters. This slavery is sanctioned by custom, prejudice, tradition, and prevailing notions of morality and purity. Intelligence is the cure for this. Man's brutality and cruelty will be buried in the same grave in which his own and woman's superstition and fixed ideas will be forever laid away.

Normal economic conditions and increased opportunities for intellectual development are in this case, as in all others related to the social problem, the indispensable agents of improvement. It would be idle to discuss the possibility of any change under the present industrial and political arrangements. Woman must now content herself with indirectly furthering the cause nearest to her heart: she must simply join her strength to that of man—and even the most selfish of us will wish more power to her elbow—in his effort to establish proper relations between capital and labor. And only after the material foundations of the new social order have been successfully built, will the Woman Question proper loom up and claim attention.

Let us attempt here to briefly summarize the problem, the remedy, and the reasoning process by which the same are formulated, so far as we understand the position of the most extreme radicals in our ranks.

"Woman must enjoy equal rights and equal freedom and must in all respects be the equal of man. They must contract on absolutely equal terms." How attain and permanently maintain this condition?

"Economical independence is the first and most important thing to women who would be and remain free. When a woman ceases to be self-supporting and begins to look to man for means of life, she deprives herself of independence, dignity, and power of commanding respect. Complete control over her own person and offspring is the next essential thing. With this right of disposing of her own favors she must never part, and to no one must she delegate the privilege of determining the circumstances under which she shall assume the function of maternity. Eternal vigilance is the price of liberty.

"Communism being the grave of individuality, woman must beware of ever abandoning her own private home, over which she exercises sovereign authority, to enter into man's dominion. Someone is bound to rule in the family, and the chances are decidedly against her gaining the supremacy, even if they be considered a more desirable issue than the other alternative.

"The ideal, then, is: independent men and women, in independent homes, leading separate and independent lives, with full freedom to form and dissolve relations, and with perfectly equal opportunities to happiness, development, and love."

Beautiful as this ideal may seem to some, I confess that it inspires me with no enthusiasm. On the contrary, it seems to me unnatural, impossible, and utterly utopian. While welcoming liberty, I do not anticipate such results . . .

"Right" is but a euphonious equivalent of "might." . . . A "right" to a thing means the capacity to profitably secure it. The rights of an individual are fixed by his powers of body and mind. He has a right to appropriate and enjoy all that he can . . .

From this standpoint, what becomes of the demands for equal rights and opportunities in the relations of men and women? "Words, words, words," without meaning or significance. Nature having placed woman at such a decided disadvantage in the path of life, of what avail are her protestations and cries for equality with man? In order to gratify one of her strongest natural desires, she is compelled to enter into relations with man of which the burdensome and painful consequences she alone has to bear. While man's part in the relation is pleasurable throughout, woman purchases her enjoyment at an enormous price. And woman's loss here is man's clear gain. Up to the moment of her contracting to cooperate with man in the production of offspring woman may be considered as man's equal,—ignoring the questions of physical vigor, weight and quality of the brain, etc., which cannot and need not be discussed here. A young girl would, under proper and normal conditions, enjoy equal opportunities with the young man in the matter of providing for her material and intellectual wants. Economic independence, education, culture, and refinement,—all these would be fully within her individual reach. But let her enter into love relations with the young man and resolve upon assuming parental obligations and responsibilities, and all is changed. She is no longer the equal of her male companion. For some time before and a long time after giving birth to a child, she is incapable of holding her independent position and of supporting herself. She needs the care, support, and service of others. She has to depend upon the man whom she made the father of her child, and who suffered no inconvenience from the new relation. With the equality of powers for self-support vanish all other equalities,—a fact of which believers in the equality of the sexes are not only well aware, but one which they continually use as an excellent argument for economic independence of women. Surely, then, they ought not to overlook this cruel, illusion-breaking fact of natural inequality of men and women resulting from the wide difference in the consequences which reproductive sexual association entails respectively upon the partners to the same. Women must either look to their male companions for making good the deficit thus occasioned in their accounts,—in which case the foundation is laid for despotism on the one side and subjection on the other,—or else find the means of support in excessive labor or in economy of consumption

during the intervals of freedom from the restraints and burdens mentioned above,—which would make the burden of life heavier to her and
so reduce her opportunities for development and recreation. In both
cases—inequality.

"Few children" will no doubt be suggested as the solution of this
difficulty. But is this desirable and compatible with our conception of a
future happy condition? Children are a joy and a blessing to parents
whom poverty, or the fear of poverty, does not transform into unnatural,
suspicious, brutal, and eternally-discontented beings. . . . But I do not
think human happiness would be subserved by carrying this limitation
to an extreme. Moreover, this control over nature can only be successfully
maintained by either the employment of artificial checks and preventives
or by the practice of abstinence,—methods which nobody will recommend except as necessary evils, but which should never be resorted to in
the absence of serious reasons.

Of course, if—as seems fairly established—mental exertion, access
to other pleasures, comfortable surroundings generally are really important factors in checking fecundity and frequency in the matter of offspring, this last problem will of itself be most happily solved under the
new conditions of life. But this prospect, while it may cheer the hearts of
believers in small families, scarcely affords relief to those with whose
position we are now mainly occupied.

Assuming sexual passion to be no stronger in women than in men
(some are of the opinion that it is much stronger), there will always be a
preponderance of forces and tendencies in favor of men in this natural
antagonism. Man has no motive to deny himself gratification of his
sexual desires except his dislike to be the cause or even the witness of
the pain and suffering of those whom he loves, whereas woman, as we
have seen, stakes her most vital interests when she follows her natural
impulse.

Leaving it for advocates of independent homes to settle these difficulties for me, I may ask here, wherein would be the evil or danger of family
life when, the economic necessity for it having disappeared, so far as the
woman is concerned, under a more rational industrial system, it should
be maintained in the higher interests and free wishes of both parties to
the contract? Why should not the love relations remain much as they are
today? With the tyranny and impertinent meddling of Church and State
abolished, would not the relation between "man" and "wife" always be

the relation of lover and sweetheart? Between true lovers who are really devoted to each other the relations are ideal. But legal marriage is the grave of love; material conditions and the current notions of virtue and morality destroy the individuality of the married woman, and she becomes the property of her husband. Remove these, and living together ceases to be an evil. The family relation in that state will continue to be perfect as long as they will continue at all.

. . . Why a man should not "make a home" for the woman he loves, I am unable to see. While he is providing the means, she is educating the children and surrounding him with comfort. When they cease to be happy together, they separate. And, as in the commercial sphere, the fear of probable competition suffices to prevent monopolistic iniquity without necessarily calling forth actual competition, so in family life under freedom the probability or rather certainty of the woman's rebellion against the slightest manifestation of despotism will make the man very careful in his conduct and insure peace and respect between them.

I am not blind to the fact that my ideal contains the element of Communism, and also involves the concentration of love upon one person of the opposite sex at a time. But, as long as these are a spontaneous result of freedom, they are no more to be theoretically deplored than especially recommended. Personally I hold, however, that some sort of Communism is inevitable between lovers, and that "variety" in love is only a temporary demand of a certain period. A certain degree of experience is just as necessary in the matter of love as it is in any other branch of human affairs. Variety may be as truly the mother of unity (or duality, rather) as liberty is the mother of order. The inconstancy of young people is proverbial. But when free to experiment and take lessons in love, the outcome might be that finally each Apollo would find his Venus and retire with her to a harmonious and idyllic life . . .

E.   "A Reply to Victor"—Zelm (Sarah Holmes)[*]

Zelm, in a lengthy reply to Victor, defends the ideal of separate households both by meeting the practical objections to separate households and by casting doubt on the desirability of "making a home" from an individualist standpoint. On practical grounds, she raises issues familiar to modern feminists, such as the need for (and legitimacy of)

* May 26, 1988 (V:21, #125), pp. 6–7.

child care, the need for family planning, and the possibility of women working during and shortly after pregnancy. All of these, of course are meant to confound Victor's central contention that maternity inevitably makes women dependent. On more theoretical grounds, she attacks the "communism" of the nuclear family, where the husband works and the wife is a homemaker, insisting that developing individuality should be paramount. Indeed, monogamy itself is inconsistent with liberty because it excludes outsiders from what to the "partners" is their most important social relationship.

"Independent men and women, in independent homes, leading separate and independent lives, with full freedom to form and dissolve relations, and with perfectly equal opportunities to happiness, development, and love" . . . . This idea. so stated, is attractive to me and completely in harmony with my idea of the course in life which will best further human happiness.

I am not sure that I quite understand Victor's position in regard to the number of children desirable in the future family, Yet this seems to me so essential an item in the consideration of the social problem of the future that it must be dealt with at the outset. If the greatest amount of happiness can only be secured by obedience to the "natural" sexual instincts, unrestrained by consideration of any other pleasures which are renounced for their sake, then I can but admit that there seems no escape from the perpetual dependence of woman upon man. Of whatever form the new organization of society may be, it is not likely to be one in which one can "have his cake and eat it too." And, allowing considerable margin for the "certain period" at which, Victor claims, "variety is only a temporary demand," it is not too much to suppose, on his theory of life, that every Apollo will find his Venus before she is older than twenty-five. She has twenty years of child-bearing possibilities before her, and the simple gratification of by no means abnormal sexual impulses might result in her giving birth to ten children. And yet his plan involves that, during this time, when, he asserts, she "needs the care, support, and service of others and is therefore unable to support herself," she is nevertheless "educating the children and surrounding her lover with comfort"! It seems to me that, if I have not misunderstood him in this, he has been looking at the subject from a man's standpoint.

But I do not see why we should let this sexual impulse lead us where it may. . . . I do not always eat whenever I see appetizing food; I refrain from sitting in a draught and drinking ice-water when I am too much heated; I sometimes get up when I am still sleepy; and I do not stay in the ocean long enough to risk a chill. And I know the consequences of following the simple sexual impulses to be more serious than any other.

I may consider many of nature's methods exceedingly wasteful and clumsy, and I may believe that, if I had made the world, I would have made it otherwise; that I would have made our simple, spontaneous, first, and most keenly-felt desires those which, if blindly followed, would result in the greatest conceivable happiness. But nature and the laws of the universe and of our own selves are facts which we cannot alter and to which we can only study to adjust ourselves. "If God exists, he is man's enemy"; woman's even more. Finding no escape from this conclusion, I no longer treat nature as my friend when she betrays me. . . . Now, for the woman, the consequences of simply obeying the sexual impulses are the bearing of children. That means risking her life. It also means the endurance of intense suffering, such suffering as she has never before been able to conceive. In the future social condition I believe every girl will be taught this. Nevertheless, I believe there will still be children in the world. I believe that, when a woman no longer looks upon bearing children as either a duty or a slave's necessity in the service of her master, it is not impossible that she will consider it the greatest privilege life may hold out to her. And with her claim to this child which has cost her so much once recognized by all men and women, why may it not be that she would *choose* this luxury rather than other "opportunities"? A woman will no longer look upon children as a more or less unfortunate natural consequence of the satisfaction of a strong desire, but as a blessing—yes, the very greatest in life to any woman with the mother-instinct—to be secured with full purpose and careful choice, with a complete understanding of all else that must be given up for its sake. Victor has not made it clear to my mind that the woman is the loser who chooses this. It is hard to find the measure of other development or luxury that will be compensation for a woman's loss of this possibility.

But I do not admit that she must needs sacrifice her independence to secure this end. Under normal conditions a woman is by no means unfitted for any productive labor during pregnancy. It would be an exceptional case in which she would be unable to perform the three hours' daily work necessary for self-support during the whole period. This is adding one hour to the limit set in the "Science of Society," in which Mr. Andrews claims that two hours' daily labor will be more than sufficient to support each individual in average comfort. I do not even admit that the woman "has to depend upon the man whom she made the father of her child for some time before and a long time after giving birth to a child." All that is needful is that she have the service and help of some one . . .

After the birth of a child, a woman may be unfitted for any productive labor for two months. And we must add to the list of expenses the support of a nurse during this time and the physician's fee. During another seven months she will nurse her child and, perhaps, will do no other work except directly caring for him. But I am taking this for granted rather from a desire not to underestimate the needful expense of child-bearing than because it seems to me surely the better way. There is a strong feeling among advanced people that a woman ought to do nothing whatever during pregnancy and child-nursing but fold her hands and look at beautiful pictures and listen to beautiful music. But I think this is largely reactionary. The pendulum has swung quite over. It is like saying: "Women have done too much; therefore they should do nothing."

It is a safe estimate, it seems to me, to say that it will cost not more than half as much to support a child for the first ten years of its life as to support an adult. That is, a woman will be obliged to work four hours and a half a day instead of three for ten years in order to support each child. And she must have previously saved money enough for the child-bearing expenses which I have just indicated. After ten years, in the new order of economic life, a child may be self-supporting.

I cannot see how all this can seem to any one an impossibility or even an undesirability. When the nursing period is at an end, the mother engages in the four and a half hours' daily employment, leaving for this time her child in the care of others. These others may be friends who assume this care because it is to them a delight and a rest. Or, in the absence of such friends, it may be simply trustworthy people who would find in it, not rest, but attractive labor, for which they would receive due remuneration. I am almost certain of encountering on this point a remonstrance in the minds of many women. A true mother will never leave a young child, they will say. But I am almost as certain that every mother who is thoroughly honest with herself will admit that it would have been better, both for herself and her child, if she could have left him in safe hands for a few hours each day. . . .

This theory of independent living does not seem to me to involve any loss of the "home" which the family relation has always, it is assumed, been alone able to secure. There would always be, for the little children, the safe, sure mother-home. And, besides this, there would be the father-home, somewhere else, and as many friend-homes as there were dear friends, to which the little children would lend their sunshine whenever their wish so to do met with the mother's consent.

I cannot really understand anyone but a communist being ready to favor "a sort of communism between lovers." In every other social relation an Individualist would have the strongest faith in every plan which conduced to the greatest development of individuality as most certain to bring happiness. But in this relation, in which, of all others in life, mistakes result in the sharpest suffering, this general principle is set aside, and the development of individuality, at least of womanly individuality, less carefully considered than the securing, for her, of certain luxuries and other material advantages. It is true that, when one is in love, it is impossible to conceive happiness in any other form than the constant presence of the loved one. Nevertheless, I believe that neither the finest nor the keenest happiness lovers are capable of yielding each other will result from following this wish blindly, without reason or thought. I am even disposed to find fault with Victor's saying that "between true lovers who are really devoted to each other the relations are ideal." I do not think that "devotion" is any element of an ideal relation between grown-up people. A mother or father or adult friend may be devoted to a helpless baby, to a child, or to a weak, sick, afflicted man or woman. But only weakness has need of devotion, or desires it. What strong men and women want, in either the relation of friendship or in that fervid, passion-full form of friendship known as love, is simply to feel the "home in another's heart"; a home not made, but found. Apollo's Venus is doubtless altogether lovely in his eyes, but that fact is only tiresome or amusing to the rest of the world, and must inevitably tend to fill Venus with a narrow vanity which effectually checks all desire or capacity for growth. I no more admire a blind love than a blind hatred. Either is below the plane on which developed men and women will find themselves. That youth is inconstant is proverbial, but not all proverbs are quite true. Youth is the age of hero-worship, and the tendency of that period is to idealize the object of love. Today young people, experimenting in love, begin by finding an Apollo or Venus in every beautiful face, and end—in what? In finding the true one at last? Not at all. In finding that they were mistaken, but in concluding that this one *will* do. Having reached this conclusion, their inconstancy hides itself from public view under the veil of married life, and these young people become *constant*, but not always constant in their *love*. My prophecy of the future is that, after love has been left free long enough (I do not mean an individual man or woman, but all men and women), Apollo will find that he has no Venus. Because it seems to me that, as human life advances and human beings differentiate, there becomes less and less possibility of finding any one with whom one is completely in sympathy.

Nevertheless, I believe there will always be love. Indeed, I believe in love. . . . Now, I am going to assume, in spite of all public sentiment to the contrary, that love is not a bad thing, but a good thing; that it is a normal, healthful, strength-giving, developing force among the conditions of human existence; that it is called forth by the perception of lovable, admirable, fine qualities, wherever they exist; that in its intrinsic nature it is a blessing, and not a curse, wherever it exists; that it does not need to be *sanctified* by a marriage rite or even by the approval of friends . . .

When a man "makes a home" for a woman in the way Victor proposes, he makes it impossible that either shall know any other love without calling upon the other to bear a certain amount of deprivation. For me, any arrangement which would involve the love of only one at a time would be sufficient to condemn it. Not to be free to love is the hardest of all slavery. But marriage is like taking a path in which there is only room for two. And a man and woman cannot take up a position before the world as dearest friends or lovers—call the relation by any name you choose— without by that action cutting themselves off from all fullness and spontaneity of other love and friendship. By the very announcement of their mutual feeling—in whatever form the announcement may be made—they have said: "Everything in my life is to be subordinated to this." To voluntarily and deliberately "make a home" is to say that nothing foreign to either can enter. The result in life today is commonly this: of the old friends of either only those enter the new home who have a sufficient number of qualities that are equally attractive to both to make them welcome and who can be content to continue friendship on the basis of those qualities. If John does not like music, Ellen gives up her musical friends. Why should he be asked to hear the piano, when it is only so much noise to him, or even hear music discussed, when it is a bore to him? Why should Ellen be called upon to breathe tobacco-perfumed air, because John and certain of John's friends feel restless and uncomfortable without their after-dinner cigar? Things are mainly either pleasurable or painful; not indifferent. If John and Ellen are honest with each other, they will discover that John dislikes music and Ellen dislikes tobacco, and that to lay aside their sensitivities on one occasion may be a slight matter, but that to be called upon to lay them aside at any time is a really serious matter. But Victor perhaps thinks the home need not be like that. John may have his smoking-room and Ellen her music-room. In that case the smoking-room would be, after dinner, John's home, and the music-room Ellen's home. The place where we are free,—that is home. That is perhaps the secret of all home feeling. The presence of our dearest friends helps it only when their mood meets ours.

But this is not "making a home." To make a home, in the popular sense, is to buy land and build a house which is *ours*, buy dishes and furniture which are *ours*, agree to have children which are *ours*, and to make no change in our life arrangements except by mutual consent.

Victor puts the case simply, and it sounds easy: "When they cease to be happy together, they separate." Is it so simple? It is not enough to say: We are not bound together one hour longer than our mutual love lasts. Mutual love does not come and go, keeping step like well-trained soldiers.

As the first flush of love passes away, people begin to *discover* each other. After all, they were not one. In very many cases it was only the blinding force of the sex element which retarded this discovery. There was no conscious deceit. But the discovery is apt to be a painful one. And the old hunger for sympathy in all things returns. If we are still free to seek it, no harm comes. There may even be no pain in the slow discovery that in no one other soul can it be found. But if we are not free, and if, by some chance, one, not both, comes to believe that the love was founded on a mistake? . . .

It is very true of love that we know not whence it comes or whither it goes. It is sometimes more sadly true, and makes one of life's problems far more intricate, that we know not when it comes or when it goes. Its death is as incomprehensible as its birth. Sometimes it is drained away, silently and unsuspectedly, by the thousand wearing trifles inevitably attendant upon that constant companionship which the torrent of new-born love so imperiously demands. Sometimes it is swept away in one instant by the discovery of some quality of character of whose existence we have never dreamed. Sometimes, as in "What's To Be Done?" the constant need of one is identical only with the temporary need of the other, and discovery can not possibly be made until the temporary need has passed. All life is either growth or decay,—that is, change. And with every change in the individual there is change in his love. In the happiest lives and the longest loves its proportion and depth and character are perpetually changing.

Victor says: Variety may be as truly the mother of duality as liberty is the mother of order. Has he forgotten that this mother does not die in giving birth to her daughter, and that this child does not thrive well without the mother?

Notes

1. For a general account of antebellum sexual reform, see Hal D. Sears, *The Sex Radicals: Free Love in High Victorian America*, Lawrence: Regents Press of Kansas, 1977. For anarchism's connections, see William O. Reichert, *Partisans of Freedom: A Study in American Anarchism*, Bowling Green: Bowling Green University Popular Press, 1976, pp. 277-314. *Liberty* itself published a year-long series of articles that well represents the antebellum connections. This was the triangular debate in 1852-53 between the anarchist Stephen Pearl Andrews, and Henry James and Horace Greeley: *Love, Marriage, Divorce and the Sovereignty of the Individual* (begins February 25, 1888 [V:15, #119] and continues through #143 [February 23, 1889]).

    On the more general topic of feminism and *Liberty*, see Sharon Presley, "Feminism in *Liberty*," pp. 158-165 in Michael Coughlin, et al, eds., *Benjamin R. Tucker and the Champions of Liberty*, St. Paul: Michael Coughlin and Mark Sullivan, n.d. [1986]. An interesting account of several prominent women in anarchism around the time of *Liberty* is Margaret Marsh, *Anarchist Women, 1870-1920*, Philadelphia: Temple University Press, 1981. See also the anthology of women anarchist writings by Wendy McElroy: *Freedom, Feminism, and the State: An Overview of Individualist Feminism*, Washington, D.C.: Cato Institute, 1982. The literature on Emma Goldman is voluminous, but these are some of the most significant biographical works: Richard Drinnon, *Rebel in Paradise: A Biography of Emma Goldman*, Chicago: The University of Chicago Press, 1961; Candace Falk, *Love, Anarchy and Emma Goldman*, New York: Holt Rinehart Winston, 1984; Alice Wexler, *Emma Goldman: An Intimate Life*, New York: Pantheon, 1984.

2. *The Word* was published 1872-1890, 1892-1893 in Princeton and Cambridge, Massachusetts. *Lucifer* was published 1890-1907 in Valley Falls and Topeka, Kansas and in Chicago. For Tucker's association with Heywood, see James J. Martin, *Men against the State: The Expositors of Individualist Anarchism in*

America, 1827–1908, Colorado Springs: Ralph Myles, 1970 (originally published DeKalb, Ill.: Adrian Allen, 1953), pp. 205–206. For more on Heywood, see Martin Blatt, *Free Love and Anarchism: The Biography of Ezra Heywood*, Urbana: University of Illinois Press, 1989.

3. F.F.K., "The Sexual Freedom of Women," March 31, 1888 (V:17, #121), p. 5. While Kelly objected to this commerce, Sarah M. Chipman ("Natural Rights," May 12, 1888 [V:20, #124], p. 1) saw this as a legitimate choice by women, holding that anarchists should be concerned rather with preventing invasion.

4. J. William Lloyd, "The Kreutzer Sonata," September 27, 1890 (VII:12, #168), pp. 5–6.

5. Victor refers here to the novel "What's To Be Done?," serialized in *Liberty* between May 17, 1884 and May 1, 1886.

9

Children as Property

Schemes and philosophies of child-rearing and education have proliferated among anarchists, for they have been especially concerned with how to raise freedom-loving and responsible individuals.[1] Not surprisingly, the status of children was examined in *Liberty* from a thoroughgoing individualistic standpoint. State control of children was clearly anathema, but so was "community" involvement. Thus, the responsibility for child-rearing and education was presumed to rest solely with the parents, or more narrowly, with the mother.

Indeed, Benjamin Tucker went even further, arguing that children, at least those still too young to emancipate themselves, were really the *property* of their mothers. How could he have come to such a conclusion? He argued that children were unavoidably dependent upon an adult for support and thus they could not enjoy an equal amount of liberty with adults (see selection A). These unequal creatures consequently could not be owners, but were instead owned by that person whose "labor" had produced them. Yet, children would eventually become free and equal individuals themselves, that is property-owners rather than owned property. In egoist theory, property was created by contract, so children became owners when they began to make contracts. In particular, as owners, they could join in contracts for mutual defense of life, liberty, and property. Until then, however, they were property. The implications of this were severe: no outsider could legitimately intervene to prevent the neglect or even the abuse of a child, for this would be invading the property right of the parent.

Tucker's argument raised a firestorm of controversy in *Liberty*. John Badcock was a particularly insistent critic, although one who shared the egoistic assumptions on which Tucker based his arguments. For Badcock (selection C), Tucker's argument treated the concept of "property" as a fetish. It was not true, he argued, that there could only be "owners" and "owned."[2] The very idea of putting children "on a par with property" was offensive to the sympathies of civilized people, he said.[3] Tucker urged Badcock not to let his sympathies interfere with logical principles such as property and equal liberty, but both men assumed that the proper relationship between parents and children was a matter of expediency, particularly a matter of what relationship would cause the least pain to children. J. William Lloyd (selection D) offered a more fundamental critique of Tucker, attacking the very idea (central to egoist anarchism) that rights were based on might or contract. If that was so, he conceded, Tucker was right and children were property. But for Lloyd rights were based in nature and could be discerned by scientific examination. For him, the logical corollaries of Tucker's egoist notion of property in children (for example, that parents could legitimately kill their children or sell them into slavery) should have led Tucker to rethink egoism as the "ethical basis of anarchism."

That is, the question of children was in many respects an extension of the debate over egoism, one that put its stakes in poignant terms. Tucker, ever the logician, refused to be swayed by such sentimental considerations and held his ground, evidently even putting his principles into practice by establishing numerous contracts with his own daughter.[4]

Further Reading in Liberty

Perhaps the best discussion of the dilemmas of education for an egoist anarchist was Clara Dixon Davidson, "Relations between Parents and Children," September 3, 1892 (IX:1, #235), pp. 2-4. Evacustes E. Phipson ("The Rights of Children," October 5, 1895 [XI:11, #323], p. 7) makes the more contemporary argument that children (and, to some extent, animals) deserve rights by virtue of their sentience, particularly their capacities to feel pain in various forms.

A.   "Compulsory Education Not Anarchistic" —Benjamin Tucker[*]

Despite its title, this early article really focuses on making a distinction between abuse and neglect of children (the latter would include denying an education to a child). Tucker clearly does not accord any rights to children, for the question he addresses is whether abuse or neglect invade the rights of third parties, children not being in a position of equal liberty with regard to their parents. On the other hand, the distinction he makes between abuse and neglect indicates that he does not yet consider children to be property in the fullest sense, for that would entail in their "owners" a "right to use and abuse." As it is, he here argues that outsiders may intervene to stop physical abuse, because such abuse poses the possibility of "certain and immediate disaster."

A public-school teacher of my acquaintance, much interested in Anarchism and almost a convert thereto, finds himself under the necessity of considering the question of compulsory education from a new standpoint and is puzzled by it. In his quandary he submits to me the following questions:

1. If a parent starves, tortures, or mutilates his child, thus actively aggressing upon it to its injury, is it just for other members of the group to interfere to prevent such aggression?

2. If a parent neglects to provide food, shelter, and clothing for his child, thus neglecting the self-sacrifice implied by the second corollary of the law of equal freedom, is it just for other members of the group to interfere to compel him so to provide?

3. If a parent wilfully aims to prevent his child from reaching mental or moral, without regard to physical, maturity, is it just for other members of the group to interfere to prevent such aggression?

4. If a parent neglects to provide opportunity for the child to reach mental maturity,—assuming that mental maturity can be defined,—is it just for other members of the group to interfere to compel him so to provide?

5. *If it be granted* that a knowledge of reading-and-writing—i.e., of making and interpreting permanent signs of thought—is a *necessary* function of maturity, and if a parent neglects and refuses to provide or accept opportunity for his child to learn to read-and-write, is it just for other members of the group to interfere to compel the parent so to provide or accept?

Before any of these questions can be answered with a straight yes or no, it must first be ascertained whether the hypothetical parent violates,

---

* August 6, 1892 (VIII:50, #232), pp. 2-3.

by his hypothetical conduct, the equal freedom, not of his child, but of other members of society. Not of his child, I say; why? Because, the parent being an independent, responsible individual and the child being a dependent, irresponsible individual, it is obviously inequitable and virtually impossible that equal freedom should characterize the relations between them. In this child, however, who is one day to pass from the condition of dependence and irresponsibility to the condition of independence and responsibility, the other members of society have an interest, and out of this consideration the question at once arises whether the parent who impairs the conditions of this child's development thereby violates the equal freedom of those mature individuals whom this development unquestionably affects.

Now it has been frequently pointed out in Liberty, in discussing the nature of invasion, that there are certain acts which all see clearly as invasive and certain other acts which all see clearly as non-invasive, and that these two classes comprise vastly the larger part of human conduct, but that they are separated from each other, not by a hard and fast line, but by a strip of dark and doubtful territory, which shades off in either direction into the regions of light and clearness by an imperceptible gradation. In this strip of greater or less obscurity are included that minority of human actions which give rise to most of our political differences, and in the thick of its Cimmerian centre we find the conduct of parent toward child.

We cannot, then, clearly identify the maltreatment of child by parent as either invasive or non-invasive of the liberty of third parties. In such a difficulty we must have recourse to the policy presented by Anarchism for doubtful cases . . .

Those of us who believe that liberty is the great educator, the "mother of order," will, in case of doubt, give the benefit to liberty, or non-interference, unless it is plain that non-interference will result in certain and *immediate* disaster, if not irretrievable, at any rate too grievous to be borne.[5]

Applying this rule to the subject under discussion, it is evident at once that mental and moral maltreatment of children, since its effects are more or less remote, should not be met with physical force, but that physical maltreatment, if sufficiently serious, may be so met.

In specific answer to my questioner, I would . . . make reply as follows:
1. Yes.

2. Yes, in sufficiently serious cases.
3. No.
4. No.
5. No.

B. "A Sound Criticism"—Benjamin Tucker[*]

*In this excerpt from the article that ignited the debate over children in
1895, Tucker claims that children must be seen as property, and that this
conclusion must guide analysis of their situation. Therefore, one should
not ask "what rights do they have?" or "what duties do parents have?"
but rather "who owns them?" His answer is that individual parents, not
the state or the community, are the legitimate owners. This leads to a
hardening of the principle articulated in the previous selection: outsiders
may not intervene in the property relationship between a parent and her
child, even if it becomes abusive.[6]*

The material with which the sociologist deals may be divided into two
classes,—owners and owned. Now, under this classification the child
presents a difficulty; for, while unquestionably belonging in the category
of the owned, he differs from all other parts of that category in the fact
that there is steadily developing within him the power of self-emancipation, which at a certain point enables him to become an owner instead of
remaining a part of the owned. But I am unable to see that this singularity
can alter his technical status pending the day of self-emancipation. Till
that day he must remain in the category of the owned, and, as a matter
of course, till that day he must have an owner. The only question is: Who
shall own him,—the parent or the community? We may decide upon one
or the other, according to our view of the requirements of a true social
life. If we are State Socialists, we shall decide in favor of the community.
If we are Anarchists, we shall decide in favor of the parent. But to
whichever of these two we award the control of the child, there the control
belongs; and thereafter to attempt to award a superior control to the other
is to disregard the principle originally chosen for our guidance.

If parental ownership and control be acknowledged, it is absurd to say
that the doctrine of equal liberty gives the community a right to deprive
the parent of control and assume ownership of the child itself whenever

[*] June 29, 1895 (XI:4, #316), pp. 3–4.

parental control is exercised cruelly. . . . The opinion which would favor displacement arises from a feeling of sympathy which blinds the person holding it to the meaning of equal liberty. The question whether such sympathy is to be heeded is simply the old question as to when and where it is advisable to deliberately and avowedly violate the rule which in general we find invaluable in the shaping of our social conduct.

C.   "L'Enfant Terrible"
—Benjamin Tucker and John Badcock, Jr.

Tucker's shift to a rigid property analysis of children was not imme-diately noticed, for John Badcock, Jr. wrote shortly after Tucker's article that even within a utilitarian framework, children should not be con-sidered property. Badcock insisted that they should be seen as objects of sympathy, to be protected by all, including the parents. Tucker objected that this would pave the way for community intervention.[7]

A central theme for critics of the "children as property" view was that it made a fetish out of property.[8] In this selection, Tucker fleshes out his theory (in response to criticisms by J. Greevz Fisher) by reiterating that only those who are able to enter into a mutual contract to protect their property have any realistic (i.e. enforceable) claim to it. Thus, children are "owned" before they can make such contracts, and become "owners" only after they begin to do so.

Badcock advances two major criticisms. First, he insists again that human sympathies have been important in expanding liberty and will continue to be important in maintaining it.[9] After pointing to some of the absurd logical corollaries of parental ownership, he attacks the vague-ness of Tucker's criterion for becoming an "owner": one's "ability" to make contracts. In particular, he suggests that there is a world of difference between the desire (or conception) to form contracts and the actual power to enter into one.

Tucker [*] *:*

Though I, as an Egoist, agree with Mr. Fisher that "even ownership in general is but a means to an end," and that I am in no wise bound to respect property (except as I bind myself by contract), and that we

---

* "L'Enfant Terrible," August 24, 1895 (XI:8, #320), pp. 4–5.

"tolerate appropriation because no better basis for industrialism has been or seems likely to be invented," it is none the less true that, having fixed upon appropriation as the best basis for industrialism that we know of, we combine to protect and maintain it; and the principle of equal liberty allows us to thus combine, if we do so voluntarily. We combine, moreover, to protect, not only property, but also life and liberty. But the life, liberty, and property *of whom*? So far as the child and its status are concerned, this is the crucial question. And I answer it that we combine to protect the life, liberty, and property only of those who have reached a stage of development which enables them to form at least some crude conception of such a combination and its purpose,—in other words, only of those in whose minds the idea of contract has taken shape. If we protect the life and liberty of organisms that are outside this limit, we do so only in the interest of their owners; we do not protect them against their owners. As for the property of such organisms, they have none; they are themselves the property of others. Were we to protect organisms outside this limit in their own interest and against everybody, we should by that very act cease in a measure to protect the property right of organisms inside the limit. All this is but another way of saying what I said in No. 316 [selection B],—that sociological material consists of two categories, the owners and the owned, and that the possession or lack of the power to contract, of the power to consciously and deliberately undertake to serve another in return for another's respect, determines the category in which any given organism belongs. No animal has this power; therefore all animals fall into the category of the owned, and are not entitled to social protection. There is a time in the life of every child whom death does not cut off in infancy when it acquires this power. As long as the child lacks this power, it remains in the category of the owned, and should not have social protection, because that would be injustice to its owner; as soon as it acquires this power, it becomes an owner, emancipates itself, and may contract for social protection. But this emancipation does not consist, as Mr. Fisher and Mr. Byington[10] seem to think, in the mere manifestation of a recognizable will. Animals have wills and can make their volitions known, but they do not thereby become owners, and members of society. The necessary qualification for social membership is the power to entertain the simple idea of the social contract.

Now a second question arises: if the unemancipated child falls within the category of the owned, who is its owner? I answer that I can see no clearer property title in the world than that of the mother to the fruit of her womb, unless she has otherwise disposed of it by contract. Certainly the mother's title to the child while it remains in her womb will not be denied by any Anarchist. To deny this would be to deny the right of the mother to commit suicide during pregnancy, and I never knew an Anarchist to deny the right of suicide. If, then, the child is the mother's while in the womb, by what consideration does the title to it become vested in another than the mother on its emergence from the womb and pending the day of its emancipation? I think that no valid consideration can be shown; and, if such is the case, then it is established that the unemancipated child is the property of its mother, of which, by an obvious corollary, she may dispose as freely as she may dispose of any other property belonging to her.

Badcock I* :

. . .In your article you state: "As long as children are unable to make contracts, I know of no reason why they should not be 'put on a par with property,' especially if putting them on a par with property tends on the whole to lessen their suffering, and if there is no method of dealing with them that does not virtually put them on a par with property." . . . You leave me in the dark as to how you consider a property-status for children can conduce to their welfare. And, in the absence of any qualifying phrases in your articles, I can only infer that the property-status contemplated by you is absolute . . .

Then I reply that, as the absolute property status of children means their total and unconditional enslavement to their parents or other owners, with the denial of their claims to any outside assistance against owners' tyranny, and the forcible prevention of outsiders from giving assistance and succor, however much the child may be tortured, meaning also a stop put to the spread of sympathetic feeling and consequently to the extension of liberty, while men's brutal feelings are allowed material upon which their brutality may be cultivated, the "par with property" status of children appears to be an invention of the devil. The czar of Russia, I believe, puts all his subjects on a par with property. This human property idea is, in fact, *the idea* with all potentates, and is really the one thing that our liberty propaganda *was* intended to abolish.

---

* "On the Status of the Child," September 21, 1895 (XI:10, #322), pp. 7–8.

If, Mr. Editor, you had proclaimed that liberty was only for your own class, or only for adult males, or only for those between sixteen and sixty years of age, leaving the second childhood of man to be enslaved like the first, you would have paralleled your utterances drawing the line of liberty *against* those who have not passed their childhood as shown by their being "unable to make contracts." As if their ability or non-ability to make contracts had anything more to do with their rightful enslavement or emancipation, or with the expediency of protecting them from ill-treatment, than their ability to smoke had.

Seeing that childhood and manhood (or womanhood) are but stages to the life history of the same animal,—which stages might, to please classifiers, be extended to a round dozen—seeing that the immature and more or less dependent boy develops *gradually* into the mature and more or less independent man, any sharp line that society draws between the status of the child and that of the adult must be arbitrary in proportion to its sharpness.

The arbitrariness of the line may be of little import for expediting small matters, like the collection of taxes or votes, or even for fixing individual responsibility for debt; but, when the line of demarcation is used to determine *between the two extremes of slavery and liberty*, the *entire* status of the individual, the sacrifice of common sense and all the requirements of individual growth and development to a mere rule is flagrant . . .

Parents are *not* producers of their children in the same sense that they may consider themselves the producers of their handiwork or brain-work. The evolution of all the complex tissues and endowments of the child goes on so independently of the parents' will that . . . "having produced my child myself" is grotesque in its impudence. Of course, if ownership rights are granted . . . these rights would be salable, and a class of child-slaves and slave-markets would follow as a matter of course. How nice for the children!

But the whole is obnoxious and unworkable, except at the cost of stunted feelings. No one can be expected to discriminate between an act of cruelty committed upon a child and a similar act committed upon one who is not a child, and to check his spontaneous help to the injured one if he finds it to be under age. . . . To discriminate in this matter *against* the child—the weakest—is only possible by the most callous or the most cowardly. It is dead against our instincts, and a system based upon this discrimination would depend upon a creed or a government for its workableness.

. . . It is because *I recognize* "that this is an imperfect world," and recognizing that between our august selves and babies, and savages, and criminals, and lunatics, there is a wide gap,—although the missing links are numerous enough,—I say that, although we cannot live on free contract terms with these inferiors, it shows a great want of the spirit of liberty and toleration in anyone who would deny the said inferiors a limited liberty. And, when the spirit goes, the form is likely to go also.

Badcock II[*]:

The mere fact of an organism being able to appreciate the idea of a social contract, or any contract, especially when strained to include those with an "idea of secession," is a wholly different thing from having "the possession . . . of the power to contract; of the power to consciously and deliberately undertake to serve another in return for another's service, and respect another in return for another's respect" which you said [selection B] "determines the category in which any given organism belongs." As if a little girl who *seceded* from her harsh parent had any *power* to entitle her to equal liberty!

The *power* to maintain one's liberty differs in degree very considerably—no two persons having *equal* powers. If individual liberty depended upon the power of the individual, *equal* liberty would be an impossibility. Nietzsche's definition of liberty as "the will to power" is not the idea of liberty which Anarchists aim at, so far as I know, although they recognize that a state in which liberty from molestation will be general can only be maintained through individual power.

The contract basis for equal liberty, as it rests upon the *power to contract on an equal footing with others*, can only be for those having *equal powers*. Adopt that basis, and you are committed to Nietzsche's ideal of a State in which a powerful aristocracy monopolize all the liberty, and keep in slavery all the proletariat.

However much the reciprocal obligations idea may have been of use in evolving the higher from the lower status, it is dispensed with whenever assistance is given by a strong person to a weak one. Although the sympathetic feelings receive satisfaction by such help given, and by the

---

[*]"On the Status of the Child," November 30, 1895 (XI:15, #327), pp. 7–8.

removal of the discordant misery or cruelty, that is only a negative benefit, and cannot be construed as a reciprocal benefit by one who wishes the sympathies left out of account in determining liberty rights.

I grant we cannot treat children and the lower animals as on an equal liberty-footing to ourselves. Nor, indeed, can we treat many men on that footing, especially those who try to cheat and rob us. It then becomes a question of expediency as to what measure of freedom we will allow those various classes of children, criminals, etc., we have in our control. To deny any protection to children would be paralleled by the denial of any protection to criminals against the cruelest possible treatment. But as with criminals, our humane instincts lead us to prevent excessive punishment being dealt out to them, and anything beyond what "fits the crime" arouses our indignation and leads us to side with the prisoner, so with children (who also are outside the full liberty status) we require that they be dealt with with at least a moderate amount of respect.

D.   "The Anarchist Child"
—J. William Lloyd and Benjamin Tucker

Badcock eventually concluded that for contract to work at all as the basis for property, human sympathy would have to be engaged. J. William Lloyd was skeptical of this line of criticism, conceding that Tucker's position was unassailable "while admitting contract as the ethical basis of anarchism." Therefore, his objection was more fundamental than Badcock's: egoistic contracts were no substitute for natural rights. Yet even from the standpoint of natural rights, the situation of children posed dilemmas, for they were still "dependent individuals." Because of this dependence, they were subject to the limited control of those supporting them. Because they were individuals, they still enjoyed some residual rights, which could be enforced, even against parents, by outside individuals.

Lloyd [*]:

. . . I do not think that Mr. Tucker's critics can successfully attack his position while admitting contract as the ethical basis of Anarchism. With so much conceded, the logic of his position seems hardly assailable. If

---

[*] "The Anarchist Child," September 21, 1895 (XI:10, #322), p. 6.

the Anarchist's only obligation is to a contract, invasion outside of that contract is no crime, and what he owns he certainly owns absolutely and may do as he will with.

I only feel that I have a right to speak on this subject because I do not accept contract as the ethical basis of Anarchism in the first place, and, in the second, do not regard children as the property of anybody.

I agree with Mr. Tucker in that it is "only on egoistic and utilitarian grounds—that is, grounds of expediency—that I believe in equal liberty." With me, happiness is the first thing, and liberty a means to that end. I base my Anarchism on Natural Right; that is, I believe there are in the nature of things certain lines of conduct and relations of man to man which are, above all others, conducive to happiness in the individual and harmony in society,—which are, therefore, above all others, expedient. Anarchists, according to my definition, are people who regard equal liberty as the greatest of these naturally right human relations, and who therefore stand for its advocacy and defence. As a means to this end a contract may often be wisely used, but, whether used or not, *an Anarchist has no right to invade any individual.* Individuals I divide into two classes,—dependent and independent. An independent individual is one who supports himself, and who is therefore absolutely free from the dictation of others,—a perfect individual. The dependent individual cannot fully support himself; therefore he is rightfully subject, to a limited extent, to the direction and dictation of those who support him, and is an imperfect individual.

What is this "limited extent"? It is the liberty of the one who supports the dependent. For example: if in free society a cripple begs me to support him for charity's sake, as he cannot earn his own, he, if I accept, at once becomes subject to me. Because I supply his food, I have a right to say what he shall eat; because I dress him, I can say what he shall wear; because I pay his doctor's bills, I direct his hygienic habits; because I am responsible, to some extent, for damages he may inflict, I control to that extent his conduct. I have a right to do all this; otherwise, I am his slave and he is my master. In short, my control over him is not that of an owner, but purely and altogether defensive.

Let it be observed that this dependent individual is not my property or my slave, even although his dependence may be the "product of my labor,"—that is, I may have broken his limbs, or staved in his skull, and so made him dependent; nor have I, according to the logic of my position, any right to invade him in any way, even if there be no contract between us; nor have I any right to prevent his seceding from my support at any time, either to the support of another or to become independent.

Now, then, I have no difficulty whatever about this child question, because I class the child as a dependent individual. The parent has the right of defensive control over the child, and no other. As the defence of equal liberty is the legitimate business of Anarchists, any Anarchist will have a right to defend an invaded child against its parent or any one else. And any child will have the right at any time to secede from any parent or guardian and adopt another or become independent altogether; at which moment the right of parental control, in the rejected parent, ceases.

Anarchist parents will know perfectly well what they do when they set about begetting a child. They will know they are not producing property, but another individual with the rights of an individual, and they will know their right relations to that individual. The child is not an invader by forcing his dependence upon the parent; but the parent, having forced dependent life upon the child, is an invader, if refusing support to this dependent individual.

That a child is property is absurd. If property, then a slave. A doctrine that establishes slavery in Anarchy is certainly sufficiently reduced to an absurdity, but this is not all. My property is mine, *always mine*. My child, if my property, is not only my slave now, but my slave for life; and not only my slave for life, but may be sold to another to be his slave, or may be willed to heirs and assigns.

This doctrine, carried out logically, poisons Anarchism to its fountainhead, and reaffirms government in its intensest and most detestable form.

Tucker [*] :

. . . Mr. Lloyd's argument is that certain rules of conduct are conducive to happiness and therefore expedient; that Anarchists view equal liberty as the principal of these expedient rules; and that an Anarchist consequently has no right to invade any individual, and hence has no right to invade a child. I might, if it were necessary, disprove here, in a direct manner, the proposition that an Anarchist has no right to invade any individual. But this is needless. I have only to call Mr. Lloyd's attention to the fact that we are discussing the question, not of what an Anarchist

---

* "What Is Property?" September 21, 1895 (XI: 10, #322), pp. 4–5, 8.

has a right to do, but of what a mother has a right to do. Apparently he has forgotten for the moment that not all mothers are Anarchists. I remind him, then, that some mothers, and even a vast majority of mothers, are Archists and do not consider equal liberty expedient. They consider authority expedient and the right rule of conduct in the nature of things; and, hence, by Mr. Lloyd's own argument, they are not called upon . . . to refrain from invading anybody. Now, as I do not suppose that Mr. Lloyd means to countenance the absurdity of denying absolute control of children to Anarchist mothers while allowing it to Archist mothers, he must, in order to prove his case, establish that it is the duty, not simply of Anarchists, but of every person, to refrain from invasion. Which he cannot do, because, while basing his own duty in this respect upon his own view of expediency, he cannot refuse to allow others to make their opposite views of expediency the basis of a right to invade. . . . It being the most obvious of truths that every one must judge of expediency for himself, no Egoist can logically deny that every organism has the right to act as it thinks best, so far as its might will allow. Might is the measure of right everywhere and always, until, by contract, each contracting party voluntarily agrees to measure his right thenceforth, not by his might, but by the equal liberty of those whom he has contracted to protect. So here we are, back again to the *regime* of contract; and, as Mr. Lloyd is logical enough to perceive that, if contract determines rights, my position regarding parents and children is invulnerable, I have no further quarrel with him, unless he shall take issue with what I have said above.

Nevertheless, before ending with him, I will consider briefly certain other features of his letter. His analogy between the cripple and the child sustains rather than overthrows me, for his cripple makes a contract, and I as strenuously defend the liberty of the child in whom the idea of contract has dawned as I defend the slavery of the child to whom contract is not yet possible. All his remarks about the child as a dependent individual apply only to what I call the self-emancipated child. He attributes to his dependent individual the right of secession. What is secession, I should like to know, if not self-emancipation? The very idea of secession implies some conception of contract, however crude. Nothing that Mr. Lloyd says meets the case of the real infant.

And again: "That a child is property is absurd. If property, then a slave. A doctrine that establishes slavery in Anarchy is certainly sufficiently reduced to an absurdity." Slavery in Anarchy an absurdity! Will not the animals be slaves under Anarchy? Wherein does the undeveloped child differ from the animals? In its possibilities, does Mr. Lloyd answer? But the ovum in a woman's body has the same possibilities. Is it not her property? Slavery in Anarchy, instead of an absurdity, is a necessity. Property in any living creature means slavery in the ordinary sense . . .

Lloyd[*] :

As Mr. Tucker seems to feel that his opponents on this child question are inclined to be too hard upon him personally, I want to state at the outset that I know Mr. Tucker to be a generous friend and believe him to be a humane man. All the more strongly do I oppose him on this account, because I believe his doctrine would cause many to regard him as inhuman, and at any rate would be used by the inhuman as a justification for their inhumanity. Knowing Mr. Tucker's almost superstitious reverence for logic, I do not wonder that he accepts all the logical corollaries of his position, but I am as surprised as any of his critics to find that, once comprehending them, he does not abandon a position whose logical corollaries are so revolting. And I confess that his arguments appear to me strange, desperate, and reactionary. Without the least excitement I must say that his position on this question, if adhered to, will strike the death-blow to philosophical Anarchism. It is suicidal. Modern civilization will never accept it.

In the beginning of his reply to me he brings in Archist mothers. "We are discussing the question," he says, "not of what an Anarchist has a right to do, but of what a mother has a right to do." What of it? The question is the same. Natural rights are not changed by names. If in the nature of things it is wrong for one man to invade another, the invader acquires no indulgence by taking the name of Archist. My contention is that right and wrong are scientific facts, and our opinion about the inexpediency or expediency of a given course decides nothing but our own action. . . . I had always supposed that Anarchists, at least, were satisfied that the invasion of one human being by another was in the highest degree wrong, foolish, dangerous, and inexpedient,—that this *was* Anarchism, and this only. It would appear that all these years I have been laboring under a great mistake,—teaching a false doctrine,—and I am now assured by the chief apostle of Anarchism that he "might, if it

---

[*] "Anarchist or Free Socialist?" November 2, 1895 (XI:13, #325), p. 7.

were necessary, disprove here, in a direct manner, the proposition that an Anarchist has no right to invade any individual."

Very cleverly, by ingeniously restating my position in his own words, he tries to bring me under the *regime* of contract, but I will none of it. . .

He says: "While basing his own duty in this respect upon his own view of expediency, he cannot refuse to allow others to make their opposite views of expediency the basis of a right to invade." But I do. Certainly in a narrow and proximate sense a man has a right to do what he *thinks* right because he can do no other. But all the same, if in his ignorance he is doing that which produces unhappiness, he is doing wrong, and nature proves him wrong by turning the consequences against him. He is not in harmony with Natural Right, and any one invaded by his ignorant action has a right to restrain it. But it must be observed that I do not base my "duty," in the true sense, upon my "own view." I base my action upon my own view, as others do, but my real duty and my real expediency are found in accordance with the natural right . . .

"Slavery in Anarchy an absurdity!" cries Mr. Tucker. ". . . Slavery in Anarchy, instead of an absurdity, is a necessity." That I should live to hear it! —and from my chief leader and teacher! "Will not the animals be slaves under Anarchy? Wherein does the undeveloped child differ from the animals? In its possibilities, does Mr. Lloyd answer? But the ovum in a woman's body has the same possibilities. Is it not her property?" . .

The ovum in the woman's body is her property. It has not the possibilities of the child. It is not a human being. When the germ of the woman and the sperm of the man have commingled and developed under certain conditions, then they have the possibilities of the child; then they become human. The precise point at which humanity commences is for physiologists to determine. I doubt if any one could say at present. . . . Border lines are always vague. What I am jealous to establish is the principle that, where humanity exists, it is to be sacredly respected and defended against invasion. Mr. Tucker makes the point "that no Anarchist will deny a mother's right to commit suicide during pregnancy." Perhaps; but I, who am now no Anarchist, do deny it *after the embryo becomes a human being*. The mother has a right to kill herself, but no one else . . .

And now to make an end. As I have clearly been mistaken as to what constitutes Anarchism; as Mr. Tucker is the accredited head of that philosophy and as he now assures the world in no uncertain tone that contract is its only basis, that an Anarchist has a right to invade, that might is the measure of right everywhere and always, that slavery in Anarchy is a necessity and children, fools, and non-contracting individuals the fit subjects of such slavery, that it is the duty of Anarchistic juries to effectually restrain those who attempt to defend children against parental cruelty, even to the finding a man guilty of murder in the first degree who should kill a parent to save a child,—in view of all this, and much more, I now wish to state with equal emphasis that henceforth I will have none of it.

Henceforth I am no Anarchist, but a Free Socialist!

Notes

1. See, for example the selections in "Section VI: The Anarchist on Education," in Leonard I. Krimerman and Lewis Perry, eds., *Patterns of Anarchy: A Collection of Writings on the Anarchist Tradition*, Garden City, N.Y.: Anchor, 1966.
2. J. Greevz Fisher ("Children as Chattels," August 24, 1895 [XI:8, #320], p. 6) argued that parents were "trustees," while William Gilmour called them "guardians" ("An Apparent Contradiction," August 24, 1895 [XI:8, #320], p. 7).
3. "The Life More than the Creed," August 10, 1895 (XI:7, #319), pp. 7–8.
4. Paul Avrich, "An Interview with Oriole Tucker," in Michael Coughlin, et al, eds., *Benjamin R. Tucker and the Champions of Liberty: A Centenary Anthology*, St. Paul: Michael E. Coughlin and Mark Sullivan, n.d. [1986], pp. 20–27. In this anthology, see also Wendy McElroy, "The Non-Economic Debates in *Liberty*," pp. 136–139.
5. Tucker clarifies this later by arguing that interference is *not* justified by the superior importance of the child's physical integrity, but because "the child is potentially an individual sovereign." ("Children under Anarchy," September 3, 1892 [IX:1, #235], p. 2.)
6. Tucker admits that outsiders (including himself) might intervene anyway, out of compassion for the child, but he insists that such interference is still an invasion of property rights and probably should be punished as such ("On Picket Duty," September 7, 1895 [XI:9, #321], p. 1).
7. John Badcock, Jr., "The Life more than the Creed," August 10, 1895 (XI:7, #319), pp. 7–8; Benjamin Tucker, "The Creed Essential to the Life," #319, pp. 4–5.
8. For J. Greevz Fisher, Tucker's discussion (in selection B) of children's "technical status" and of sociological categories "has a flavor of artificiality which ought to raise suspicion." ("Children as Chattels," August 24, 1895 [XI:8, #320], p. 6)
9. This is familiar not only from Badcock's earlier arguments here, but from the debate over egoism in 1890, where J.M.L. Babcock made similar points in discussing the motivations of and necessity for reformers.
10. Stephen Byington, "The Status of the Child," August 24, 1895 (XI:8, #320), pp. 6–7.

10

Literature and Anarchy

At various points during the nineteenth century, the relationship between the most progressive tendencies in literature and the arts and anarchistic tendencies in politics and reform was very close. Examples include the Godwin-Shelley-Wollstonecraft circle in early-1800s England, the Transcendentalists and early anarchists in the United States in the 1830s and 1840s, and the Impressionists and anarchist terrorists and anarcho-syndicalists in fin-de-siécle France. Thus, Tucker's aim to make *Liberty* "a mouthpiece, to some extent, for the exponents of Anarchism in art"[1] was not just one editor's idiosyncrasy. Although *Liberty* did not publish as much poetry as many reform journals, Tucker did serialize several novels over the course of its twenty-seven year run, including Tchernyshevsky's *What is To Be Done*[2] and Felix Pyat's *The Ragpicker of Paris*.[3] Nor was *Liberty* Tucker's only instrument for promoting literature. In 1889, he began publishing *The Transatlantic: A Mirror of European Life and Letters* and in 1906, he opened a book shop in New York.[4] His aim in the latter project was to carry a large stock of "advanced literature," by which he meant "the literature which, in religion and morals, leads away from superstition, which, in politics, leads away from government, and which, in art, leads away from tradition."[5] As far as possible, he sold such literature under the moniker "Tendency Novels" (see selection D below) and it was these criteria that substantially guided Tucker's editorial choices in opening *Liberty*'s columns to discussions of modern literature.

Although primarily referring to prose, "advanced literature" could also include poetry, plays, and even opera; the roster of authors considered was impressive: Emerson, Whitman, Ibsen, Zola, Nietzsche, Tolstoi, and Wagner. Whitman and Emerson were both admired by

Liberty's contributors, but it was very late in their careers before *Liberty* appeared, so the focus was understandably on up-and-coming authors, particularly Ibsen and eventually Nietzsche. Tucker in particular was fond of Ibsen, ranking him with Stirner and Proudhon as one of "the three great Anarchistic figures that stood preeminent in the literature of the nineteenth century."[6] Nietzsche was a somewhat different matter. Initially calling attention to him in 1892 as "another great Egoist, who [was] now rising into prominence in the wake of Ibsen and Stirner," Tucker published a long series of excerpts from Nietzsche, translated by Tucker's close friend George Schumm.[7] By 1897, however, Tucker had become critical of Nietzsche, noting that he did not support the anarchist axiom of equal liberty. Nevertheless, his writings could prove useful: "Nietzsche says splendid things,—often, indeed, Anarchistic things,— but he is no anarchist. . . . He may be utilized profitably, but not prophetably."[8] The selections below concerning Whitman, Ibsen, and Nietzsche (A, B, and C respectively) illustrate the role that "advanced literature" could play in furthering the aims of anarchism, and of reform generally.

Probably the best expression of this political approach to culture, although much too long to excerpt here, was an article that Tucker solicited from George Bernard Shaw. Reacting to Max Nordau's lengthy attack on modern art, *Degeneration*, Shaw defended avant-garde tendencies in art, music, and literature.[9] Tucker sent copies of the issue containing Shaw's review (eventually published as the pamphlet *The Sanity of Art*) to every major publisher and newspaper in America. Despite this tactical alliance, Shaw and Tucker were political enemies, Shaw's Fabianism being explicitly at odds with Tucker's anarchism, as for example in Shaw's pamphlet "The Impossibilities of Anarchism."[10] However, Tucker always claimed that Shaw had anarchist tendencies, illustrated most forcefully in a pseudonymous excerpt Tucker had taken from a London anarchist paper, *Freedom* in 1885.[11] Criticism of Shaw for his adherence to "State Socialism" thus fell mostly to Victor Yarros, represented here by the selection (F) opposing municipal theatres.

Municipal support of theatres was obviously an example of state promotion of culture and thus taboo to anarchists. While this manifestation of a *laissez-faire* approach to culture might please modern critics of the National Endowment of the Arts, the individualist anarchists' vehement opposition to censorship, even of obscenity, clearly would not.

Although sexuality itself was seldom explicitly discussed in *Liberty* (see chapter eight), the right to do so, particularly in works of fiction, was staunchly defended. The most controversial episodes had to do with two writers whose lives and writings dealt not merely with sexuality, but even with homosexual themes: Walt Whitman and Oscar Wilde. Whitman's *Leaves of Grass* was under attack again in 1882 by the state of Massachusetts. Under pressure from the district attorney, the prospective publishers demanded deletions from Whitman, which he refused. They returned the plates to him, and Tucker printed an edition from these, offering it for sale and challenging the district attorney to arrest him. Tucker's attitude toward "obscenity" may have been ambivalent, but his objection to censorship was emphatic: "disgusting as is the perversion of moral passion which finds expression in obscenity, it is much less dangerous to the public morals than the perversion of moral passion which finds expression in government."[12] In 1894, the censorship issue rose again in a court case and this time, Victor Yarros expanded on Tucker's argument, insisting that censorship had to be resisted, not only in the name of "quality" literature, but even in the case of "obscenity" (see selection E below). In 1895, Tucker criticized Oscar Wilde's conviction, stating that nothing he had done was invasive, and thus that his jailers, not he, were the criminals. Nevertheless, something good came out of Wilde's ordeal, the poem "The Ballad of Reading Gaol," which Tucker praised as "a terrific portrayal of the soul of man under Archism."[13]

Further Reading in Liberty

An interesting reprint is G.K. Chesterton's "A New View of Whitman," (December 1904 [XIV:24, #386], p. 6), which criticizes Whitman's abandonment of metre and modesty in his poetry. Also illuminating is an exchange over the "message" of Ibsen's plays, one author finding it confusing (Mrs. Howard Udell, "Ibsen's Latest Utterance," June 29, 1895 [XI:4, #316], pp. 6-7) and the other finding it clearly egoistic (Herman Kuehn, "Ibsen's Real Teaching," ibid, p. 7). One of the most interesting of George Schumm's translations of Nietzsche is "Aphorisms from Nietzsche," July 1899 (XIII:12, #362), p. 6.

A.   "A Poet of Nature"—J. William Lloyd[*]

Although full of praise for Whitman, for his egoism, his universality, and his inclusiveness, Lloyd finds inconsistencies in Whitman's embrace of "evil." While "evil" may be part of the universe, it can be costly to the individual. For an alleged egoist to celebrate his own decadence strikes Lloyd as a flaw, but one which Whitman in the end could not square with his own admiration for the healthy human body. Lloyd also applies political standards to Whitman's poetry in complaining of his patriotism and pro-Union sentiment, which seem to contradict the poet's "anarchistic" tendencies.

Walt Whitman, the poet of Nature, has joined the unseen majority. The mysterious compact of forces which we term the human organism has in his case dissolved, and we are told that he is dead. To himself dead, perhaps, yes, but to us, who remain and remember, he is *not* dead. A figure so great, so conspicuous, so picturesque, standing alone like a native mountain in the midst of the citied plain of modern conventionality, can never die out from memory-view of man.

Never, perhaps, since the days of Ossian, or of the author of the Kalavela, has there existed a poet who was so thoroughly the poet of rude, basic, barbaric Nature—or a man who so desired to be, and who so nearly succeeded in becoming, Nature in himself. With him we are brought down to the skeleton and seed of things, the first principles, the primeval granite, the primitive motives and passions. He not only sings the very soil from which the human plant springs, but, with inspiring genuineness, the very *manures* by which that plant is fertilized. . . . Even as he sings always of primal nature, so the human-nature he celebrates is that of the natural, basic man,—the laborer, the peasant, the pioneer, the warrior, the hunter,—the rude, blunt man of simple ideas, direct action, and untamed loves and hates. Never, perhaps, since poetry began was there a poet so consistent in matter, manner, and himself. Saturated with the conviction that Nature was perfect and without fault, equally to be celebrated in all that we call evil and all that we call good, he not only strove to be the mouthpiece of Nature, but to be identified with it, to be a "Kosmos." Perceiving freely that egoism is the great fact and Keynote of Nature, and of every nature, he fearlessly celebrates it—

---

[*] May 7, 1892 (VIII:38, #220), pp. 3–4.

> One's self I sing.

and stands erect with the grand challenge:

> I celebrate myself . . .
> Walt Whitman, an American, one of the roughs, a Kosmos.
>
> Toward all,
> I raise high the perpendicular hand—I make the signal. . . .
> I need no assurance—I am a man who is preoccupied of his
>   own Soul. . . .
> I will effuse egotism, and show it underlying all—and I
>   will be the bard of Personality. . . .
> And nothing, not God, is greater to one than one's self is. . . .
> Solitary, singing in the west, I strike up for a new world.

Yet he never, in this worship of individuality, forgot the correlative fact of solidarity, never forgot that every nature is but a part and modification of Nature, that the individual is but a unit of Society. Remembering this, he continually found occasion to—

> Yet utter the word Democratic, the word En Masse,

and the beautiful word, "Comrade," is forever on his lips—

> And who but I should be the poet of comrades?

Indeed, as with Ingersoll, friendship, warm, and sunny, and genial, is the most charming characteristic of the man.

How tremendously helpful, healthful, and inspiring all this is to the sickened sojourner in modern conventionalism goes without saying. It is like the strong air of the high hills, the brine of the ocean, or the strong light of one of Olive Schreiner's "shimmery afternoons" in the desert.

> Divine am I inside and out, and I make holy whatever I
>   touch, or am touched from.
> The scent of these arm-pits are aroma finer than prayer.
> This head more than churches, bibles, and all the creeds. . . .
> I do not trouble my spirit to vindicate itself or to be
>   understood,
> I see that the elementary laws never apologize, I reckon I
>   behave no prouder than the level I plant my house by,
>   after all.

I exist as I am—that is enough.
If no other in the world be aware, I sit content.
And if each and all be aware, I sit content.

One world is aware, and by far the largest to me, and that is
  myself.

With Walt one of his most constant and sublime thoughts was his unity
and identity, one might almost say his equality with the universe.

I do not doubt but the majesty and beauty of the world are
  latent in any iota of the world; . . .
I do not doubt I am limitless—in vain I try to think how
  limitless; . . .
Earth! my likeness!
A vast Similitude interlocks all. . . .
To be this incredible God I am. . . .
I have the idea of all, and am all, and believe in all. . . .
The Many in One—what is it finally except myself?

And this oneness of feeling is even greater toward humanity; he
returns continually to the theme that he is to include all, embrace all, and
himself with all. In this he is one in spirit with Christ and Buddha, and
even excels them in the eloquence and intensity of its expression. The
"Neither do I condemn thee" is not equal to—

Not till the sun excludes you, do I exclude you. Not till the
  waters refuse to glisten for you, and the leaves to rustle
  for you, do my words refuse to glisten and rustle for you.

And the sentiment of brotherhood has never been expressed with such
virile eloquence as in—

I do not ask who you are—that is not important to me.
You can do nothing, and be nothing, but what I will infold
  you.
To a drudge of the cotton-fields, or cleaner of privies I lean,
On his right cheek I put the family kiss, And in my soul I
  swear, I never will deny him.

In his conception of poetry Walt returns to antique ideals. Poetry is
not to sing of beauty, but to be filled with religious earnestness. A poem

is a great meaning, and a poet one who sings of great meanings with positive intuition.

> The maker of poems settles justice, reality, immortality; . . .
> Divine instinct, breadth of vision, the law of reason, health,
>   rudeness of body, with drowsiness, gayety, sun-tan,
>   sweetness—such are some of the words of poems. . . .
> The words of poems give you more than poems,
> They give you to form for yourself poems, religions,
>   politics, war, peace, behavior, histories, essays, and
>   everything else,
> They balance ranks, colors, races, creeds, and the sexes, . . .
> Whom they take, they take into space to behold the birth of
>   stars, to learn one of the meanings,
> To launch off with absolute faith—to sweep through the
>   ceaseless rings, and never be quiet again.

The irregular rhythm of the wind and the waves is his model. Like Emerson, and that greatest of woman-poets, Emily Dickinson, he is one of the wind-harp singers. He clearly perceives that the heart of Nature's remedy is rhythm, full of infinite, mysterious meaning, not a polished and rigid form, but perpetually varying, recurring pulses.

Not so musical as Ingersoll, who is a poet of the same school, he is truer, and infinitely more picturesque and sublime. He knew and felt the charm of the great monotonies—the deserts, oceans, snowfields, processions of days and seasons which occur in Nature, and did not hesitate, on occasion, to make his verses correspondingly broad, and monotonous in the repetition and procession of facts and phrases. Shallow critics rebuke this, and tell us how many lines he commences with "Where" and "I see," too small and lacking in critical sympathy, themselves, to perceive its merit and meaning. When he writes such anatomical lines as:

> Wrist and wrist-joints, hand, palm, knuckles, thumb,
>   forefinger, finger-joints, finger nails,

he really writes that which is beautiful and strong, no matter how few can appreciate it . . .

Like all great men who greatly love Nature, he was enthused by the beauty of what more limited natures call *ugliness.*

> Of ugliness—to me there is just as much in it as there is in
>   beauty—And now the ugliness of human beings is

> acceptable to me; . . .
> And mossy scabs of the worm fence, and heaped stones,
>   elder, mullen, and pokeweed. . . .
> I do not doubt there is far more in trivialities, insects,
>   vulgar persons, slaves, dwarfs, weeds, rejected refuse,
>   than I have supposed.

A nature so broad, generous, serene, striving to love as men dream that God loves; so healthful, helpful, manly, and virile,—can hardly be over-valued or praised enough. We are too close to this great man yet to appreciate him; but he wrote of the bases of things, he wrote for all time, and the future will comprehend him. Ingersoll did well to call him "the brother of mountains," but the phrase is hardly sufficient. He *is* a mountain, a continent, a world, a universe, and he can hardly be said to have exaggerated when he called himself "a Kosmos" and "a God."

But nothing that we know, imagine, or have heard described, is without impersonation, and Walt was sometimes mistaken and inconsistent. Two of these lapses need notice. Continually identifying himself with the universe, he sometimes forgot that he was an egoist. From the outlook of the universe there is no evil, but from the standpoint of the individual there is nothing which may not assume the relation of evil . . .

Or if there is evil, he affirms that "it is just as important as anything else," and there, also, affirms a half-seen truth. Evil *is* important, and how—simply in this, that it gives strength to the man who resists it. Vice, crime, ignorance, and physical hardships are all evil, and are all valuable merely because by resistance to them man becomes virtuous, just, wise, and manly. Walt seems never to have exactly comprehended this, and in his large charity felt that he had not only to include the victim of vice but vice itself, not only the criminal but the crime. The motive was a large and noble one, and the attempt in a certain way does him credit, but it is more to his credit that it so largely failed. As regards crime the failure was complete. With all his identifications he never was able to identify himself with a tyrant, a sneak-thief, a cut-throat, or a ravisher. The most he can do is to place himself at the bar for sentence, but that means sympathy with the man, and not his crime. In fact, when we remember that crime means the invasion of someone's liberty, the attempt of such a one as Walt Whitman to celebrate it becomes laughable. It was like trying to turn himself inside out. But he had set himself to "make the poem of evil also," "to be the poet of wickedness, also," and something had to be done. At last he makes a bold break, at the point of least resistance, and we hear:

> Give me now libidinous joys only!
> Give me the drench of my passions! Give me life coarse
>   and rank!
> To-day, I go consort with nature's darlings—to-night too,
> I am for those who believe in loose delights—I share the
>   midnight orgies of young men,
> I dance with the dancers and drink with the drinkers,
> The echoes ring with our indecent calls.

Here was success indeed, but from the standpoint of sane egoism it cannot be called creditable. To the egoist self-injury is the unpardonable sin, and the *only* sin, and here was an egoist celebrating his own rot. . . .

It is plain, then, that if Walt could sometimes, and momentarily, celebrate the beginnings of vice, he could not even for a moment celebrate the results . . .

Now hear him when the egotist was sane in him:

> If anything is sacred, the human body is sacred,
> And the glory and sweet of a man is the token of manhood
>   untainted, . . .
> Do you not see how it would serve to have such a body and
>   soul that when you enter the crowd an atmosphere of
>   desire and command enters with you, and every one is
>   impressed with your personality? . . .
> This man was of wonderful vigor, calmness, and beauty of
>   person, . . .
> He drank water only—the blood showed like scarlet
>   through the clear-brown skin of his face, . . .
> I henceforth tread the world, chaste, temperate, an early
>   riser, a gymnast, a steady grower.

But it is unnecessary to proceed. This man whose tastes were so pure and simple, whose manhood was so loving and complete, who was so intoxicated with the human body, "natural and nonchalant," its health and beauty, and the glow and glory of its clean, free sex, could only by violence make himself the chanter of "libidinous joys" and the "drench" of the passions which rot manhood from the surface to the core.

Another lapse is even more striking, though it occurs but seldom. How Anarchistic Walt was I need not try to prove. I should have to quote two thirds of his work. But is it not a strange commentary on human illogic to hear a man who could write—

> Fall behind me, States!
> A man, before all—myself, typical, before all,

invoke, in another place—"a shrill song of curse on him who would dissever the Union," and thereby deny secession, that most sacred of individual rights. And here and there, elsewhere, that old prejudice of patriotism makes him blind to the logic of world-citizenship.

But when he chants—

> I swear I am for those that have never been mastered! . . .
> For those whom laws, theories, conventions, can never
> master,

we forgive him instantly, and when he adds—

> By God! I will accept nothing of which all cannot have
> their counterpart on the same terms.

we are compelled to love him.

Although Walt calls himself "one of the roughs," by a natural law of attraction he drew to himself the gentlest and most refined natures, and we are not surprised to find among his friends and admirers such names as Emerson, E.C. Stedman, John Burroughs, Tennyson, George Eliot, and Edwin Arnold. But his roughness was all on the surface, it was like a hairy breast, broad and sunburned, but full of the warmest and tenderest love. No saint or saviour ever preached a love so broad, charitable, and inclusive as he.

Gentle and genuine, rugged and stately as an elk of the true wilderness, and as completely natural, his was one of those rare and typical natures which enthuse and inspire men for all time merely by the power and picturesqueness of their personality.

He was, and will always be, one of the natural leaders.

B. "Ibsen's Power and Weakness"—Florence Finch Kelly[*]

Like Lloyd, Kelly praises the realism and radicalism of her subject, in this case the Norwegian playwright, Henrik Ibsen. She also finds political gripes, in particular the lack of realism in expressing the economic causes for the modern social ills that Ibsen so eloquently describes. In the end, she too finds reason to admire her subject, primarily for the power in his presentation of the psychological dilemmas of modern "rebels." The theme of contradiction, inevitable when political ideologues try to claim an artistic genius for their own, is even more typical of the assessments of Ibsen in Liberty *than it was of critiques of* Whitman.[14]

Ibsen is usually called a "realist," but, to my mind, he is rather rebel than realist, and as much prophet as rebel. He rebels, with intense convictions, against the accepted forms of his art, against present conditions, against the life of today. With prophetic clearness and strength of vision he looks far into the future, seizes upon its possibilities, transports them into the immediate present, and surrounds them with the severest actualities of his own time.

Great, unto genius, he undoubtedly is. But, with all his greatness, one is forced to wonder why could not this mighty man have been a little broader, a little clearer-sighted, a little greater? He gathers together the elements in the problem of life,—the position of women, commercial relations, the obligations of social and family ties, the restraints of religion, and the power of conventional ideas; with magnificent scorn he tells off his indictments against them, holds them up to shame and loathing, and sweeps them off the stage. But he has not solved his problem. It is still there, as puzzling as ever. For he has not even touched the primary element of the whole matter,—the economic question.

And it is just here, in his blindness to the potency of economic conditions, that Ibsen's philosophy fails, and he himself falls short of being one of the mightiest of his time. He is a realist—and a most matter-of-fact one—mainly in the setting of his scenes. When it comes to inspiring his chief characters with motives, he is usually an idealist of the most extreme type. He refuses to consider why men sink into that mire of hypocrisy and dishonesty and double-dealing which arouses his contempt. He finds them there, and with one jerk sets them far up on the mountain-tops of spiritual regeneration. Surely, if he were a little more, or very much less, of a genius, he would see that most of that commercial trickstering and lying and deceiving which he mirrors so truly that society

---

*April 19, 1890 (VII:1, #157), p. 6.

winces at the portrait is due more to an economic system which makes it pay—which even makes it necessary—to lie and evade and deceive, than to innate and acquired dishonesty. And surely he would see, too, that as long as economic conditions are as they are, men will continue to be dishonest and shifty and untruthful in business—because it pays.

This, to my mind, is the worst fault that can be found with Ibsen's work, whether considered from its artistic or its philosophical side. And, surely, much can be pardoned to so great a mind, which understands so clearly, up to that point, and voices so powerfully the most potent spirits of his century. He is the only purely literary man of his time who hears and understands and dares to interpret what they are trying to do. No other has understood and seized upon the awakening consciousness of individuality among women as he has done. Those few hours of Nora's life in "A Doll's House" typify woman's history during the whole of this nineteenth century. Possibly he did not intend it so,—when an author's pen is tipped with genius, there is always more in his words than he is conscious of when he writes them,—but, whether or not he did, a century of progress is there, in letters of fire. . . .

Ibsen has not fully expressed, but he is the only author who has conscientiously attempted to express, that restlessness and those half-hushed threats of revolt against conventional bonds and restraints and illogical customs which are part of the signs of the times. The spirit of rebellion against this dead-weight heritage from past generations and the benumbing fear of it—the one forcing men to think and the other refusing to let them act—seem to me to be the principal idea, rather than sexual relations, or heredity, in "Ghosts." That dead-weight heritage and the spirit of rebellion against it form one of the pitiful tragedies of this closing part of the nineteenth century, and Mrs. Alving is the embodiment of it all. She no longer believes in these ghosts of dead ideas, which others respect as living entities, but she does not dare proclaim her unbelief, she does not dare act upon it. She inwardly despises them; they have wrecked her life; but she pays to them the outward respect which general usage demands. Her life has been one long sacrifice to the ghosts of duty and obligation. She has lied unremittingly to her son in order that he may respect his father's memory; and, when he comes home with his inherited disease, "worm-eaten from his birth," she will not tell him, until the last necessity is put upon her, that not he, but his father, has been to blame, even though the boy's self-reproach adds to his sufferings. And when she does finally tell him of his father's dissolute life, she takes the blame upon her own shoulders and shields the dead man, in order that the son may retain some portion of filial love and respect. And all the time she knows that she is doing homage to "ghosts."

Is she not very like the spirit of the time, which bends the knee and bows the head before each one of a thousand ghosts, though in secret thought despising them all?

C.   "Nietzsche and His Compeers"—"Egoist"[*]

Although shedding little light on Nietzsche's thought, this article follows the pattern of ambivalent embrace of a modern genius for the cause of anarchism. At best an egoist, and certainly no anarchist, Nietzsche was admired by individualist anarchists primarily for his corrosive attacks on conventional morality, including occasionally the state. What distinguishes this article is its general thrust, a "Zeitgeist" explanation of genius, and its concluding remarks on Wagner, another culture hero ambivalent to anarchists.

Parallels, like comparisons, lead to distinctions, which are invidious, and thus, according to legend, are odious. But any one who has taken the full scope of revolutionary ideas into his view, must see that in each age, or century, or even in each generation, there have been—and there are—minds between which, though essentially diverse in character and differing greatly in bent, are still to be found certain connecting links, which seem almost to point to a connection, in some mysterious manner, of the life threads of these individuals.

In every division of the realm of advanced thought there are supreme intellects, which tower above all others in their vicinity. Yet, in the various divisions, these mighty minds seem to have been pushed upward by the same general force or impulse. Call that impulse what we may, or attribute it to what source we will, the result of its movements is unquestionable. Looked at rationally, and without any superstitious awe, this force is nothing but the influence of the thought of past ages acting as a sort of leaven in minds ready to receive, yet so differently constituted as to produce results in great variety, but all seemingly reaching toward the same goal—the progress of mankind . . .

---

[*] June 1904 (XIV:21, #383), p. 6. Originally published in *Freeland*.

No one person, perhaps, has caused such universal commotion among the students of ethics, in this generation, as has Friedrich Nietzsche. Nobody has so baldly and clearly stated his thoughts and arguments in contravention of the Christian and time-honored system of morality, and so invariably carried consternation and dismay into its camps. No man who could say that "both nature and history are fundamentally immoral," and also that "true virtue consists in thirst for danger and courage for the forbidden," could avoid bringing upon his head the anathemas of both the church and the State. Nothing could be more revolutionary to their codes of ethics. But Nietzsche reaches these positions by cold and philosophical reasoning. He produces the facts of history and facts of natural science to prove the latter. The tendency of all Nietzsche's thought is toward the upbuilding of the individual, rather than toward the support of the collectivity. This controverts the human brotherhood idea, and thus incurs the enmity of all the dominant forces in modern society. Indeed, "human brotherhood," in its general and indiscriminate sense, was as abhorrent to Nietzsche as was the supernaturalism of theologists.

Nietzsche, it may be said, stands near the pinnacle of his generation in the conception of rational ethics. Yet, not far from him, either in altitude or distance, stands another commanding figure—Max Stirner. How evident that the same impulses and emotions, to a certain extent, governed these two men! Then, as fruits of the same period, though different in trend of thought (still, however, toward the same general ideal), we have Proudhon in France, Ibsen in Norway, Spencer (though not so close) in England, and Thoreau and Emerson and Walt Whitman in America. If we take the short step from the drama and poetry to music, we might also name Wagner and Richard Strauss, who have taken positions far in advance of their contemporaries, and who, I firmly believe, have been actuated by the same general impulse of progress that has manifested itself in other branches of human thought.

It is true that we must not forget that Nietzsche himself, after once being a great admirer and friend of Wagner, later in life turned and actively opposed him. But, while we may recognize this difference between two giant intellects, and while undoubtedly in its latest phases Wagner's work was to a certain extent reactionary, we must not lose sight of the fact that *in the main* Wagner's music stands—if it stands for anything—for rebellion against established forms and ideals; and, further, that one of the greatest creations of his intellect—the character of

Siegfried—is the embodiment, in more than one essential respect, of the idea of Nietzsche's "overman." Siegfried was a breaker of idols and superstitions, and was the incarnation of "thirst for danger and courage for the forbidden."

While Nietzsche was not an Anarchist, he has, in more than one instance, shown his contempt and disgust for the State, and I can do no better in closing this article than by quoting one of his most scathing arraignments of it: "Whatever the State speaks is falsehood, and whatever it possesses it has stolen. Everything is counterfeit in it. The biting monster—it bites with stolen teeth. Its very bowels are counterfeit."

Nietzsche had little use for cant and hypocrisy, and the cowardice of which they were bred. His ideals were courage, strength and honesty— superb trinity!

D. "Tendency Novels"—Benjamin Tucker[*]

These were books offered for sale by Tucker. With the exception of Schreiner's book, he translated all of them from the French. In this long-running advertisement, he indicates the literary and political qualities that defined "tendency" novels.

My Uncle Benjamin. Claude Tiller.

A humorous, satirical, and philosophical novel . . . It is one of the most delightfully witty works ever written. Almost every sentence excites a laugh. It is thoroughly realistic, but not at all repulsive. Its satirical treatment of humanity's foibles and its jovial but profound philosophy have won its author the title of "the modern Rabelais." My Uncle Benjamin riddles with the shafts of his good-hearted ridicule the shams of theology, law, medicine, commerce, war, marriage, and society generally.

The Story of an African Farm. Olive Schreiner.

A romance, not of adventure, but of the intellectual life and growth of young English and German people living among the Boers and Kaffirs; picturing the mental struggles through which they passed in their evolu-

---

* May 7, 1892 (VIII:38, #220), p. 4.

tion from orthodoxy to rationalism; and representing advanced ideas on religion and social questions. A work of remarkable power, beauty, and originality.

The Rag-Picker of Paris. Felix Pyat.

A novel unequalled in its combination of dramatic power, picturesque intensity, crisp dialogue, panoramic effect, radical tendency, and bold handling of social questions. Probably the most vivid picture of the misery of poverty, the extravagance of wealth, the sympathy and forbearance of the poor and despised, the cruelty and aggressiveness of the aristocratic and respectable, the blind greed of the middle classes, the hollowness of charity, the cunning and hypocrisy of the priesthood, the tyranny and corruption of authority, the crushing power of privilege, and, finally, of the redeeming beauty of the ideal of liberty and equality that the century has produced.

The Kreutzer Sonata. Count Leo Tolstoi.

This novel, dealing with the questions of love and marriage, urges a morality that is more than puritanical in its severity, while handling the delicate subject with all the frankness of the realistic school. This book, so far as the central lesson to be drawn from it is concerned, is of a reactionary character, and should not be regarded as a part of Liberty's propaganda. Yet it is a work of interest, almost a masterpiece of art, a romance not without sociological importance. No lover of independent thought can fail to admire its rare unconventionality, the fearless way in which the author addresses polite circles upon a subject which they generally taboo.

What's To Be Done? N.G. Tchernychewsky.

Written in prison. Suppressed by the Czar. The author over twenty years an exile in Siberia. The book which has most powerfully influenced the youth of Russia in their growth into Nihilism. Whoever comes under its influence will fall in love with high ideals.

E.   "Liberty and Literature"—Victor Yarros[*]

Victor Yarros here reacts to a New York Supreme Court decision regarding the sale of books deemed obscene by Anthony Comstock, the crusading censor of the late nineteenth century. While many had praised the decision for its resistance to Comstock, Yarros objected to the distinction the judge had drawn between the classics, or "standard literature," which was out of Comstock's bailiwick, and cheap, obscene novels, which were the fit subjects of censorship. Yarros objected that such a distinction would not protect modern classics such as Zola, that it empowered judges to act as literary critics, and that, in practice, this would enforce the censorious opinions of "hypocrites and bigots" in the community. Were this referring to popular music rather than literature, it could have been written yesterday—the threats to liberty of expression endure and Yarros's conclusion is still relevant.

Thinkers and reformers who ought to know better have hailed with joy the decision of Justice O'Brien, of the New York supreme court, in the application made some time ago by Receiver Little, of the Worthington Publishing Company, for instructions concerning the disposition of certain books which Anthony Comstock sought to suppress as indecent and immoral . . .

Judge O'Brien is praised as a wise and enlightened judge . . . I cannot swell the volume of praise, the decision appearing to me essentially reactionary and dangerous. Doubtless under the language of the statute covering the subject the court was as liberal in construction as it is possible to be without nullifying the intent and purpose of the statute, but to suppose that the decision will encourage literature or promote any progressive tendencies in it is to take an erroneous and superficial view of things. Judge O'Brien is less objectionable as a censor than the vulgar and idiotic Comstock, but the cause of literature and liberty demands freedom from all censorship. To allow anybody to divide literature into classes is to open the door to the gravest abuses and most outrageous discrimination. The rule by which our courts are guided is well stated in the "Evening Post's" comment upon this Comstock assault upon Fielding and other classical authors: "It is as literature," says the "Post," "that all such books should be weighed. If the literary element is by far the

---

[*] September 22, 1894 (X:9, #296), p. 2.

predominating one, and the indecency is only an incident, or an expression of the manners of the time of publication, letting Anthony Comstock pass on their merits would make us very ridiculous. His proper field is books in which the pornographic purpose is the main or only one, but he ought to be ashamed to ask any tribunal to suppress a classic. He may depend upon it that works which five or six generations have admired are out of his bailiwick." Under this rule, the judges are to determine whether the literary or pornographic element predominates in a given work, and whether any alleged indecency is an expression of the manners of the time or a deliberate pandering to depraved taste. Is literature safe under such censorship? Our judges are not distinguished for literary culture and critical acumen, and it is by no means certain that even the classical authors would be uniformly held to be outside the Comstock bailiwick. . . . There are few judges in England or America who, even if they had the literary qualifications, would have the courage to protect the right of publishers to put on the market complete, unabridged translations of Zola's masterpieces. Is there any question that the literary element predominates in Zola's books, and that their "indecency" is an expression of the manners of the time? The hypocrites and the bigots care nothing about the interests of literature, and judges are apt to give effect (even if they do not share the sentiments) to the notions of the hypocrites and bigots in the community. A judge might shrink from ordering the suppression of a work which "five or six generations have admired," but experience has taught us to expect very little consideration and appreciation of works admired by the educated and progressive elements of one generation only. And what is the effect of such ignorant treatment of modern writers? . . . A rule whose operation kills genius is not one that lovers of literature can rejoice over. Far better the temporary sway of the fool, Comstock, whose very audacity, born as it is of vulgarity and ignorance, would hasten our literary emancipation.

Reformers should demand the utter abolition of Comstockism, not in the name of classical literature, but in the name of liberty, which is higher than any literature. Just as in the administration of justice the powerful can protect themselves and the poorest and meanest citizen's rights are the ones requiring vigilant defence, so, in literature, the classics will never suffer for lack of friends, while in the so-called indecent and pornographic authors liberty is in danger of being crushed out. It is the extreme cases which need the aid and support of the fearless and logical advocates of fundamental principles.

F. "The Municipal-Theatre Absurdity"—Victor Yarros[*]

One of the many articles by or about Bernard Shaw in Liberty,[15] *this one is characteristic in combining artistic and political issues. Yarros objects not only to Shaw's proposal for municipal theatres, but also to the glib way in which he advocates them. In particular, Shaw's diatribe against private enterprise and hope for public enterprise draws Yarros' ire. After offering a general defense of private enterprise against public, Yarros turns to the impact of state sponsorship of theatre on theatre itself. He claims that Shaw's problem is not with theatre-owners, who are merely providing what the public demands, but rather with the public taste, which Shaw hopes to "educate" through municipal theatres. This elitist goal is not likely to be effected, for the same reason that censorship is unlikely to promote "quality" literature: government officials are either too stupid themselves or too subject to the crass desires of their constituents to really be "educators."*

One of the things which do not in themselves deserve any serious consideration, and about which it is difficult to write with any degree of patience, is the proposal for State theatres. Yet circumstances render it necessary to overcome one's profound repugnance, and reason about this absurdity. When William Dean Howells offers the alderman-controlled theatre as a cure for the moral and artistic defects of the modern theatre, it is easy to dismiss the suggestion with an indulgent remark or two. . . . When, however, a man of real intellectual power, G. Bernard Shaw, advocates the same scheme, and advocates it in his peculiar, positive, dogmatic, breezy, and extravagant manner, benevolence is out of place. Mr. Shaw is a fighter, and, when he is wrong, he is recklessly wrong. He makes the most amazing assumptions with the air of a man who states incontrovertible mathematical truths, and fairly takes one's breath away by his audacious defiance of facts . . .

It is not only when dealing with such an old subject as factory legislation that he throws moderation and accuracy and philosophic fairness to the winds; even on so disputable and *fin-de-siècle* a question

---

[*] May 2, 1896 (XI:26, #338), pp. 2–3.

as State theatres, Mr. Shaw is absurdly dogmatic and question-begging. The man who once distinctly declared that his tendencies and natural inclinations are all Anarchistic, and that he is a State-Socialist only because he can see no other alternative to monopoly and inequality and robbery, is now illogical and inconsistent enough to deplore "anarchical" protests against legal marriage and to advocate State theatres. True, he does not go the length of demanding the total suppression of private theatres; he is satisfied with less . . .

Mr. Shaw is anxious to popularize and decentralize the theatre; he wishes to make the English a nation of playgoers. This, he thinks, cannot be accomplished under private management or commercialism . . .

Any one who appreciates and loves liberty must be opposed to the absurd scheme. It means that Mr. Shaw and his Philistine majority will tax everybody in order to provide amusements for this same Philistine majority. Whether the minority wants the amusements provided by this majority, or any amusements at all, is not deemed material. If Mr. Shaw and his majority want to be amused in a certain way, everybody is to be compelled to contribute. Is it "obsolete nonsense" to ask Mr. Shaw and his majority to pay for their own pleasures? Is it a mark of idiocy to refuse to support artistic paupers?

Is there any reason, asks Mr. Shaw, for abandoning so important an institution as the theatre to private speculation? Translated into intelligible and direct English, it means: is there any reason for letting people choose their own amusements and support such theatres as please them? Mr. Shaw's question is simply childish. What he really means is that, since, as a Fabian Socialist, he intends to abolish *all* private enterprise, and put the State in control of *every* important industry, institution, and interest, he naturally looks forward to the nationalization of the stage as part of the great scheme. He sees no reason for making an exception of the theatre, and he is right. Nobody does. But it clearly would have been more straightforward for him to say to the readers of the "Saturday Review" that he favors municipal theatres because he is a State Socialist and would municipalize or nationalize everything.

What Mr. Shaw finds it possible to say, with a perfectly straight face, about the inferiority of private enterprise (he prefers the term speculation) to public enterprise cannot be taken seriously. A professional humorist like Gilbert could not have put it more strongly. Bad as private enterprise is, it is integrity itself compared to public enterprise. The main thing that makes for efficiency and honesty is competition, the fear of being outdone, and the necessity of attracting and holding public favor against a number of active rivals. All such motives and incentives disappear when public enterprise annexes a given institution, and nothing else emerges to take their place. Some innocent reformers talk about honor and duty as motives, but the man of the world knows better. When the daily life of nations abounds in illustrations of political stupidity, corruption, ignorance, jingoism, and idiocy, it is rather cool for Mr. Shaw to wave these facts aside . . .

But enough about the political aspects of the matter, and a word or two about the artistic. That such an acute critic and discriminating judge of the drama should propose municipal theatres as a remedy for dramatic decadence is truly astonishing. The theatre, he complains, is dying of commercialism. This clearly means that the "speculators" do not find true art very profitable. They naturally give the public what it appears to want,—farce and melodrama. To blame them is absurd. They are no better and no worse than dramatic critics, editors, writers, saloon-keepers, and preachers. No one will supply things for which there is no demand,—no one except reformers and pioneers. Business is not reform. If the artistic dramas which the elect prefer had a market value, managers would tumble over each other in their eagerness to produce them. . . . As a general thing, the "speculators" may be trusted to do exactly what the public taste renders it profitable to do. Mr. Shaw's quarrel, then, is with the public taste. He thinks, and rightly, that the public ought to enjoy true art and turn away in disgust from clap-trap and sham and vulgarity. His proposal, therefore, really is that municipalities shall *educate* the public in matters dramatic,—give them the finest plays, regardless of their artistic development, as a means of elevating them. But is there any reason to believe that municipal officials, elected by the respectable voters, will agree with Mr. Shaw and the elect as to what plays are fine, artistic, and elevating? Are not all the facts rather against such a belief? Would municipalities produce Ibsen or Jones (at his best) or Sudermann? Would not the rule of the absurd censure be even more arbitrary, "moral," and irritating than now? In truth, the notion that municipal theatres would promote the interest of art and realism and dramatic progress is worthy of one of Gilbert's heroes . . .

Notes

1. Editor's introduction to Jean Jullien, "Ibsen's 'Master Builder,'" June 2, 1894 (X:2, #288), pp. 6-8.
2. Serialized May 17, 1884 (II:16, #42) to May 1, 1886 (IV:2, #80).
3. Serialized March 10, 1888 (V:16, #120) to March 8, 1890 (VI:26, #156).
4. [advertisement], October 5, 1889 (VI:21, #151), p. 8; "On Picket Duty," February 1906 (XV:1, #391), p. 3. See also Wendy McElroy, in *Literature of Liberty*.
5. "On Picket Duty," February 1906 (XV:1, #391), p. 4.
6. Tucker, "On Picket Duty," June 1906 (XV:3, #393), p. 11.
7. Tucker, [editorial column], October 1, 1892 (IX:5, #239), p. 3. These are some, but by no means all, of Schumm's translations: "Extracts from the Works of Nietzsche," December 17, 1892 (IX:16, #250), pp. 1, 4; "Religion and Government" [from "Menschliches, Allzumenschliches"], January 7, 1893 (IX:19, #253), pp. 1, 3-4; "The Philosopher and Old Age," November 30, 1895 (XI:15, #327), pp. 6-7; "The Morality of Custom," March 21, 1896 (XI:23, #335), p. 6; "Nietzsche on Egoism," April 18, 1896 (XI:25, #337), pp. 7-8.
8. Tucker, "On Picket Duty," December 1897 (XIII:7, #357), p. 1.
9. Shaw, "A Degenerate's View of Nordau," July 27, 1895 (XI:6, #318), pp. 2-10.
10. Shoshana Edwards, "The Worthy Adversaries: Benjamin R. Tucker and G. Bernard Shaw," in Michael E. Coughlin, et al, eds. *Benjamin R. Tucker and the Champions of Liberty*, St. Paul: Michael E. Coughlin and Mark A. Sullivan, n.d. [1986], pp. 92-100.
11. "What's In a Name?" April 11, 1885 (III:8, #60), p. 5. See also Edwards, "The Worthy Adversaries," p. 92.
12. Tucker, "Obscenity and the State," May 27, 1882 (I:21, #21), p. 2; [advertisment for "Leaves of Grass"], July 22, 1882 (I:24, #24), p. 4; "On Picket Duty," August 19, 1882 (I:25, #25), p. 1. See also A.E.G., "Walt Whitman's 'Fleshly Pieces,'" September 16, 1882 (I:26, #26), p. 1.
13. Tucker, "The Criminal Jailers of Oscar Wilde," June 15, 1895 (XI:3, #315), pp. 4-5; "The Ballad of Reading Gaol," March 1899 (XIII:10, #360), p. 5.
14. See, for example: C.L.S., "The Letters of Ibsen," February 1906 (XV:1, #391), pp. 36-43; Georg Brandes, "Henrik Ibsen," August 1906 (XV:4, #394), pp. 50-55; Henry Arthur Jones, "The Influence of Ibsen," December 1906 (XV:6, #396), pp. 58-60.
15. See, for example, the articles cited above, especially Shaw's critique of Nordau. A few years later, Yarros wrote a critique of Shaw's "The Perfect Wagnerite" ("Shaw, Wagner, and Siegfried," May 1899 [XIII:11, #361], pp. 3-4) which restated the critique of Shaw's State Socialism and prefigured "Egoist's" admiration for the character of Siegfried (see selection C).

PART FOUR

Strategies for Advancing Anarchism

11

Preferred Strategies:
Agitation and Passive Resistance

All social movements debate strategy and tactics, and American individualist anarchism was no exception. In the pages of *Liberty*, this debate was grounded in several assumptions about revolutionary change and the nature of the individualist anarchist movement. Although these assumptions can only be gleaned from the many articles about particular strategies and tactics, their centrality is clear. First, the revolutionary change that would lead to anarchy was to be a gradual and mostly nonviolent one. This was partly a reaction to the furor surrounding the Haymarket bomb and subsequent trial, partly influenced by Spencer's evolutionary sociology, and partly a matter of consistency with anarchist ideals of non-invasion and equal liberty. The aim of anarchist strategy, therefore, was not the state's *abolition*, but rather, as Proudhon put it, "its dissolution in the economic organization."[1] That is, the state would be gradually undermined as its various interventions in economic and social matters were successfully resisted.[2] This strategy was well-suited to the nature of the individualist anarchist movement: a small, but intelligent and pluralistic minority. Organizing such a "movement" into a large-scale, violent force was not only implausible, but also unnecessary and inconsistent with the ends of anarchism.[3] This band of individualists could not possibly overthrow the state, nor would they wish to, for this would force other individuals into the paradox of obedience to a new anarchist system. What they could do, gradually and nonviolently, was to make the state progressively more irrelevant, by freeing individuals both physically and mentally from its invasive demands.

This broad strategic thrust could encompass a wide variety of strategies and tactics. These can be divided into three general categories,

247

depending upon how consistent the strategy or tactic is with the end of individual sovereignty and equal liberty. The first category, covered in this chapter, are the "preferred strategies," those that are completely consistent, namely "agitation" and "passive resistance." These have the potential to become full-blown praxis, where practices that will be central to the future individualist anarchy are applied *now* to move a statist society in the direction of anarchy. For example, just as individuals in an anarchy would have to be persuaded not to invade the liberties of others (since no state would exist to restrain them), so agitation could be effective in the present to convince people not to rely on the state. The question when considering preferred strategies, then, was not whether but how to employ them. The second category, covered in chapter twelve, are the "acceptable strategies," encompassing practices that could legitimately occur in an anarchy, and thus could be acceptable anarchist strategy, *so long as* they remain consistent with anarchist principles. For example, unions would not be a necessary feature of individualist anarchy nor of its strategy under statism, but could be effective in either, *so long as* they do not contradict equal liberty. The third category, opportunistic tactics, are those inconsistent with anarchist principles. Although generally frowned upon, such tactics as violence and voting might be useful in very limited circumstances. The very existence of this category in anarchist strategy indicates the strategic flexibility and pluralism of the individualist anarchists. Although ultimately ineffective in their goal (so far), their failure is not the result of their being utopians. They were neither unconcerned nor unrealistic about strategy, though they may of course have been wrong.

A foundational question, even for "preferred strategies," is the one addressed by the first two selections in this chapter: How are anarchists to live in a statist society?[4] Since anarchy was not to come immediately or cataclysmically, some accommodation had to be made. In a sense, anarchists had to figure out how to be "in the world, but not of the world." Would anarchists act, as Byington suggested (selection B), as if they were "citizens of the future society" or would they try, as Yarros suggested (selection A), to maximize their freedom as individuals, hoping that this would lead eventually to anarchy. That is, would strategy tend to emphasize the principles of anarchy or the opportunities for reform? This question had ramifications for both the major preferred strategies.

In terms of agitation, was the point to get across a well-defined, strict program of individualist anarchism or would anarchists cooperate in pushing for any reform that might whittle away at the state? Tucker seems to have preferred the former, accepting without apology the term "plumb-line" anarchism, while other writers criticized *Liberty* for being too critical of reformers whose hearts if not their heads were in the right place. This also raised the question of coalitions, particularly with communist anarchists. Simpson and Tucker (in selections C and D) suggest that broad coalitions should be avoided, since this would involve individualist anarchists with rash or emotional reformers, thus threatening the attempt to build up an intelligent minority of anarchists. Others, notably Holmes and Labadie (selections E and F) argued for as broad a coalition as an opportunistic agitation might allow.

In terms of passive resistance, were anarchists to resist the state primarily for propaganda reasons, to demonstrate their commitment to anarchism, or was this a philosophy of life, essential to the acquisition and maintenance of freedom for individuals? Tucker (selections G & H) seems to have seen passive resistance in primarily strategic terms: if done by individuals, it could only be propaganda, but if by a substantial minority, it could be truly subversive (as in the case of the Irish Land League's "No-Rent" campaign). In either case, he felt that such non-cooperation with essential functions of the state (e.g. tax-gathering) was the only effective action that radicals could take against the massive violence of the modern state. Victor Yarros (selection J) saw passive resistance in terms of praxis: it was a strategy to subvert the state that was also the embryo of the social dynamics of anarchy.

Further Reading in Liberty

Yarros wrote a long, ambivalent, and sophisticated discussion of strategy in "Ideas and Conduct" (December 15, 1888 [VI:9, #139], p. 7). A scathing critique of *Liberty*'s lack of "constructive" strategy was offered by an Appleton, a frequent contributor in the early years: "L'Etat, c'est L'Ennemi" (February 26, 1887 [IV:16, #94], pp. 4–5).

In 1892, a dispute broke out on the question of whether anarchist reformers ought to be "enthusiastic." William Bailie made the egoist case against self-sacrifice and for anarchist struggle as "self-realization" ("Bursting a Bubble," June 25, 1892 [VIII:45, #227], pp. 2–4.). Tucker called for an enthusiasm without froth, "settled down into quiet, patient, steadfast, unshakeable determination" ("On Picket Duty," August 20, 1892 [VIII:52, #234], p. 1). Miriam Daniell accused Tucker of thus preferring bores to fanatics ("Enthusiasm Again," September 10, 1892 [IX:2, #236], p. 3).

A.   "Methods and Results"—Victor Yarros[*]

In this general assessment of anarchist strategy, Yarros offers a pessimistic, opportunistic, and ultimately egoistic approach. Rather than offering religious enthusiasm and individual "perfectionism," he insisted that anarchism was a politico-economic reform unconcerned with individual anarchists' personal conduct. Thus, as he concluded in an earlier article, one had to be a "moderate," one concerned "to practise no more of the ideal than is compatible with maintaining a firm hold upon the real, and no less than is required to make the real worth the effort of maintaining that hold."[5]

Melancholy as the present situation is, the task of remedying and improving it would not be found a discouragingly difficult one if only a considerable number of intelligent citizens once arrived at a general agreement as to the needful measures and proper methods of reform . . .

But it is well to realize the fact that the progress of truth and reform, even if sure, is very slow and by no means steady. While there seems to be overwhelming evidence in favor of the view that humanity must and will proceed in the right direction, there is no reason to suppose that we are guaranteed against temporary relapses and periods of stagnation. We may have to pass through another century of reaction and retrogression, and witness some extraordinary developments in political and social and industrial relations before the forces of progress begin to assert themselves in practical life and to mould institutions in conformity with the generalizations of social science. There is abundant reason to think that we are very far from the time which will mark the turning point in the career of governmentalism, notwithstanding the increasing signs of popular discontent. . . .

These considerations, I say, it is well to bear in mind, for they guard us against certain untenable positions and impracticable conclusions

---

[*] December 13, 1890 (VII:17, #173), pp. 4–5.

which our earnestness and valor might tempt us to jump at. Because some of our Anarchistic allies are losing sight of the difference between the abstract and the concrete, the ultimate and the initial, the absolute and the relative, and are led into grave errors and misrepresentations of Anarchism, it is of the highest importance that it be made clear just what we promise, demand, profess, as well as what we do not. We do not hold out hopes of a speedy deliverance and sudden emancipation. We do not, like religious enthusiasts, ask people to seek salvation in perfect obedience to the truth as we see it and pay no heed to the surroundings. We do not demand from anybody the carrying out of "the perfect law," and we do not profess to be holier and purer than others. We do not offer to the sufferers any specifics with which they can at once proceed to heal themselves. We are not free from disease ourselves and we do not undertake to cure anybody. We readily admit our incapacity for treating individual cases. . . . For my part, I repudiate, with most Anarchists, the new version of the old "be-good-and-you'll-be-happy" gospel as a thing wholly composed of emotional ingredients, with no trace of thought to give it definiteness and force.

Anarchism is a politico-economic doctrine, which (at least partially) must be made the basis of political and economic relations *in order* to give individuals opportunities for intellectual and moral development. Under present unfavorable conditions sacrifice can result in no benefit, but must remain sacrifice,—that is, pure loss and waste. Under favorable conditions no sacrifice will be required. Sensible people know better than to expect a miraculous conversion of the powerful, such as would impel them to surrender their privileges and devote themselves to ethical culture . . .

Rational Anarchists do not concern themselves with questions of private conduct; nor do they discourage attempts at temporary material improvement on the part of those who are oppressed by the prevailing system. Labor organizations will never achieve justice to labor by the means now in vogue; yet no rational Anarchist would advise them to disband and desist from all efforts to better their condition. Cooperative homes may prove advantageous to individuals, and may be recommended despite the certainty that therein does not lie the solution of any very pressing modern problem. And so throughout. It is a silly and preposterous notion that, because Anarchists entertain decided views with regard to the deepest questions of human progress, they are to give no thought to the morrow, but become fanatical imitators of religious cranks, who think of nothing but salvation, apostles in rags, unwashed, homeless wanderers. Yet this is the logic of the position that reform should begin at home!

Reform must begin, not at home, but in the market, in the labor and money market. To tell the workingmen that the labor problem will be solved by their refusing to take interest on their savings and rent for their land is to make one's self a proper subject for ridicule. What the workingmen and small struggling employers must be told is that certain economic reforms would kill the usurious powers of capitalists and put an end to exploitation of man by man. What the starving Irish tenant must be told is that by a proper method of resistance it is possible for him to defy the robber-landlord and keep the lion's share of his product, now abstracted under various pretences from him, in his own pocket. Anarchists must tell the laborer, the farmer, the small merchant, that legal privilege and artificial monopoly are the cause of their hardships, and that economic liberty alone can lift them into a position where the fruits of their skill and toil will be theirs to enjoy, and where the only suffering they will be condemned to endure will be that resulting from personal faults. Those Anarchists who conduct themselves thus, who understand the needs of the hour and the language of their contemporaries, do all that it is possible for them to do. If they are listened to and followed— well; if not, well also, though not *so* well. Whatever tendencies prevail, each of us will have done his share and will have contributed his influence. In the end the right view must obtain supremacy. But those Anarchists whose talk stands in no discoverable relation to time, place, and circumstances, who fail to distinguish between narrow, false opportunism and wise, philosophical opportunism; between short-sighted expediency and broad expediency; between absolute and ultimate principles, and relative, concrete truths,—those cannot even justly claim the merit of intelligent and well-directed effort in behalf of their cause. Whether the cause which they try to serve in their peculiar fashion fails or succeeds, *they* will have wasted their energies to no purpose.

And let no one be disquieted at the thought that, in spite of our struggles, slavery may be our lot instead of freedom, darkness instead of light. After all, we do not work for the future and in expectation of palpable results. Those results are desirable, and no chances should be thrown away; but we fight because therein lies our peace and contentment, because fight we must, because daily, hourly, are we thus impelled to struggle. Not to fight would mean not to live out our individual nature, not to be what we are; and this is impossible.

B.   "Beginning Anarchy Now"—Steven T. Byington[*]

Byington, one of the few professing Christians to write for Liberty, *here analyzes how anarchists can live "in, but not of" the statist world. His suggestions are guided by the general idea that anarchists should practice what they preach, for example by refusing to use the government as a tool, or by implementing voluntary alternatives to government programs. Byington became one of the most prolific contributors and activists in the* Liberty *camp after the turn of the century, coordinating an "Anarchist Letter-Writing Corps" and several other educational projects, as well as translating Stirner's* The Ego and His Own.[6]

There can be few things more useful to our cause than that men should live by its principles. In the first place, there is nothing like practice for producing belief, whether in one's self or in his neighbors. In the second place, there is nothing like practice for giving a correct understanding. In the third place, whenever the time comes for giving general effect to our ideas, and we begin to live under the new conditions and to make the mistakes that are natural to beginners and to see Anarchism getting discredited by the mistakes that are associated with its realization, it will then be of the highest importance that there be as many as possible who have had, in advance, such experience of Anarchic life as has been possible. And, finally, it seems as if it must be pleasanter for us to live as citizens of the society we desire, subjugated by an alien conqueror, following his fashions as much as we must and our own as much as we may while we hope and plan for liberation, rather than as citizens of a society which we hate and desire to destroy.

What, then, will be a reasonable life under the domination of government, for an Anarchist patriotically loyal to his free society in embryo?

He will avoid governing. He will not accept the office of sheriff; he will not protect his licensed business by prosecuting the unlicensed competitor in the next block; he will not, as a striker, call in the anti-trust law against his employer. The reasons against doing these things

---

* July 1904 (XIV:22, #384), pp. 2–4.

hereafter are reasons against doing them now, and have no validity for the future that they have not for the present. The argument that the world is now run on a basis of violence and dishonesty, and therefore one must take care of himself by being as unscrupulous as the rest in order not to be trodden under foot, is a compound falsehood. . . . The man who uses this argument becomes a worse rascal than those whom he set out to equal, and is consequently an especially pernicious factor in making the general situation worse.

It is a different case when governmental methods are used in a purely defensive way against an aggressor. The anti-trust law is like a club: its use in general is anti-social, but when a man comes at you with a club it is hard to set limits to your dangerous liberty of hitting back. So, in what I said just now about strikers, it is to be assumed that the employer in question has not got out an injunction against the paying of strike benefits. But, if you say that the social order gives the employer a general unfair advantage, and that this employer as a republican voter is responsible for the social order; therefore it is all right to apply the anti-trust law to him,—then you fall back into the fallacy I spoke of just now . . .

Our Anarchist will disregard the laws of the State, so far as they are not forced upon him: he will do what he thinks best, no matter whether it is legal or illegal, as far as his fear of prosecution permits—and, on the average, a little bit further . . .

He will disfellowship the State in thought and language. He will not feel or talk as if he and his had won or lost a battle when it is the United States that has won or lost. He will not speak of the government's doings with a first person plural pronoun, but with a third person. He will not talk of "our" troops in the Philippines, though he may speak of "our government" in the same sense as he speaks of "our climate," "our mosquitoes," "our tramps." This is harder than it looks, but it is useful. It is all right that he should sympathize with the United States in an international dispute in the same way as he may perhaps sympathize with Japan against Russia, but he should throw up his hat for them as a looker-on and not as a member. He will discriminate between nations and States, as do the best text-books of international law. He will not say "nation" when he means "government" or "union," nor "national" when he means "governmental" or "federal" . . .

He will boycott the government when he can. He will prefer not to hold a government office and draw his pay from stolen money. He will employ the express rather than the post-office when the expense and the convenience are the same. But an all-around boycott of government is doubtless as impossible as an absolute disregard of the government's laws.

When he sees a thing to be done, he will try to get it done without the government's help. Here is a difficult point, but one of cardinal importance. It is a weak point of ours at present. They ask us, "What substitute will you put in the place of government?" and we answer, "What substitute would you give a man for a disease when you cured him of it?" which is apt to seem to our critics more epigrammatic than convincing. Reformers of the Riis type scoff at "scientific" sociologists who oppose the positive action demanded by the Riises. "The science of doing nothing!" they cry; and we are among those who get hit by the sarcasm. . . .Our attitude in public affairs is purely that of obstructionists. This is a cheap, conspicuously cheap, attitude. Everybody knows that it is easy to sit back and refuse to help, and find fault with those who are at work; and, however just the fault-finding and however sound the reasons for disapproving the work, there will be no general impulse to respect those who are doing nothing but this. The world will overlook our being eccentrics, extremists, doctrinaires, Utopians; it will not pardon our being inactive talkers.

There is a great future for the man who will set the Anarchists to work as such. An energetic push for the actual establishment of a private currency, or a private post-office, or even a large and successful smuggling agency, would put a wholly new face on our propaganda. But it is not only in defying or evading legal restrictions on commerce that there ought to be opportunities. Because government is such a big, overgrown, complicated mass, we do want "substitutes for government" in many respects. We shall still want not only mails, but a census, weather reports, and lots of other things that the government is now furnishing. We shall still want boards of health. Doubtless "care for the public health is the favorite excuse just now for tyranny." A favorite excuse for tyranny is likely to be something useful; for useless things do not serve well as excuses. The purity of the milk supply, the plumbing of tenements, the adequacy of fire-escapes in hotels,—these are things that it pays to have somebody in the middle to look after; it does not pay to leave it to each individual to look out separately for his own safety, nor to leave it to the self-interest of the trader in a commercial society, or to the carefulness and intelligence of the producers in a communistic society. Now do not go off with the notion that I want to give somebody the powers of the present boards of health. I am talking Anarchism. Within the sphere of purely voluntary action there is a great field for the kind of work I speak of. The work has been so largely left to government that the possibilities of non-governmental action in these lines has not been explored. And public utilities of this sort ought to offer a fine field for Anarchist activity, because some of them are being done miserably, and none are being done without the characteristic inelasticity which hobbles all governmental action. We ought to be able to step in while the governmentalists are waiting to get an act through the legislature; we should go right to work, put ourselves in the lead, get these Riises—whose only care is to see something done—to help us, and have the laugh on the public authorities who were practising "the science of doing nothing" . . .

To displace the government from its useful functions by doing these things better, is surely very nearly the ideal way of establishing Anarchy.

C.   "The Wail of the 'Whoop-Her-Ups'"—A.H. Simpson[*]

Recriminations between the individualist and communist anarchists were rife after the Haymarket incident and trial. The obvious ideological differences were compounded by strategic and class differences. The communists, such as William Holmes, preferred mass meetings and fiery rhetoric[7] to the "dilettante radicalism" of the individualists, with its calm discussions in "carpeted rooms." Simpson retorts here that it's better to have a "clear head" than a "big heart," for this will attract and maintain an intelligent anarchist minority, rather than an ephemeral radical majority.[8]

William Holmes, an old comrade of Parsons, and a devoted follower of the revolutionary and salvation method of reform, and a serious and earnest worker, is sorely troubled that the old days of banner-carrying, street-preaching, and picnic-revivals of the hungry *proletaire*, etc., are no more. He looks with longing for a renewal of those "momentous times," and, when he thinks of the present method of spreading ideas, he gets scornful and calls it dilettante radicalism. "The philosophic Anarchists," he says, "discuss the evils of monopoly and Government, whilst

---

* February 7, 1891 (VII:21, #177), p. 3.

they turn a deaf ear to the pitiful cries of the poor victims thereof. They meet in carpeted rooms about cheerful grates to argue questions of political and social economy; they discuss the woman question, the land question, the questions relating to finance and government,—in short, they philosophize on all the evils of an admittedly infamous system; but little is done to enlighten the masses; the old-time enthusiasm is gone; agitation on the streets and in the slums is foolish and vulgar. We must train our own intellects, develop our Ego,—and to the devil with the poor *proletariat*, with his rags, his hovels, his bad odors, and his misery."

Unfortunately it is not quite true that philosophical Anarchists meet in carpeted parlors, though occasionally one may be invited to a representative gathering or a private club. But what if they did meet in pleasant places? . . . Why deplore a tendency that carries the truth to those who need it?

"At one time," says Mr. Holmes, "great halls were filled weekly to overflowing by multitudes who came to hear glad tidings, but this is in a great measure changed." Well, how is that? Why don't the multitudes show up now? Have they all gone into carpeted rooms with cheerful firesides to discuss philosophic Anarchism? Unfortunately, no. The fact is that the shining lights of those noisy days of strong denunciation, when big hearts were more in demand than clear heads, have disappeared. Some of the noble and brave ones, like Parsons and Spies,[9] have been eclipsed forever. Others have drifted into all sorts of side shows, and appear to have forgotten the little they ever did know. Some, like our friend Holmes, are as serious and solemn as ever, but Bourbon-like, never learn anything new. Some have retired into privacy altogether, and though at one time they were prominent figures at the lake front and weekly gatherings where the glad tidings were dispensed, they are now never seen or heard of, not even at the Eleventh of November Anniversary meetings. Some of the less noisy but more thoughtful ones have become philosophic Anarchists . . .

It is narrow-mindedness to say that because one does not see the wisdom of talking expropriation to crowds of ignorant and unfortunate workmen, that he turns a "deaf ear to the pitiful cries of the poor victims, or that he has no sympathy with their sufferings." Occasionally I feel as doleful and almost as hopeless as Mr. Holmes, but a little reflection will show that the dreadful condition he deplores is due to the lack among the agitators of an intelligent understanding of the problem to be solved, or the method of solving it. Agitation is a very necessary work, but, if the agitators have nothing but communistic dreams or Bellamyism to offer the multitudes, they had better cease their altruistic agitation awhile and "train their intellects" and "develop their Ego," regardless of the sneer in the last quotation from Mr. Holmes. . . .

D.   "On Picket Duty"—Benjamin R. Tucker[*]

Closer to the individualist anarchists were the free-love anarchists such as Moses Harman and Ezra Heywood. Although Tucker supported free-love, he was hardly enthusiastic about it and saw it, like communist anarchism, as a potential threat to the educational efforts of individualist anarchists.[10] Tucker's criticisms of reformers and radicals were notorious (see next selection), but this one is notable in that he criticizes not the content of Harman's views, but rather the rashness of his attempt to flout the obscenity laws.

Moses Harman, the editor of "Lucifer,"[11] has been arrested again for printing a letter which the Kansas authorities are pleased to pronounce obscene. I somehow missed the number that contained the letter, and so do not know whether the opinion of the authorities is well or ill founded. And furthermore I do not care. Obscene or not, it was Mr. Harman's right to print it, and, even if I thought it obscene, I should not feel it necessary to foam at the mouth over the character of the letter . . . before proceeding to condemn the prosecution as the outrage that it undoubtedly is. But it seems to me, nevertheless, a proper time to say that, judging from all accounts of the letter, Mr. Harman's act was a rash one, and that he has no business to be disappointed if Liberals do not rally to his defence. It is questionable whether determined and cool-headed men who are pushing a plan of campaign which they think the only one likely to succeed are called upon to endanger that plan of campaign and therefore their cause by sallying forth to the aid of every rash comrade who precipitates an ill-timed and misplaced conflict. Up to a certain point there is a chance to win the liberty of printing directly and on its merits; but . . . to precipitate a struggle on the issue of liberty to print the most extreme "obscenity," and suffer defeat on it, would be to lay a foundation for more

---

[*] April 19, 1890 (VII:1, #157), p. 1.

serious invasions of the liberty of printing that would be likely to interfere with the achievement of economic liberty.

E. "Pity for Our Quaking Victims"—Lizzie M. Holmes*

The criticisms expressed here about Liberty *were standard fare in contemporary anarchist papers such as* Alarm *and* Freiheit, *where Tucker was often referred to as the Censor or the Pope of anarchism. Tucker's tolerance in printing such a criticism in* Liberty *is of course balanced by the contemptuous title he gave it.*

One cannot help admiring the ability displayed in the general make-up of Liberty, and were it not for one fault a lover of freedom might be quite enthusiastic over it; but, as it is, liberal readers can but feel displeased and pained over its spirit of intolerance, severity, and invective toward any radical person, paper, or movement not in strict line with Liberty's teachings. It seems to use a special fierceness against other reformers, as the real enemies of liberty never catch a tithe of the scathing that unfortunate radicals who differ from Liberty's writers must tremble under.

I realize that the intellectual writers of Liberty who have studied deep and long, and are sure of their ground, feel they have a right to call a man a fool who shows that he does not reach the conclusions they have reached. But it seems to me real wisdom is simple, modest, not over-confident. Because the higher we go, the more we find there is to know,—the clearer we see that every line of intellectual research reaches into the unknowable, and every step is debatable ground.

When it comes to close definitions, even the editor and writers in Liberty have been known to flounder, and are not always consistent. I believe there is a great deal in the Universe we none of us know yet, and no one can be so positively sure he is right that he can *afford* to call another student a fool. It sounds so vain, so harsh, so cruel, so like the old believers in the infallibility of the church, to call people who have proved by years of devoted work their sincerity and intelligence, "ignorant," "brutal," "destitute of knowledge, common sense, style," etc.

It is simply the opinion of Liberty's editor that the "Beacon"[12] is "no friend of labor; that it has all the 'vices' of the 'Alarm'[13] and none of its

---

* July 26, 1890 (VII:7, #163), p. 3.

merits; that it shows ignorance and brutality, is insignificant and wild," etc. But it is in poor taste, looks spiteful, narrow-minded, bigoted, to express such an opinion so severely. Many others have been delighted with the bright little "Beacon." It is *interesting*, which Liberty in its profundity is not. It is a paper one can hand to any ordinary person with the assurance it will be understood,—which Liberty is not . . .

Other workers and writers, whose known devotion, self-sacrifice, and ability should "protect them from their friends," have been glibly dubbed by Liberty's staff "fools," "ignoramuses," "grovelers," etc. Why should a lover of liberty show such a pugnacious disposition? I like to believe all "our kind of people" are kind-hearted, liberal, tolerant, fraternal in their feelings; it pains me to learn they are not. The closest, strictest reasoning is commendable; but harsh names only evince a vindictive spirit. Argue as well as possible; then let readers judge who is the fool.

F.   "Liberty, and Why We Want It"—Joseph A. Labadie[*]

Labadie, a labor activist and anarchist based in Detroit, argued for a broad and opportunistic agitation for anarchism. His justification for this is that people can be attracted to anarchism in many different ways and that cooperating with communist anarchists, and even statist reformers, recognizes the individuality of human needs and wants. This opportunistic strategy also parallels the pluralism of the anarchist future.

. . . As liberty can exist only by mutual agreement, I must give reasons which my fellows deem good before they will agree to grant my claim to liberty. . . . Our reasons may differ very widely, and still be "good" reasons. What would be a good reason to one person may not be the reason for which the other wants his freedom . . .

One person may want his liberty to go to church and practise his religious faith. Another may want it to stay away from church and proclaim against all religions. Both are equally good reasons, and yet they are for the purpose of doing wholly unlike things.

One may want liberty to advance the interests of Communism, another to further the cause of individualism and voluntary cooperation.

If it can be shown to the satisfaction of the people (and it must be shown to them before they will accept it) that Anarchism will not dictate

---

[*] May 30, 1896 (XII:2, #340), pp. 6-7.

to them any explicit rules as to what they must do, but that it opens to them the opportunities of putting into practice their own ideas of enhancing their own happiness, then, it appears to me, real propagation of Anarchism has been made . . .

The strongest point to me about Anarchism is that it permits every kind of experiment, not only in the field of "economics," but of every branch of social science. It invites competition in all things. It gives a fair field to all, and permits the best to win. I cannot say that the establishment of liberty will necessarily be followed by the universal application of mutual banks, competition, and private enterprise. And he is rash indeed who dogmatically insists that Communism will be universally applied under Anarchy. I believe the society of the future will be composed of every imaginable kind of associations for the betterment of mankind, and that the competition among them will lead to the survival of the fittest. Given equal freedom, the true need have no fear of being overcome by the false . . .

I am willing to join hands with anybody that will help me to free the land from the grasp of the monopolist; that will permit me to trade wherever I choose; that will permit me to use whatever kind of money I want; that will keep his hands off me entirely, so long as I do not attempt an act of aggression.

Anybody is an Anarchist who will agree not to do my person violence, not to take my property without my knowledge and consent, and not to prevent me from doing whatever I choose, unless I choose to do him personal violence, or take his property without his knowledge and consent, or prevent him from doing whatever he chooses. And I ask the assistance of every such person to abolish every law and custom, and, where there is a fair probability of success, to resist every person, that stands in the way of the accomplishment of these aims.

Individualist Anarchist that I am, believing in the economic doctrines advocated by Comrade Tucker, I am ready to join with the Communists, the State Socialists, the Populists, the Democrats, the Republicans, or anybody else, whenever I see an opportunity to gain a larger degree of liberty. You see, I am thoroughly utilitarian and opportunist. Let me give a practical illustration. Some years ago there was submitted to the voters of Michigan an amendment to the constitution prohibiting the manufacture and sale of intoxicating drinks. Notwithstanding the fact that I am a temperance man, believing the saloon is a bad element in society, that it leads to the excessive use of intoxicants, and that its influence is anything but elevating, I joined with the saloon keepers and others to defeat the amendment, and we were successful. The baneful effects of the saloon I did not consider as bad as the destruction of that much liberty. The prohibition amendment was invasive; the saloon, even with its evil influences, is not. Evidently, the majority of the voters thought it to their benefit to defeat prohibition; but the reasons for doing so were as conflicting and irreconcilable as you could imagine, and as thick as dandelions in the spring time. The great majority of these voters were, of course, authoritarians. If, therefore, an Anarchist could, without violation of any fundamental principle, or without doing violence to anything for which he stands, join with Archists to advance liberty, what can seriously stand in the way of his uniting with other Anarchists who believe in Communism to get more liberty? . . .

If the Communists convert a considerable number to Anarchism, and the individualists convert another goodly number to Anarchism, I can see nothing standing in the way of "pooling their issues" on Anarchism pure and simple, and let the economic results to each side take care of themselves.

Comrade Tucker puts his questions in several different ways, and I will answer in several different ways. He asks me to say "(1) whether, in struggling to get liberty, we should sink our differences as to the results of liberty and simply shout 'Give us liberty,' or (2) whether it is of high importance that those of use who think that liberty will work in a certain way should try to show that we are right, and that those who think that it would work in an opposite way are wrong" . . .

(1) No; we should not sink our economic differences, any more than I sank my differences with the saloon-keepers while combatting the Prohibitionists.

(2) It is of high importance to be honest. To try to show that our way is the right one is certainly honest. But those whose views upon economics are opposed to ours may be as honest as we are, and it is just as important to them that they try to show that we are wrong. There are so many sides to the human mind that it takes many different kinds of arguments to reach it. What is reasonable to one seems unreasonable to another; what will convert one may not convert another . . .

G.   "On Picket Duty"—Benjamin Tucker[*]

In this enthusiastic description of the Land League, Tucker gives one of the clearest vision he ever provided of the structure of an anarchist society, based upon its origins in a strategy of passive resistance. The No-Rent movement in Ireland against absentee landlords remained Tucker's model of the possibilities of passive resistance carried out by an intelligent minority. Although no "movement" for passive resistance developed among the individualist anarchists, Tucker singled it out for attention when it cropped up in other countries.[14]

Ireland's true government: the wonderful Land League, the nearest approach, on a large scale, to perfect Anarchistic organization that the world has yet seen. An immense number of local groups, scattered over large sections of two continents separated by three thousand miles of ocean; each group autonomous, each free; each composed of varying numbers of individuals of all ages, sexes, races, equally autonomous and free; each inspired by a common, central purpose; each supported entirely by voluntary contributions; each obeying its own judgment; each guided in the formation of its judgment and the choice of its conduct by the advice of a central council of picked men, having no power to enforce its orders except that inherent in the convincing logic of the reasons on which the orders are based; all coordinated and federated, with a minimum of machinery and without sacrifice of spontaneity, into a vast working unit, whose unparalleled power makes tyrants tremble and armies of no avail.

Ireland's shortest road to success: no payment of rent now *or hereafter*; no payment of compulsory taxes now or hereafter; utter disregard of the British parliament and its so-called laws; entire abstention from the polls henceforth; rigorous, but non-invasive "boycotting" of deserters, cowards, traitors, and oppressors; vigorous, intelligent, fearless prosecution of the land agitation by voice and pen; passive, but stubborn resistance to every offensive act of police or military; and, above all, universal readiness to go to prison, and promptness in filling the places made vacant by those who may be sent to prison. Open revolution, terrorism, and the policy above outlined, which is Liberty, are the three courses from which Ireland now must choose one. Open revolution on

---

* October 29, 1881 (I:7, #7), p. 1.

the battle-field means sure defeat and another century of misery and oppression; terrorism, though preferable to revolution, means years of demoralizing intrigue, bloody plot, base passion, and terrible revenges,—in short, all the horrors of a long-continued national vendetta, with a doubtful issue at the end; Liberty means certain, unhalting, and comparatively bloodless victory, the dawn of the sun of justice, and perpetual peace and prosperity in future for a hitherto blighted land.

H.   "The Power of Passive Resistance"—Benjamin Tucker[*]

"Edgeworth," a frequent writer in the early years of Liberty, *had become skeptical of the strategy of passive resistance, particularly the utility and possibility of resisting taxation. Tucker acknowledges that it poses difficulties, but, when possible, individual passive resistance has significant agitational benefits. When undertaken by an "intelligent minority," passive resistance threatens to make state violence impotent, a strategy similar to that eventually implemented by Gandhi.*

"Edgeworth" makes appeal to me through "Lucifer" to know how I propose to "starve out Uncle Sam." Light on this subject he would "rather have than roast beef and plum pudding for dinner *in secula seculorum.*" It puzzles him to know whether by the clause "resistance to taxation" . . . I mean that "true Anarchists should advertise their principles by allowing property to be seized by the sheriff and sold at auction, in order by such personal sacrifices to become known to each other as men and women of a common faith, true to that faith in the teeth of their interests and trustworthy for combined action." If I do mean this, he ventures to "doubt the policy of a test which depletes, not that enormous vampire, Uncle Sam, but our own little purses, so needful for our propaganda of ideas, several times a year, distrainment by the sheriff being in many parts of the country practically equivalent to tenfold taxes." If, on the other hand, I have in view a minority capable of "successfully withdrawing the supplies from Uncle Sam's treasury," he would like to inquire "how any minority, however respectable in numbers and intelligence, is to withstand the sheriff backed by the army, and to withhold tribute to the State."

---

* October 4, 1884 (II:26, #52), p. 5.

Fair and pertinent questions these, which I take pleasure in answering. In the first place, then, the policy to be pursued by individual and isolated Anarchists is dependent upon circumstances. . . . It is not wise warfare to throw your ammunition to the enemy unless you throw it from the cannon's mouth. But if you can compel the enemy to waste his ammunition by drawing his fire on some thoroughly protected spot, if you can, by annoying and goading and harassing him in all possible ways, drive him to the last resort of stripping bare his tyrannous and invasive purposes and put him in the attitude of a designing villain assailing honest men for purposes of plunder, there is no better strategy. Let no Anarchist, then, place his property within reach of the sheriff's clutch. But some year, when he feels exceptionally strong and independent, when his conduct can impair no serious personal obligations, when on the whole he would a little rather go to jail than not, and when his property is in such shape that he can successfully conceal it, let him declare to the assessor property of a certain value and then defy the collector to collect. Or, if he have no property, let him decline to pay his poll tax. The State will then be put to its trumps. Of two things one,—either it will let him alone, and then he will tell his neighbors all about it, resulting the next year in an alarming disposition on their part to keep their own money in their own pockets; or else it will imprison him, and then by the requisite legal processes he will demand and secure all the rights of a civil prisoner and live thus a decently comfortable life until the State shall get tired of supporting him and the increasing number of persons who will follow his example. Unless, indeed, the State, in desperation, shall see fit to make its laws regarding imprisonment for taxes more rigorous, and then, if our Anarchist be a determined man, we shall find out how far a republican government, "deriving its just powers from the consent of the governed," is ready to go to procure that "consent,"—whether it will stop at solitary confinement in a dark cell or join with the Czar of Russia in administering torture by electricity. The farther it shall go, the better it will be for Anarchy, as every student of the history of reform well knows. Who can estimate the power for propagandism of a few cases of this kind, backed by a well-organized force of agitators without the prison walls? So much, then, for individual resistance.

But, if individuals can do so much, what shall be said of the enormous and utterly irresistible power of a large and intelligent minority, comprising say one-fifth of the population in any given locality? I conceive that on this point I need do no more than call "Edgeworth's" attention to the wonderfully instructive history of the Land League movement in Ireland, the most potent and instantly effective revolutionary force the world has ever known so long as it stood by its original policy of "Pay No Rent," and which lost nearly all its strength the day it abandoned that policy. . . . But it was pursued far enough to show that the British government was utterly powerless before it, and it is scarcely too much to say, in my opinion, that, had it been persisted in, there would not today be a landlord in Ireland. It is easier to resist taxes in this country than it is to resist rent in Ireland, and such a policy would be as much more potent here than there as the intelligence of the people is greater, providing always that you can enlist in it a sufficient number of earnest and determined men and women. If one-fifth of the people were to resist taxation, it would cost more to collect their taxes, or to try to collect them, than the other four-fifths would consent to pay into the treasury. The force needed for this bloodless fight Liberty is slowly but surely recruiting, and sooner or later it will organize for action. Then, Tyranny and Monopoly, down goes your house!

"Passive resistance," said Ferdinand Lassalle, with an obtuseness thoroughly German, "is the resistance which does not resist." Never was there a greater mistake. It is the only resistance which in these days of military discipline resists with any result. There is not a tyrant in the civilized world today who would not do anything in his power to precipitate a bloody revolution rather than see himself confronted by any large fraction of his subjects determined not to obey. An insurrection is easily quelled, but no army is willing or able to train its guns on inoffensive people who do not even gather in the streets but stay at home and stand back on their rights. Neither the ballot nor the bayonet are to play any great part in the coming struggle; passive resistance and, in emergencies, the dynamite bomb in the hands of isolated individuals are the instruments by which the revolutionary force is destined to secure in the last great conflict the people's rights forever.

J.   "Passive Resistance"—Victor Yarros[*]

If anything, Yarros is even closer to Gandhian nonviolent strategy, portraying passive resistance not simply as a political strategy, but as

---

[*] October 13, 1888 (VI:5, #135), p. 4.

*the means by which anarchists will resist evil in the future. Yet both Tucker
and Yarros make the case for passive resistance on expedient rather than
moral grounds. That is, if it entails too much sacrifice in a particular
situation, it is not worth pursuing, even if generally it is preferable.*

Generally speaking, there are no fixed rules by which to go in the
matter of resisting evil and invasion. Wise resistance can, in any particular case, be determined only upon a full and thorough acquaintance
with all the circumstances attached and involved. Methods good in one
case may be utterly unavailing in another, and vice versa. Where the right
of resistance is once conceded, the question of method becomes simply
one of expediency, safety, certainty, and speed. To judge of the most
effective means of resistance to a given act is possible only when the
nature of the act, with all its attending influences, is completely understood. To say, apropos of nothing in particular, that this or that method
of resistance is futile or bad is to make one's self ridiculous. And to
illustrate the correctness of the claim by referring to the evident unfitness
of the method in a special case is to carry absurdity even farther; for the
thing to examine is whether the method serves in the case in which its
adoption is urged, and not in cases not at all under discussion.

Passive resistance is not always possible. What we maintain is that,
where it is possible, it is superior and preferable to all other methods. It
must be borne in mind that we are treating the question of defensive
warfare, of just resistance to unwarrantable encroachments. And it may
be laid down as a rule in such cases that the best method of resistance is
that which secures fully the rights of the injured without causing any
unnecessary harm to the guilty. Unnecessary harm is invasion, and is sure
to provoke resistance on the part of (immediately) disinterested witnesses. If our rights are denied us, we should set about restoring them
and compensating ourselves for whatever loss we were subjected to, but,
this accomplished, it is time to stop. As a matter of abstract right,
individuals and free communities are entitled to make any and all
offences, great or small, committed against them equally punishable by
death, but such action would be unwise and imprudent: their neighbors
would rebel against such Draconian barbarism and indignantly suppress
a community which hangs men for stealing handkerchiefs and umbrellas.

Let us suppose a few cases.

A man attempts to murder you. It is not necessary to kill him (though it would be no violation of right), if you can safely escape. Killing is unwise in such a case. The sympathies of the public would be with the slain ruffian, and you would be rebuked for cruel and unnecessary violence. Only when there is no escape possible is the extreme measure expedient. But, whether you kill or run away, you have equally resisted the invader. Running is not non-resistance.

The tax-collector calls to get from you something for nothing. He threatens you if you refuse to do his bidding, and you are naturally enraged. But are you justified in knocking him down? Clearly not: simply persist in your refusal to pay the tax. Such refusal is passive resistance, and is not a paradox.

Likewise with the landlord. He demands rent, and you may quietly ignore him, while continuing to reside on what he calls his land. Again nothing paradoxical about this passive resistance.

You are not in love with so-called representative government; you do not think it has any rights you are bound to respect. Still this is no sufficient reason for shooting down legislators, or blowing up senate-chambers. Stay at home, abstain from voting, and there will be no legislators.

Just these cases have been discussed by the Kellys. They have argued that to abolish the State,—protector of the trinity of usury,—passive resistance on the part of the people is perfectly sufficient, and therefore immeasurably more rational than violence. Men make the State, as they do God, in their own image; it does not come from above or below, any more than children are "sent from heaven." It is the offspring of the marriage of ignorance to the ballot-box, and depends upon the periodical renewal of the marriage-contract for the perpetuation of its earthly career. It logically follows that, when men once become intelligent, mere passiveness and abstinence will cause the death of the monstrous offspring. Dynamite will then be entirely useless, and till then it is folly to talk of any *method* of abolition. The people must first be brought to the point of conceiving an idea of, and desire for, the *fact* of abolition. At present they think their marriage a glorious success and take great pride in their progeny, and would rather abolish us . . .

Notes

1. Benjamin Tucker, "Voluntary Cooperation," May 24, 1890 (VII:2, #158), pp. 5–6.

2. [editor's comment to] Egoist, "Protection, and Its Relation to Rent," October 27, 1888 (VI:6, #136), p. 4.

3. Tucker, "The Power of Passive Resistance," October 4, 1884 (II:26, #52), p. 5; Victor Yarros, "A Confession and a Suspicion," August 4, 1888 (V:26, #130), p. 4.

4. This question has always been of concern to anarchists (and to radicals of any stripe). See, for example, Blaine McKinley, "'The Quagmires of Necessity': American Anarchists and the Dilemmas of Vocation," *American Quarterly*, Winter 1982, pp. 503-523.

5. Yarros, "Ideas and Conduct," December 15, 1888 (VI:9, #139), p. 7.

6. Byington, "An Anarchist Letter-Writing Corps," March 24, 1894 (IX:49, #283), p. 3. Tucker praised this effort, calling it "a striking forecast of what associative effort will be when compulsion has disappeared from the world" (ibid, p. 4). See also Byington, "Publicity for Anarchism," April 1903 (XIV:8, #370), pp. 2-3 and "The Theory of Stickers," April 1904 (XIV:20, #382), pp. 6-7.

7. See Bruce C. Nelson, *Beyond the Martyrs: A Social History of Chicago's Anarchists, 1870-1900* (New Brunswick: Rutgers University Press, 1988) for an excellent description of the "movement culture" of Chicago's anarchists, both before and after Haymarket.

8. Tucker made the same point in 1907, arguing that a *Liberty* more concerned with intellect than emotions would be "a periodical which many intelligent persons read regularly and thoroughly for information, edification, and profit." ("On Picket Duty," April 1907, [XVI:1, #397], pp. 6-7)

9. Albert Parsons and August Spies were two of the four anarchist activists executed by the state of Illinois on November 11, 1887 for conspiracy to murder in the bombing deaths of four policemen at the Haymarket protest meeting on May 4, 1886.

10. As he put it a month later, "There are occasions when the blood of martyrs, far from acting as the seed of the church, furnishes the necessary taste that inspires the tyrant to a wholesale massacre and fills the witnesses thereof wth a spirit of indifference, if not of approval." ("Shoot Folly As It Flies," May 24, 1890 [VII:2, #158], p. 6.)

11. *Lucifer, the Light Bearer* was published in Valley Falls and Topeka, Kansas and Chicago, from 1890 to 1907.

12. Published San Diego and San Francisco, 1890-1891.

13. Published in Chicago and then New York, 1883-1889.

14. Tucker, "On Picket Duty," February 1906 (XV:1, #391), pp. 6-7 (Russian general strikes); "On Picket Duty," April 1906 (XV:2, #392), pp. 8-9.

12

Acceptable Strategies:
Colonies, Boycotts, and Unions

While the "preferred" strategies of passive resistance and agitation were clearly individualistic in nature, the "acceptable" strategies (colonies, boycotts, and unions) necessitated cooperation and were thus more collectivistic. As such, they were potential threats to the freedom of individual anarchists. Because of this, they received qualified, or even ambivalent, support from those who discussed anarchist strategy in *Liberty*. This theoretical distinction also suggests a historical difference. The preferred strategies are more characteristic of antebellum reform, whose roots in religious radicalism led to strategies that stressed individual efforts and even individual perfectionism. Passive resistance paralleled the anti-institutional tendencies of Come-Outers, while an agitational strategy paralleled the religious phenomena of revivalism and individual conversion. The acceptable strategies, on the other hand, reflect the more opportunistic and larger-scale strategies of the postwar labor movement. When the individualist anarchists supported boycotts and unionization, they were in the mainstream of the labor movement, although their reasons for doing so were not typical.

Thus, there seems to have been a generational shift occurring in the strategy of individualist anarchism. While the more established strategies were "preferred," the newer, more labor-oriented strategies were receiving considerable attention, and some support. Nevertheless, the lines between antebellum, religious, and perfectionistic reform on the one hand and postwar, labor, and opportunistic reform on the other should not be too strongly drawn. In particular, the conflict between perfectionistic and opportunistic orientations to strategy informed the debate over colonies, boycotts, and unions. Were these strategies acceptable if they

271

could *lead* toward anarchism (an opportunistic approach) or could they be supported only if they were *themselves* anarchistic (perfectionistic)?

When it came to colonies (what would be called "communes" today), most writers in *Liberty* agreed that forming separate, isolated, and ideal communities presumed too much and accomplished too little (see selection A). That is, colonies could only work with already perfected (or nearly perfect) anarchists, and thus did little but preach to (and possibly comfort) the converted. They therefore had little impact on the lives of those suffering under the state and its monopolies.

Boycotts were the subject of much more debate. At least one writer saw them in "perfectionistic" terms (Byington, selection C): boycotts were not merely a strategy for advancing anarchism, but a primary method of maintaining social peace under anarchy. Most writers discussed whether boycotts were inconsistent with anarchist principles and whether they could be effective tools. For Tucker, boycotting was consistent with equal liberty because it was basically passive: "You do not *interfere* with a man by *ignoring* him."[1] "The very foundation stone of equal liberty must be the freedom not to do—the right to do nothing. The boycott, either individual or collective, is nothing but the exercise of this freedom."[2] Joseph Labadie stressed that boycotting was an effective strategy because the "exploiting classes" didn't know how to respond effectively to "weapons that do not need force or violence to be effective."[3] Others, notably Hugo Bilgram (selection D), disputed that boycotts could be effective without threats of violence, citing the actual boycotts carried out by unions at the time. Issues such as the acceptability of secondary boycotts or employer blacklists also helped to clarify the anarchists' position on boycott (selection B).[4] Occasionally, non-labor boycotts, such as when the Chinese boycotted American products to protest exclusion of Chinese immigrants, were cited as evidence of the broad potential of boycotts.[5]

Unions, like boycotts, were typically defended as theoretically sound, but were sometimes criticized for their actions in particular labor struggles. Victor Yarros saw unions positively, insisting that they were voluntary organizations seeking to promote the mutual interests of their members.[6] Moreover, because their interests usually pitted them against monopolists, they often ended up opposing the government directly, as the American Railway Union did in the Pullman Strike of 1894. This made them unwitting allies of the anarchist movement. Yarros and others felt that, with some skillful agitation by anarchists, they could become conscious allies.[7] Other individualists, including Tucker (selection E), were more skeptical, seeing unions (workers' trusts) as little better than the trusts formed by businessmen. This debate came to a head with a long exchange between two trade unionists, A. H. Simpson and Henry Cohen (selection F), on whether trade unions were "anarchistic."

Further Reading in Liberty

J. William Lloyd and Benjamin Tucker sparred over whether colonies required perfected human beings: Lloyd, "Shall We Colonize?" February 18, 1893 (IX:25, #259), pp. 2-3; Tucker, "Still Preaching Goodness," March 4, 1893 (IX:27, #261), p. 2.

A.S. Matter criticized boycotts as coercive, and thus little better than courts and jails: "Is the Boycott Invasive?" October 6, 1894 (X:11, #297), pp. 3-4.

Victor Yarros and Dyer Lum both advocated anarchist support for ongoing union struggles: Yarros, "The Great Strike," July 14, 1894 (X:5, #291), p. 3; Lum, "The Knights of Labor," June 19, 1886 (IV:4, #82), p. 7. In 1896, the secretary of the American Federation of Labor, August McCraith, was sympathetic to individualist anarchism and contributed a nearly-egoist defense of unionism: "Why I Am a Trade Unionist," March 7, 1896 (XI:22, #334), p. 6.

A. "Free Societies"—E. C. Walker vs. Benjamin Tucker[*]

Walker defends the "free societies" set up by reformers on two major grounds: (1) they don't take people out of the struggle, but rather offer a refuge for activists and their families; (2) they provide a practical demonstration of anarchism, a more effective strategy than agitation. Tucker responds by conceding the first point, but arguing that anarchy needs to be demonstrated, not in isolated, rural communities, but in the midst of industrial cities.[8]

To the Editor of Liberty:

_____

[*] July 26, 1884 (II:21, #47), p. 8.

In the able article from the pen of Elisee Reclus which you republish from the "Contemporary Review," our author, speaking of the various small societies organized by reformers, says, among other things:

"Yet even were they perfection, if man enjoyed in them the highest happiness of which his nature is capable, they would be none the less obnoxious to the charge of selfish isolation, of raising a wall between themselves and the rest of their race; their pleasures egotistical, and devotion to the cause of humanity would draw back the best of them into the great struggle."

The fundamental error in the above is the idea that men who have become members of such societies have thereby ceased to participate in the "great struggle." . . . They may have erred—indeed, most of them have erred—in the methods chosen through which to realize their dreams of a bettered humanity, but theirs has been a rocky and thorn-strewn pathway, the labor has been arduous, the light of hope dim and flickering; the contumely, hatred, and persecuting opposition of the world have been theirs, and small indeed the reward they have earned by their "selfish isolation."

Most cordially could I concur with Elisee Reclus in condemnation of any movement looking to the withdrawal of good brain and earnest purpose from the field of active conflict, for I keenly realize that there is needed in every community a portion of the leaven of Liberty,—a missionary of the gospel of Justice. But what we most need today is a practical application of the principles of Anarchy upon a scale that shall challenge the attention of the slothful masses. By this I do not mean a large organization, but small groups here and there formed upon the principles of voluntary mutualism, held together alone by the affinity of common interests and kindred aspirations. We believe that all forms of compulsive government are usurpations, that it is possible to have peace and order and prosperity where no man is called master and where Liberty compels the observance of all reciprocal duties by the force of its own beauty and desirableness alone. Theorizing is all well in its place, but practical application of principles is infinitely better. The apostle of Anarchy, in preaching that gospel, is doing a grand educative work, but the man who lives it in a free group of men and women exerts a tenfold power for good. In every department of human activity, in the gratification of every impulse of our mental, emotional, and physical natures, is

needed an immediate exemplification of the beautiful truths of Anarchism, of self-government.

In no other way can such free groups be made immediately useful; in
fact, it is the imperative necessity for free social life which forces them
into existence. In ordinary society the companions and children of
radicals are ostracized to the fullest possible extent. Their sensitive
natures are wounded at every turn by the stinging gibes and cold neglect
of those with whom they are compelled to associate if they have the
companionship of their fellows at all. They are made to feel that they are
the associates of social pariahs, of men who are at war with the cherished
institutions of a barbaric past. . . . These women and children must either
starve their social natures or drift with the stream of popular prejudices,
and so drifting they often—nay, in most instances—carry with them the
men to whom they are bound by the various ties that build up and
conserve the family life. It is this that has lost to the cause of reform the
services of more men than can be easily numbered. . . . They must either
give up their progressive work or sacrifice all home attractions and duties.

All this is sad, but it is all true. And the only possible remedy that I
can see is in the formation of such societies as those condemned by Elisee
Reclus, societies which shall be at once refuges for the non-combatants
and coigns of vantage for the warriors of freedom.

Tucker[**]

The excellently-written article by E.C. Walker printed in this issue sets
forth considerations in favor of isolated communities for reformatory
purposes which are forcible and weighty, especially that of preventing,
by the avoidance of social ostracism, the constant and serious drain upon
the radical forces. Nevertheless, Reclus is right, all things considered. It
is just because Mr. Walker's earnest desire for a fair practical test of
Anarchistic principles cannot be fulfilled elsewhere than in the very heart
of existing industrial and social life that all these community attempts
are unwise. Reform communities will either be recruited from the salt of
the earth, and then their success will not be taken as conclusive, because
it will be said that their principles are applicable only among men and
women well-nigh perfect; or, with these elect, will be a large admixture
of semi-lunatics among whom, when separated from the great mass of

---

* "On Picket Duty," July 26, 1884 (II:21, #47), p. 1.

mankind and concentrated by themselves, society will be unendurable, practical work impossible, and Anarchy as chaotic as it is generally supposed to be. But in some large city fairly representative of the varied interests and characteristics of our heterogeneous civilization let a sufficiently large number of earnest and intelligent Anarchists, engaged in nearly all the different trades and professions, combine to carry on their production and distribution on the cost principle and to start a bank through which they can obtain a non-interest-bearing currency for the conduct of their commerce and dispose their steadily accumulating capital in new enterprises, the advantages of this system of affairs being open to all who should choose to offer their patronage,—what would be the result? Why, soon the whole composite population, wise and unwise, good, bad, and indifferent, would become interested in what was going on under their very eyes, more and more of them would actually take part in it, and in a few years, each man reaping the fruit of his labor and no man able to live in idleness on an income from capital, the whole city would become a great hive of Anarchistic workers, prosperous and free individuals. It is such results as this that I look forward to, and it is for the accomplishment of such that I work. Social landscape gardening can come later if it will. It has no interest for me now. I care nothing for any reform that cannot be effected right here in Boston among the every-day people whom I meet upon the streets.

B.   "The Boycott and Its Limit"—Benjamin Tucker[*]

Responding to a criticism of the boycott, Tucker lays down his basic principle on when boycotts are legitimate: "A man has a right to threaten what he has a right to execute." For Tucker, it was the substance of the threat, not its intent, that determined its legitimacy. Thus, one could rightfully threaten to boycott anyone for any reason, but could not rightfully threaten physical invasion under any circumstances.

London "Jus" does not see clearly in the matter of boycotting. "Every man," it says, "has a perfect right to refuse to hold intercourse with any other man or class from whom he chooses to keep aloof. But where does liberty come in when several persons conspire together to put pressure upon another to induce or coerce him (by threats expressed or implied)

---

* December 3, 1887 (V:9, #113), pp. 4–5.

to refrain also from intercourse with the boycotted man? It is not that the boycotted man has grounds of legal complaint against those who voluntarily put him in coventry. His complaint is against those who compel (under whatsoever sanction) third persons to do likewise. Surely the distinction is specific." Specific, yes, but not rational. The line of real distinction does not run in the direction which "Jus" tries to give it. Its course does not lie between the second person and a third person, but between the threats of invasion and the threats of ostracism by which either the second or a third person is coerced or induced. All boycotting, no matter of what person, consists either in the utterance of a threat or in its execution. A man has a right to threaten what he has a right to execute. The boundary line of justifiable boycotting is fixed by the nature of the threat used. B and C, laborers, are entitled to quit buying shoes of A, a manufacturer, for any reason whatever or for no reason at all. Therefore they are entitled to say to A: "If you do not discharge the non-union men in your employ, we will quit buying shoes of you." Similarly they are entitled to quit buying clothes of D, a tailor. Therefore they are entitled to say to D: "If you do not cooperate with us in endeavoring to induce A to discharge his non-union employees,—that is, if you do not quit buying shoes of him,—we will quit buying clothes of you." But B and C are not entitled to burn A's shop or D's shop. Hence they are not entitled to say to A that they will burn his shop unless he discharges his non-union employees, or to D that they will burn his shop unless he withdraws his patronage from A. Is it not clear that the rightful attitude of B and C depends wholly upon the question whether or not the attitude is invasive in itself, and not at all upon the question whether the object of it is A or D?

C. "Quasi-Invasion and the Boycott"—Stephen T. Byington[*]

Byington here considers a common objection against anarchism, the problem of "quasi-invasion," or what might be called the "externalities" of non-invasive behavior. "Quasi-invasion," however, can be resisted by boycott, a simple, natural, and effective social sanction. Unlike Tucker's logical delineation of the limits of boycott, Byington offers his characteristic vision of anarchist social dynamics, in which the extent of boycott

---

[*] May 19, 1894 (X:1, #287), p. 2.

will be limited by the intensity of repulsion with which individuals or groups react to obnoxious individuals.

The great objection to Anarchism in some people's minds is that there is a class of *quasi*-invasive actions in which my neighbor's business indirectly but inevitably affects me, so that if he is allowed to carry it on in his own way, undesirable circumstances are forced upon me. If he is allowed to sell liquor, drunkards make the streets unsafe for me; if he is allowed to run a gambling den, my clerk is tempted to steal from me; if he drives a cart on Sunday, the noise disturbs my worship; if he walks down the street naked, the innocence of my daughter's mind is destroyed; if he refuses to answer the census enumerator, science is injured and all the world suffers; if he enjoys the street lights without helping to pay for them, others are encouraged to sponge on me for such public benefits . . .

Even if you laugh at all the complaints I have cited, you cannot deny that a man can, without being invasive, make himself such an unutterable nuisance that no normal man can be happy near him. If such men could be less restrained under Anarchy than under government, it is at least a drawback to the advantages of Anarchy.

But we shall not be left so helpless. There is one weapon whose use is strictly non-invasive, yet whose disciplining power cannot be surpassed by government itself. It is the boycott.

It is the most natural thing in the world that, when a man, without using force, makes social intercourse with him unpleasant or undesirable, I should, without using force, cut myself off from social intercourse with him as far as may be convenient. This is the boycott. Its germ is seen when I refuse to call on an impolite man. Its full development appears when a whole community, finding a man's course to be such as they positively cannot stand, unite in refusing greeting, trade, or help in danger to him and to all who associate with him.

It is the simplest, most harmless, and most accessible means of making a man use his liberty reasonably. Surely, it is better to let an objectionable man severely alone than to bring a policeman's club down on him. Yet it has a bad name. The reason is plain; the State is afraid of it. The boycott offers a means for making another do as you wish without calling in the State's aid. Of course, it tends to bring the State into contempt. In opposing the boycott the friends of the State are protecting the State from a competitor who would soon take away the bulk of the business.

The boycott has another advantage. It cannot be used in any strong form without putting the boycotter to an inconvenience which increases with the inconvenience caused to the boycotted. Hence it cannot be used to its full strength except for something that men really care about. But if the boycotters are determined and persevering, they need not wait for a majority to bring success. On the other hand, the boycott could never (unless somehow backed by monopoly) compel a man to give up any of the things he cared most for. Thus the boycott would decide questions partly in accordance with the intensity of the desire on the two sides, not merely in accordance with numbers.

D. "Is the Boycott Invasive?" —Hugo Bilgram vs. Benjamin Tucker[*]

Bilgram, a prominent advocate of mutual banking, here casts doubt on the boycott, contrasting the rosy picture drawn of it by anarchist theorists with the actual practice of union boycotts. He makes a set of charges, culminating in an indictment of boycotts as basically despotic. In his response, Tucker reiterates the principle that boycotts are not invasive, and thus that Bilgram's various charges are irrelevant. Bilgram's most serious objection, however, is that boycotts attack individual capitalists, not the system of monopoly capitalism, and are thus fundamentally ineffective. Tucker responds opportunistically, supporting them even if they benefit only a few workers.

1. Boycotts proper are never spontaneous, but either are imposed by some authority or are the tacit accompaniment of strikes, which in their turn are instituted by some authority. They are imposed and raised by commands, and are obeyed by persons who have no earthly grievance against the subject of the boycott. When the said authority raises a boycott, the former relations are again assumed as if nothing had happened. The names of those placed under the ban are published or otherwise made generally known, and individual judgment is not accepted as an excuse for disobeying a boycott-order.

---

[*] April 1903 (XIV:8, #370), pp. 3–4.

2. Boycotts are invariably intended as a punishment, inflicted by some authority, and they are a most effective form of punishment. To be put under the ban in the former German Empire was a form second only to capital punishment, and the ban of the boycott is practically equal to it. In a district in which a boycott is firmly established, the victim is unable to obtain the very necessaries of life. He cannot walk the streets without exposing himself to cowardly insults, against which he cannot protect himself. Like an escaped slave, he can exist only by the secret assistance of some friends.

3. This punishment is meted out not only to members of that organization from which the authority to declare boycotts emanates, but is extended to all those inhabitants of the district in which the boycott rules who happen to displease that authority. A large minority, if not a majority, of the inhabitants of such a district obey the command for fear of being boycotted themselves, although they owe no allegiance whatever to the organization that declares it, and often are personally opposed to it.

4. It is invariably imposed as a punishment for an imaginary wrong. The principal sufferers are those non-union workmen who dare to disobey a strike order, or those men and women who have the temerity to disobey an order to boycott. Individual liberty is as completely suppressed as it is in time of war.

5. As a remedy for the social evil, they, like strikes, are absolutely futile. They are based upon the fallacious notion that the unjust distribution of wealth is due to the greed and rapacity of the capitalists. The instigators of boycotts have not advanced sufficiently in civilization to know that egoism, in the absence of inequitable authority, is the very cornerstone of ethics, justice, and equity, and that it should be cultivated, not suppressed. Every encouragement of efforts to right a wrong, if those efforts are misdirected and therefore futile, will have the effect of misleading the would-be reformers and of delaying the inauguration of a radical remedy.

Taking into view all these characteristics of the modern boycott, it is simply incomprehensible to me how an advocate of equal liberty can find a single word in their defence. . . . Boycotts have every ear-mark of offensive despotism, and the authorities that impose and raise them constitute typically invasive governments.

I presume Liberty will concede that, if we had free competition, the general rate of wages could not be aught but just, and that the present injustice in wages is due, not to individual greed, but to legal interference with free competition. If this is so, then no pressure brought to bear upon the greed of individual employers can raise wages in general; the only possible remedy consists in resistance to the government's interference with equal freedom in general, and with the freedom of exchange in particular. . . .

Tucker

. . . He says that boycotts are not spontaneous. I answer that, the spontaneity of an act not being a test of its invasive or non-invasive quality, it makes no difference to the matter we are discussing whether boycotts are spontaneous or not. Anarchism itself is not spontaneous. One man, perhaps, discovers the truth of it by himself; so far, it is spontaneous. But this man goes out as a propagandist, making numerous converts, some of them very much against their prejudices and inclinations; now it is no longer spontaneous, but deliberately concerted. Has it therefore become invasive?

He says that boycotts are imposed by authorities, either expressly or tacitly. This is more serious. If this is true, then boycotts are invasive. But is it true? A comes to B, a grocer, and says: "If you don't sell groceries at prices fixed by me, I will burn your store down." Here A is exercising authority; he is threatening what he has no right to execute. But suppose A simply says to B: "If you don't sell groceries at prices fixed by me, I will not buy of you, and I will advise my friends not to buy of you." In that case A is not exercising authority; he is threatening only that which he has a perfect right to execute. When any trade union or other body conducting a boycott threatens what it has no right to execute, it becomes invasive, and may with propriety be restrained. But, so long as it threatens only that which it has a right to execute, any one attempting to restrain it becomes an invader himself.

He says that boycotts are invariably intended as a punishment. I answer that no more than spontaneity is intent the test of the invasive or non-invasive quality of an act. In the case above supposed, A's withdrawal of his trade from B may be prompted by malice, but that fact does not make his withdrawal an invasive act. A doctor who spontaneously declines to treat a man dangerously ill does not, in so declining, violate the principle of equal liberty; neither does the trade union which threatens to boycott him if he does not so decline. Call both doctor and trade union cruel and malicious, if you will; perhaps I will agree with you; but neither is invasive.

He says that boycotts are directed not only against members of the organization conducting the boycott, but against outsiders. I answer that any organization has a right to threaten either outsider or insider with the adoption of any course concerning him which it has a right to adopt.

He says that boycotts are imposed as punishment for an imaginary wrong. I answer that an act does not have to be reasonable in order to be non-invasive. Take again the case of A's attitude toward B, the grocer. B's prices may be perfectly equitable, but that does not affect A's right to object to them and to withdraw his trade as a means of inducing B to change them.

He says that the boycott is not a remedy for the social evil. I answer that I have never said to the contrary. Nevertheless the boycott may, and often does, raise the wages of an individual or of a body of individuals, and I know of no reason why these should not, by all legitimate means, indulge that egoism which Mr. Bilgram and I agree in commending . . .

I conclude with the remark that boycotters are subject to all the failings that afflict human beings in general. They are sometimes cruel, sometimes malicious, sometimes short-sighted, sometimes silly. But it is one of the beauties of the boycott that, if employed unwisely, it tends to become a boomerang. The less need, therefore, is there to restrain it, even were such restraint justifiable . . .

E.   "Trades-Unionism"—Benjamin Tucker[*]

In this early article, Tucker offers ambivalent support for unionization. Although no higher than capitalist unions, they were a "crude step" toward anarchism because they at least fought the state and could, by agitation, be turned completely against it. Twelve years later, his assessment was not so sanguine: "to be ready to fight is well, but the people neither know what to fight nor what to fight for. Alas! between the rich knaves and the poor fools there is little to choose. I hate the former as much as I pity the latter, but I fear them both alike."[9]

---

[*] June 10, 1882 (I:22, #22), p. 3.

Of late there has been a remarkable activity on the part of all classes of working men in this country in the way of combining for mutual protection and well-being. And not only has this activity been pushed among the obnoxious "foreigners," but simon-pure American mechanics have been forming trades unions in all quarters.

Liberty rejoices at the rapidly increasing numbers of American trades unions; not that the animus of a labor union is on a one whit higher plane than that of a capitalist union, but because labor combinations are a crude step in the direction of supplanting the State. The trades unions involve a movement for self-government on the part of the people, the logical outcome of which is ultimate revolt against those usurping political conspiracies which manifest themselves in courts and legislatures. Just as the Land League has become a formidable rival of the British State, so the amalgamated trades unions may yet become a power sufficiently strong to defy the legislatures and overthrow them.

The capitalists and their tools, the legislatures, already begin to scent the impending dangers of trades-union socialism, and initiatory steps are on foot in the legislature of several states to construe labor combinations as conspiracies against commerce and industry, and suppress them by law. They have already boldly shown their hand in New York and New Jersey, and the capitalistic organs are putting out adroitly disguised feelers in order to ascertain how American sentiment would receive the introduction of Russian and Bismarckian methods into the United States
. . .

How plain it ought to be to an unprejudiced workingman that the legislature itself is the really dangerous and lawless conspiracy! It is in supplanting this political conspiracy by an intelligent and self-governing socialism that the trades unions develop their chief significance. In this view we are willing to temper somewhat, for the time, our criticism of the fact that the trades unions themselves are generally largely imbued with the element of force and authority. Perhaps they could hardly be expected to be otherwise, when we remember that the newborn labor organizations are plants growing out of the old political order. But, imperfect as they are, they are the beginnings of a revolt against the authority of the political State. They promise the coming substitution of industrial socialism for usurping legislative mobism. While we hail the growth of labor combinations as a potent sign of emancipation, we invite workingmen to study the methods of Liberty, throw overboard the State, repudiate all politicians and their services, and go straight forward about their business . . .

F.   "Is the Trade Union Anarchistic?"
—A.H. Simpson vs. Henry Cohen

Tucker's ambivalence of 1882 became a full-blown debate in 1895, as the individualist anarchists reacted to dramatic events in the labor movement. In particular, they celebrated the defeat of the "State Socialistic" Plank Ten of the American Federation of Labor's platform at its 1894 convention in Denver.[10]

Here, A.H. Simpson takes the negative, arguing that trade unions are despotic and ultimately ineffective in solving the labor problem. Cohen praises the anarchistic tendencies of unions and urges anarchist unionists to agitate to commit unions to anarchist, rather than state socialist, principles. Ultimately, the debate comes down to the question of how voluntary unions really are in practice. Cohen acknowledges that they may seem coercive, but this is because of the struggles they're engaged in and that "the conditions, and not the union men, are to blame." Simpson concludes from this that unions really aren't anarchistic because they don't respect equal liberty. Again, opportunistic and perfectionistic strategies clash.

Simpson[*]

. . . I maintain that a trade union is a despotic, tyrannical, arbitrary, and ignorant body; that its individual members are as selfish, overbearing, and intolerant of opposition as any other organization to be found in our present society; and that a trade union is no more worthy of respect than any other monopoly,—like Sugar trust or Pullman trust,—*except that its members are the under dogs* in a cannibalistic fight. A trade union has no more sense of equity or justice or liberty than any other organization, political, religious, or social. I do not say it is worse; it is sufficient to say that it is no better than any other organization . . .

---

* "Anarchism and the Trade Union," October 5, 1895 (XI:11, #323), pp. 6–7.

As an economic factor a trade union is next to worthless. If the ideal of the Federation could be realized and every wage-worker enrolled as one of its members, the condition of the laborer as a class would scarcely be changed . . .

Cohen[*]

. . . When I say trade unions are the most thoroughly Anarchistic organizations in our present society, I mean they are more nearly Anarchistic than any other. They are not so because the men who started them believed in freedom, but because the State allies itself with capital in fighting the unions. Thus it happens that, in most of the skirmishes between capital and labor, labor finds itself arrayed against the State.

A voluntary association formed for the mutual benefit of its members, using the boycott and other passive weapons in its fight against capitalism and the State, certainly seems to me very near the Anarchist idea.

When men pledge one another to buy union-made goods and thus mutually strengthen their unions, it is evident that they expect to get as much as they give. It is not a desire to sacrifice, and I never pretended that it was.

The trade unions that have been successful—a result of years of hard work—are now in danger of having their work undone by the State Socialists, who are trying to introduce politics into the unions and ram their doctrines down the throats of the union members, whether they are willing or not. Those unionists who are not ready to jump into heaven *via* the State are dubbed "pure and simple" trade unionists. In defence, they point to the work they have already done when the State Socialists find fault; but, when they (the trade unionists) talk of the future, they are weak, and their answer to the politician is only a negative one.

If these men understood Anarchism and could bring up the positive arguments against authority and restriction, they would make short work of the State Socialists. Besides, the educational work of Anarchism could be done side by side with their regular union work without their hindering each other in the least. Politics, on the other hand, will break up a union in no time.

---

* "Anarchism and the Trade Union," November 16, 1895 (XI:14, #326), p. 7.

By showing the "pure and simple" unionist that the voluntary idea is a much more valuable one than even he supposes, and that, in opposing the Statists, he is in the right, much valuable work can be done . . .

Simpson[*]

Just a few words in reply to Mr. Cohen. I will not exploit your space by touching on any of the "ifs" and "may bes" that are not essential to the main point under discussion, which is: "Are trade unions the most thoroughly Anarchistic organizations in our present society?" Mr. Cohen, in his reply, says they are,—not because the men who are in them believe in freedom, but because the State allies itself with capital in fighting the unions, and so it often happens that labor finds itself arrayed against the State. This is a curious bit of reasoning for a plumb-liner. If to fight against the State, not necessarily because one believes in freedom, but because of something else (religious fanaticism, for instance), is Anarchistic, then the New York saloon-keepers are Anarchists, and the Seventh Day Adventists, and the woman suffragists, and the criminal classes, etc., and even the corporate monopolies when they resist interstate commerce and anti-trust laws. Doesn't that prove too much? . . . This assumption that organized laborers are soldiers of freedom, whether consciously or not, and that capitalists and "scabs" are opposed to freedom, only needs developing to lead to demagoguery . . .

But, says Cohen further, "a voluntary association for the mutual benefit of its members, using the boycott and other passive weapons in its fight against capitalism and the State, is *very near* the Anarchist idea." Here the assumption is that trade unions are intelligently formed for the purpose of fighting capitalism and the State, in the sense that Anarchists use those terms, whereas Cohen knows that the trade unionist body is thoroughly orthodox, and believes in the extension of the functions of the State, accepts the teaching of orthodox political economy, and utterly opposes Anarchism. It is only a minority in that body who reject orthodox economy,—e.g., the Single Taxers and Socialists. So orthodox and stupid are the trade unionists that they resist the logical extension of their own principles by the State Socialist, and Cohen commends them for refusing to have these dogmas rammed down their throats. Cohen will not say that trade unions oppose State Socialism intelligently in the light of Anar-

---

[*] "Is the Trade Union Anarchistic?" December 14, 1895 (XI:16, #328), p. 6.

chism, when they indorse nationalization of railroads and telegraphs, and all the rest of the A.F.L. platform . . .

Another assumption in that voluntary association illustration is that a union is voluntary, like an insurance society or base-ball club or fraternal or religious bodies, and that one can secede at will, join or not join, as interest or pleasure prompts. There is no comparison in the cases. As well say that the government of New York or even of the United States is voluntary, and, if you don't like New York Sunday laws, etc., you can secede and go to—South Carolina. In what is called a strong union town a man cannot choose to join or secede. It is compulsory, unless he confines himself to some workshops which the trust has not reached. Today the right of a man to work in certain places, unless he consents to pay for the privilege and to submit to certain conditions which he (rightly or wrongly) considers unjust and outrageous, is much nearer Tammanyism than Anarchism . . .

In joining the A.P.A., or the Catholic church, or the Grand Army, or a protective tariff club, one joins an organization for mutual benefit, using passive resistance and sometimes the boycott against outsiders, and in that sense are these Anarchistic organizations? They are certainly more free in their policy than unions: first, a man knows precisely what to expect, and, even if he miscalculates, he can secede without being hunted out of town,—except perhaps in rare instances, and then they are more like unions. To say that a union that levies compulsory taxes to support itself, and assessments for labor parades, badges, receptions, etc., and combines compulsory sick benefits and death benefits with support of "Homes," assessments for committees on government ownership of telegraphs, fines for non-attendance at meetings, fines for not parading on Labor Day, and penalties and assessments for anything that a majority may vote to be "for the good of the union,"—to say that such an organization is more Anarchistic than the Catholic church or the A.P.A. or the American Tobacco Company is to use misleading language . . .

I am afraid I have occupied too much space, and so I will not take up the economic argument, seeing that Cohen has nothing further to say than that trade unions have raised the wages of *some* men in *some* trades. I don't deny it; that is why I am union cannibal myself. But that they have any effect on the law of rent, or rate of interest, or tend to decrease profits,—this I deny . . .

Cohen[*]

The pretence that a secret society or base ball club is a voluntary association, and that a trade union is not because the latter uses the boycott, doesn't go; and to compare a union to the State of New York is absurd. Mr. Simpson had better read the numbers of Liberty that contain the editorials on the boycott.

The assumption is that a member of a secret society is liberal and tolerant, whereas, if he joins a union, he immediately becomes arbitrary. If the need of a benevolent society were as great as that of one whose aim is to increase wages, the same means would be used to keep it going. A workingman who wants to join a benevolent association can take his pick from a number of societies. After he has decided which society he wishes to join, he can select the particular lodge or branch he wants. This same workingman, if he joins a union, must join that of his trade, and he cannot choose for fellow-members those he likes and reject those he dislikes. In fact, to be at all successful, every worker at that trade must be brought into the fold.

This makes the union a less harmonious body from the beginning. The benevolent society is not antagonized and fought by capital, and, as its existence is less important, such a bitter struggle is not, and need not, be made for it.

The demands for government control of railroads and telegraphs are, of course, the result of political superstition, but boycotting non-union men out of town, and enforcing certain arbitrary rules, are necessary to the life of the union.

The conditions, and not the union men, are to blame for this. Even Anarchist officers of a union must act like the conservatives . . .

Simpson[**]

Mr. Cohen started out by affirming that trade unions were the most thoroughly Anarchistic organizations to be found in our present society. I asserted that trade unions are as despotic and arbitrary as any other organization, and no more Anarchistic than the Pullman or Carnegie companies, etc., and maintained that one was as ignorant of the principle

---

[*]"In Answer to A.H. Simpson," March 7, 1896 (XI:22, #334), p. 8.
[**]"Trade-Union Despotism," March 21, 1896 (XI:23, #335), pp. 7-8.

of liberty as the others . . . In No. 334 Cohen has taken the position of justifying the tyranny of "enforcing arbitrary rules and driving non-union men out of town," such actions being "necessary to the life of the union," and he says that the "conditions" are to be blamed, and not the union men. How does that prove that unions are the most Anarchistic organizations in our present society? An organization is more or less Anarchistic in proportion as it attempts to maintain or enforce the law of equal liberty, either among its own members or outsiders. A trade union is neither based on or regardful of equal liberty. It takes advantage of the despotic conditions that make men dependent on their own trade, and then enforces further despotic conditions, which makes some Anarchists and Socialists feel that "rat" or "scab" conditions are hardly the less evils . .
.

Notes

1. [editor's comments to] A.S. Matter, "Is the Boycott Invasive?" *Liberty*, October 6, 1894 (X:11, #297), pp. 3-4.
2. Tucker, [editorial column], December 1904 (XIV:24, #386), p. 4.
3. Joseph Labadie, "Why They Hate the Boycott," February 1903 (XIV:6, #368), p. 6.
4. On secondary boycotts (boycotting individuals or businesses that do business with those under a primary boycott), see Victor Yarros, "The Stupidity of the Anti-Boycotters," September 1899 (XIV:1, #363), pp. 2-3; Tucker, "On Picket Duty," February 1903 (XIV:6, #368), p. 1. Logical to a fault, the individualist anarchists tended to support not only secondary boycotts, but also blacklists: S.R., "Logic and Liberty," May 1903 (XIV:9, #371), pp. 2-3; Labadie, "Why They Hate the Boycott," February 1903 (XIV:6, #368), p. 6.
5. Tucker, "On Picket Duty," August 1905 (XIV:27, #389), p. 1. See also C.L.S., "The Solution of the 'Negro Problem,'" December 1906 (XV:6, #396), pp. 44-47.
6. Victor Yarros, "Are We Fit for Freedom?" April 7, 1894 (IX:50, #284), p. 2.
7. Victor Yarros, "The Great Strike," July 14, 1894 (X:5, #291), p. 3. For a similar argument about the Knights of Labor, see Fair Play, "Do the Knights of Labor Love Liberty?" February 20, 1886 (III:24, #76), p. 4.
8. In a later response, Walker concedes Tucker's point, but insists that rural communities are necessary as refuges and in order to address the concerns of farmers (Walker, "Free Societies Again," September 6, 1884 (II:24, #50), pp. 5, 8).
9. Tucker, "On Picket Duty," August 28, 1894 (X:8, #294), p. 1.
10. See Tucker, "State Socialism's Discomfiture," December 29, 1894 (X:17, #303), p. 4 and Cohen's speech there, "Against 'Plank Ten,'" December 29, 1894 (X:17, #303), pp. 4-5.

13

Possible Tactics: Voting and Violence

Individualist anarchists considering strategy were ambivalent about voting and violence, especially the latter.[1] Voting was clearly cooperation with the state, while violence seemed to be a clear case of invasion of individual liberty. On the other hand, voting could conceivably be a decision-making mechanism in an anarchy, if it were part of a voluntary institution from which individuals could freely secede.[2] Violence, for its part, was quite acceptable as a defense against invasion, whether under anarchy or government. The dilemmas posed by voting and violence, then, could not be resolved theoretically and, like all questions of strategy, were ultimately a question of expediency and utility. That is, could a tactic of voting or violence accomplish an advance toward anarchy in a particular situation? Generally speaking, voting was almost never acceptable as a tactic, whereas violence was unacceptable as a strategy ("it can never accomplish the Social Revolution proper; that can never be accomplished except by means of agitation, investigation, experiment, and passive resistance"[3]), but was understandable as a reaction to oppression.

Opposing the vote, as the anarchists did, seems antidemocratic, while opposing the extension of suffrage to previously disfranchised groups, as the anarchists did for women, seems positively reactionary. Yet the writers for *Liberty* suggested that participating in a "democratic" system subjected one to the same evils as existed in any government: "The oppressor housed in ballot-boxes is the same deadly genius that lurks in the palaces."[4] The "progress" that was leading to universal suffrage, then, was not anything to be especially thankful for, a point made forcefully by Elisee Reclus in selection A. This argument applied specifically to demands for female suffrage: "There is no freedom that I would grant to man which I would refuse to woman, and there is no freedom that I would refuse to either man or woman except the freedom to invade. Whoever has the ballot has the freedom to invade, and whoever wants the ballot wants the freedom to invade."[5] Interestingly, female suffrage was also opposed on grounds of utility, on the assumption that women would use the vote more invasively, to support moralistic legislation (see selection B).

Individualist anarchist strategy, however, was basically opportunist, so the utility of voting as a tactic came up at least twice. Specifically, Victor Yarros raised the possibility in 1892 and 1896, when dramatic presidential elections stirred the passions of many. In 1892, he argued that an election that featured monetary issues so prominently could bring attention to anarchist agitation for free banking. Tucker was much more skeptical, arguing that the cause of free banking had nothing to gain from a sympathetic plank in the Democratic platform. Yarros retorted that even the failure of Democratic banking policy would be instructive, but Tucker had the last word, insisting that free banking would not "ooze up to us from hell."[6] In 1896, Yarros went even further, suggesting that anarchists might consider voting themselves, if the election of a particular candidate or party would advance some portion of the anarchist program. This optimistic assessment of the utility of voting was again shot down by Tucker's thorough and consistent skepticism (see selection C).

The last two decades of the nineteenth century saw a string of assassinations and many of the assassins were, or claimed to be, anarchists. This put the individualist anarchists in an unenviable position: they had few qualms about violence in theory, but opposed it as a strategy; on the other hand, they did not want to play into the hands of repression and hysteria. Surprisingly, what emerged from this dilemma was a relatively consistent line on assassins and "propaganda by deed." The motives of assassins were seen as an understandable reaction against oppression,[7] for their targets generally deserved the attempt.[8] In assigning "sympathy," moreover, the benefit of the doubt went to the underdog, to the assassin rather than the politician, especially after public hysteria had set in.[9] Yet, after the Haymarket incident, Tucker and his writers expressed considerable criticism of the strategy of violence. Tucker argued that violence was only acceptable as a last resort in attempting to regain the right to free speech and press.[10] As Gertrude Kelly concluded (see selection D): "an economic revolution can never be accomplished by force." By the time that the communist anarchist Alexander Berkman attempted to assassinate Henry Clay Frick, manager of the Homestead Works during the dramatic strike of 1892, the various threads of the individualist anarchist line on propaganda had come together in Tucker's pungent phrase: "No pity for Frick, no praise for Berkman" (selection E).While much of the discussion of violence in *Liberty* was related to specific incidents (there were plenty), occasionally the issue was discussed in more general terms, as in the lengthy article by Auberon Herbert (selection F).

Further Reading in Liberty

Victor Yarros' early view of voting was pessimistic: "Light for a Light-Bearer," December 3, 1887 (V:9, #113), p. 4, while he later became more enthusiastic: Yarros, "Corollaries," October 22, 1892 (IX:8, #242), pp. 2-3; Tucker, "The Temptations of Politics," ibid, p. 2; Yarros, "Corollaries," October 29, 1892 (IX:9, #243), p. 3; Tucker, "Political Salvationists," ibid, pp. 2-3. In 1882, Tucker reprinted and highly praised an 1877 article by Lysander Spooner: "Against Woman Suffrage," June 10, 1882 (I:22, #22), p. 4.

The earliest expression in *Liberty* of Tucker's ambivalence about violence was "Liberty's Weapons," September 17, 1881 (I:4, #4), p. 2. Gertrude Kelly wrote one of the best articles on Haymarket: "The Wages of Sin Is Death," May 22, 1886 (IV:3, #81), p. 5. Tucker was critical of an article by Lizzie Holmes that seemed too apologetic for violence: Holmes, "That 'Color Line,'" August 11, 1894 (X:7, #293), p. 8; Tucker, [editorial column], September 22, 1894 (X:10, #296), p. 4.

A. "Anarchy and Universal Suffrage"—Elisee Reclus[*]

The French anarchist Reclus here argues generally against voting and indeed against republican government. Voting, he says, has not helped solve economic oppression, partly because politicians are inevitably corrupted by power. Nor is voting useful for agitating revolutionary views, since elections are seen as horse races. Consequently, voters are dupes and anarchists should not descend to choosing their masters.

---

[*] March 4, 1882 (I:16, #16), p. 3.

. . . French males and majors vote in vain; they can only choose masters, petty kings who can avenge themselves for a single day of humiliation by years of insolence and irresponsible government. The elections over, the government makes war and peace without consulting the rabble of its subjects; notwithstanding the elections, millions of laborers remain at the mercy of capital, which pens them up in mines and factories, the uncertainty of the future is a load upon all. Has universal voting dispersed the corporations of robbers who speculate on labor and gather in all the profits? Has it diminished the number of merchants who sell by false weights and of advocates who plead indifferently for the just and the unjust? The plainest result of the substitution of so-called universal suffrage for restricted suffrage and suffrage exercised at the royal will is the increase of that hideous class of politicians who make a trade of living by their voice, paying court first to the electors and then, once in office, turning to those above them to beg for offices, sinecures, and pensions. To the aristocracy of birth, capital, and official position is added another aristocracy, that of the stump. Of course men are to be found among the candidates who are moved by good intentions and who are firmly resolved not to prove false to the programme which they have mapped out during the campaign; but, however good their intentions, they none the less find themselves on the day after the voting in circumstances different from those of the night before. They are a part of a privileged class, and, in spite of themselves, they become men of privilege. Invested by their fellow-citizens with the power to know everything and decide everything, they imagine themselves, in fact, competent to deal with all questions; their science is universal; they are at once *savants*, engineers, manufacturers, merchants, generals, admirals, diplomats, and administrators, and the whole life of the nation must be elaborated in their brains. Where is the individual strong enough to resist this flattery of the electors? Heir of kings and, like kings, disposing of affairs with a supreme comprehension, the deputy ends like kings, seized with the vertigo of power; proportionately he lifts his whims into laws, surrounds himself with courtiers whom it pleases him to despise, and creates self-interests directly antagonistic to those of the multitude which he is reputed to represent.

So far, our profession as electors has consisted only in recruiting enemies among those who call themselves our friends, or even among those who pretend to belong, as we do, to the party of social revendication. Must we untiringly continue this task of dupes, incessantly fill this cask which empties as rapidly, forever try to climb this rock which tumbles back upon us? Or should we busy ourselves with our own work, which is to establish, by ourselves and without delegation, a society of free and equal men?[11] To justify their participation in electoral intrigues, some revolutionary socialists claim to have no object in view except agitation. Passions being more excited during electoral struggles, they would take advantage of this fact to act more forcibly on the minds of the people and gain new adherents to the cause of the revolution. But does not the election itself mislead all these passions? The interest excited by elections is of the same order as that felt at the gaming-table. The course of the candidates at the balloting is like that of the horses at a hippodrome; people are eager to know who will win by a length or half-length; then, after the emotions excited by the struggle, they think the business finished until the races of the following year or decade, and go to their rest as if the real work was not yet to do. The elections serve only to start the revolutionists on a false scent and concurrently waste their strength. As for us Anarchists, we remain in the ranks, equals of each other. Knowing that authority always results sadly to him who exercises it and to those who submit to it, we should feel ourselves dishonored were we to descend from our condition of free men to enroll ourselves on the list of mendicants of power. That business let us leave to the prideless people who like to crook the spine . . .

B. "Woman-Suffrage and Anarchism"
—Victor Yarros vs. John B. Robinson[*]

Yarros here assumes that, in principle, women have as much right to the vote as men (that is, none), but argues that, in practice, women are likely to use the vote moralistically (e.g. for prohibition), thus threatening individual liberty. This argument was common among the writers for Liberty, *both men and women, though few shared Yarros' appeal to Spencer for evidence.*[12] *On the other hand, few bought Robinson's argument that extending the suffrage to women, as an egalitarian and progressive move, would indirectly further the cause of liberty.*

---

[*] Yarros, "Woman-Suffrage and Anarchism," August 11, 1894 (X:7, #293), pp. 2–4; John Beverly Robinson, "Woman-Suffrage and Liberty," August 28, 1894 (X:8, #294), p. 2.

Yarros

. . . From the view-point of current political doctrine and prevailing political practices, there is no rational objection to woman suffrage. It is impudence, self-stultification, and contemptible meanness for those who really believe that suffrage is a right, an attribute of sovereignty, a function of responsible and conscious citizenship, to deny the fitness of woman for the exercise of the suffrage. . . . Liberty is not arguing from the standpoint of current political belief, however, but from that of perfect individualism, equal freedom, no-government; or, more correctly, from the standpoint of men who, believing in individualism or equal freedom, wish to do and promote everything making for that ideal of political life, and to discourage and hinder everything calculated to obstruct progress and strengthen vicious tendencies and institutions. We do not believe that men are entitled to vote; we do not regard the ballot as a corollary of equal freedom. We do not believe in government, in majority-rule, in enforced cooperation. The ballot is a weapon of coercion, compulsion, government, and as such we condemn it. We seek to deprive men of this weapon, to abolish all coercive government of man by man. Now, while thus fighting coercion and government, we are called upon to deal with a practical movement in favor of extending the suffrage to women,—that is to say, in favor of arming a few additional millions with the dangerous weapon of voting. Our first and natural inquiry is, will the women use this in the interest of progress or of reaction? The question is not one of right, but of expediency. The women are not entitled to the ballot not because they are women, but because the ballot is not something which can be claimed by any one under the highest law of social existence,— equal freedom. Is it well for society, for progress, that women should obtain this weapon and wield it pending the realization of the new ideal of a free society? This is the only pertinent question, and it is a question which can only be answered in the light of woman's work and endeavors in the fields that are open to them. The Anarchists and individualists oppose woman suffrage simply and solely because they are convinced that woman's political activity would be directed tyrannyward and would arrest the political emancipation of all of us. If we thought otherwise, we would aid women in their present efforts, for, our object being the increase of liberty, we naturally favor the use of every method that leads to that result.

Robinson

"Y's" argument against woman suffrage, on the ground that women, being more tyrannical than men, will still further restrict our liberties when they obtain the ballot, seems to me to be in the wrong direction.

Women possibly may be more tyrannical than men, but if they are, it would seem to be correlated with the separation and subordination of women, which has retarded their development compared with that of men.

By mingling with people at large, at the ballot box and otherwise, men learn toleration; so, by mingling with men as companions at the ballot box, as well as in all the walks of life, women gain comradeship with men, which means equality, which means liberty.

Of course, for the ballot itself I care nothing, but that women should care to do at all what men do, on the ground of their common humanity and as equal individualities, that is wherein woman suffrage tends liberty-ward.

Besides, I am not so sure that women are naturally more tyrannical than men. Two things tend to make them artificially so: one the cant that is current among men about "woman's influence," holding them up as creatures altogether too bright and good to do anything but be bullied; the other, the excessive censoriousness of women toward each other upon the question of chastity. Both of these will go when men and women are comrades; the men will learn that women do not enjoy having to pose as etherial stage fairies any more than men would, and the women will mind their own business as men do with regard to each other's private affairs.

But surely the ballot, as well as the bicycle, tends toward liberty.

Yarros

. . . It is doubtless true that "by mingling with men at the ballot box, women gain comradeship with men," and this is a desirable result, both in itself and on account of its bearing on the struggle for freedom, but the question is whether the result will not have to be purchased at too dear a price,—whether the loss will not more than offset the gain. You propose to give women the ballot because indirectly and gradually their political experience and association with men will liberalize them and make them a progressive force in politics; but if the direct and immediate result of their "enfranchisement" will be a crushing blow to progress and liberalism, it is obviously foolish to invite certain disaster for the sake of remote and uncertain benefits. The question whether women really *are* more tyrannical than men, is thus seen to be very important. All *a priori* considerations lead to the conclusion that women's faith in the efficacy of coercive legislation and regulation is far more blind and absolute than that of men. Spencer has attempted to demonstrate, on biological and psychological grounds, that women naturally are and must always be extremely conservative, but it is not necessary to seek support in disputed theories. Woman's "separation and subordination" have certainly made her narrow, illiberal, and short-sighted. Her "excessive censoriousness upon the question of chastity" is simply one of the special manifestations of her illiberality and conservatism . . .

But let us admit for the sake of the argument that women are *not* more tyrannical then men; certainly no one will claim that they are *less* tyrannical. On what ground, then, can Mr. Robinson, whose efforts are directed toward "disfranchising" men,—toward abolishing majority rule (the only political system under which the ballot has significance and vitality), favor the extension of the suffrage to women? The ballot is inconsistent with equal freedom, and *therefore* Mr. Robinson would deprive men of it. Now he proposes to give it to women in the hope that it will prove a liberalizing and civilizing agent in their hands. Manifestly these two positions are inconsistent. If the ballot will liberalize women, it will continue to liberalize men, and there is no propriety in attempting to take it away from them. If, on the other hand, it is productive of more evil than good in the hands of men, it will have the same tendency in the hands of women.

It is important that women should "mingle with men as companions," but the ballot-booth is not the only place creating an opportunity for such mingling; in all "the other walks of life" mingling is not only possible, but wholly advantageous. The objections I have raised are not against *mingling*, but against *mingling at the ballot-box*. The difference between the bicycle, the office, the school, the parlor, on the one hand, and the ballot-box on the other, is just this: all the former indirectly tend toward political liberty without in any way neutralizing or offsetting or over-balancing that tendency, while the ballot tends toward coercion and tyranny strongly and directly, and but slightly and indirectly in the opposite direction.

C. "Tactical Voting"—Victor Yarros v. Benjamin Tucker

The possibility that voting could be an anarchist tactic is explored in some detail in this debate between Yarros and Tucker. For Yarros, voting had become purely a question of expediency, since anarchists have "no religious or moral objection" to it. The question is simply whether the immediate gain of voting in a particular situation outbalances the cost to anarchist principles or to the distinctiveness of anarchism as a political force. If not, then voting for non-invasive purposes is completely acceptable. Tucker reminds Yarros, none too gently, that voting is itself an aggression, in all imaginable cases where a coercive government exists. Thus, voting can never be non-invasive.

Yarros[*]

No question seems to be simpler at first blush than that of the proper attitude of Anarchists toward political struggles. Absolute non-participation is obviously the clear deduction, the inevitable corollary from the general Anarchistic philosophy. Yet so much human nature is there even in Anarchists that during exciting and stormy campaigns abstract principles are easily lost sight of by many, and some uncertainty is felt with regard to the propriety of holding entirely aloof. Of course, no difficulty arises when all of the contending parties are equally bad and reactionary, or when such superiority as one of the parties may have refers to a matter in which no particular interest is felt. But when class feeling runs high, and one's sympathies and antipathies are aroused, he is tempted to make an exception to the rule of rigid abstention, and to "go into politics" for the occasion.

A friend and reader of Liberty recently put this query to me: When some practical, immediate good can be accomplished by the election of a particular man or the victory of a particular party, is it not the part of wisdom and propriety for the most determined opponent of government and politics to aid and abet such election? Admitting that but little good can be accomplished in and through politics, should not that little be secured by temporary excursions into practical partisan affairs?

Now, the first thing to remark concerning this problem is that it overlooks the fact that the Anarchists themselves are a political party

---

[*] "Anarchists in Politics," November 1896 (XII:9, #347), pp. 2–3.

fighting for political ends. They have a platform and are "enlisted for the war," employing such methods as seem to them most efficacious and best adapted to the objects in view. Surely it is not without reason that ordinary political methods have been abjured by them, and surely it is no new or surprising discovery, originally neglected, that occasionally some good can be accomplished by political action. The real question is whether the immediate and practical good which, by our hypothesis, can be secured is not overbalanced by indirect and remote injury to the essential aims and purposes of Anarchism. Answer this question in the negative, and all reasons for boycotting politics vanish. It is to be borne in mind that there are no other considerations than utilitarian ones to be considered. Anarchists have no religious or moral objection to voting and party warfare, and, although they regret the fundamental principle of government and insist on doing away with all coercion of the non-invasive, they would not deem it ethically improper to use the ballot (which means aggression) for the purpose of furthering the cause of freedom. . . . This is not because the end justifies the means, but because, from the rational and evolutionary point of view, we are entitled to use the ideas and sentiments of the present as a stepping-stone to higher ideas and sentiments.

Here the fundamental difference between the Tolstoi philosophy and the utilitarian view plainly emerges. Coercion, government, legal violence, says Tolstoi, are sinful and ungodly, and hence the man who in any way countenances or identifies himself with these things is guilty of immorality. That which is sinful today was sinful two thousand years ago, and the sinners of the past and present are equally guilty. The scientific view, on the other hand, is that the ethical propriety of men's acts must be determined by the requirements and possibilities of the situation. In addition to the absolutely right, as Spencer would put it, there is the relatively right. We may think that society is ready to relinquish government altogether, and that the greatest happiness would now be secured by the complete observance of equal freedom; but the fact is that society, through ignorance or inertia, adheres to governmentalism, and we must abolish this evil as gradually and slowly as popular intelligence permits. In enlarging men's freedom, in diminishing the amount of governmental coercion, we may, without impropriety, use the political methods in vogue. It is not inconsistent to use government to abolish government, to invoke majority rule for the purpose of weakening and restricting the power of the majority.

The real question is whether this policy is safe and successful from the standpoint of what may be called Anarchistic politics. If more can be accomplished by holding aloof from party activity, by carrying on a strictly Anarchistic propaganda and declining to have anything to do with existing government agencies, by boycotting politics, in short, then it is manifestly reactionary and unwise to neglect the work of greater utility and importance for the sake of work of lesser utility. There are plenty of conservatives to attend to conservative work, plenty of moderate reformers to do the work called for by the moderate platforms, and it is essential that those who have their own distinctive, and peculiar, and special mission should concentrate their energies on that mission. The real question is not whether Anarchists can properly help free-traders to obtain free trade, or anti-monopolists of any kind to secure the repeal of a special law establishing a given monopoly, but whether they can do this without sacrificing larger and greater interests.

Theoretically, it is possible to conceive and approve of the following attitude: Let Anarchists promulgate their platform in full, and emphasize at all times the fact that they seek to abolish government altogether; and let them, in addition to their present methods of propaganda and activity, go into politics and cooperate with the more progressive elements, helping them to secure such minor reforms in the direction of liberty as they may from time to time put forward as practical issues . . .

Of course, abstention does not prevent them from expressing sympathy with progressive politicians and making war upon the more objectionable type. They can applaud the effort to secure free trade without voting and working for free-trade candidates. But, my correspondent objects, suppose that it actually depended on a single vote, or on the vote of an Anarchistic group, whether a congressional majority favorable to a free-trade bill should be elected or not; suppose that they had it absolutely in their power to decide, by throwing their political influence on the right side, whether the country should have free banking or the perpetuation of the present financial system: what would you advise?

Such a situation is logically not inconceivable . . . It seems to me, however, that no general answer can be given. Temperament would govern in each individual case. I think *I* should vote in the case supposed, but I am not at all sure that Mr. Tucker would. . . . Some would unhesitatingly make an exception to their general rule, while others would adhere to the rule.

In saying that I should vote under the peculiar circumstances supposed, I do not intend to convey the impression that I should consider myself inconsistent. My belief in guiding principles is as firm as ever, my distrust of "exceptional cases" as profound as ever. But, as I have indicated above, non-participation in politics is not enjoined by any high ethical principle; it is simply, in my judgment, a necessary condition of successful Anarchistic propaganda under ordinary circumstances. In an extraordinary situation the very interest of Anarchism might call for different behavior.

Tucker[*]

. . . It is true that Anarchists, once convinced that freedom could best be furthered by the use of the ballot, would not deem its use to that end an impropriety. But it seems to me that, in asserting this truth,—which is almost a truism,—Anarchists should be careful to make it plain that to them the use of the ballot is in itself something more and worse than a trivial act of inutility. Mr. Yarros, to be sure, declares parenthetically that use of the ballot is aggression, but certainly the tendency of his article as a whole is to make light of it in its aggressive aspect.

For my part, when I say that I would use the ballot if I thought that thereby I could best help the cause of freedom, I make the declaration in precisely the same sense and with precisely the same conception of the gravity of my utterance as when I declare, as I sometimes do, that I would use dynamite if I thought that thereby I could best help the cause of freedom. But I am as reluctant to use one as the other. If, however, I were to decide to use either or both, I would not try to deceive myself with phrases, or resort to euphemism by talk of stepping-stones, but would base myself, in that matter as in all others, squarely on the excellent doctrine that the end justifies the means,—a doctrine which Mr. Yarros substantially asserts by his article, despite his verbal disclaimer. In declaring that he would vote if absolutely sure that his vote would decide the fate of a libertarian measure,—that is, would commit an aggression,—that is, again, would violate equal liberty,—he surely acts upon the doctrine of "exceptional cases". . . His utterances, moreover, are a confession that in practice he would find exceptional cases oftener than I . . .

---

* "Principle, Policy, and Politics," November 1896 (XII:9, #347), p. 5.

*Yarros****

    . . . Do I make light of the aggressive aspect of the ballot? I deny this impeachment. I contented myself with a parenthetical allusion to the aggressiveness of the ballot, instead of enlarging and dwelling upon the matter, simply and solely because I never dreamed that special emphasis or amplification was necessary. To argue in Liberty that majority rule is aggression is to burst an open door. I passed over the question as too well settled for argumentation.

    But, says Mr. Tucker, the tendency of the whole article is in conflict with this position. I deny it, and am really surprised that so keen and logical a thinker as Mr. Tucker should have fallen into so egregious a blunder as that which prompted his criticism. He lost sight of a most vital and all important distinction,—of the essential difference between form or appearance and actual substance. I distinctly stated that I should not use the ballot and the machinery of government except for the purpose of enlarging liberty and diminishing aggression, and Mr. Tucker accuses me of favoring aggression, of violating equal freedom! Here is his own language, truly astonishing:

    "In declaring that he would vote if absolutely sure that his vote would decide the fate of a libertarian measure,—that is, would commit an aggression,—that is, again, would violate equal liberty,—he surely acts upon the doctrine of 'exceptional cases,' etc."

    Now this is a most comical lapse. . . . A vote for any measure in the direction of equal liberty cannot be a violation of equal liberty. The form is the same, the content different. The ballot is generally employed for purposes of aggression, but those who should employ it for the purpose of preventing the perpetuation of aggression and securing an extension of personal liberty could not possibly become guilty of aggression. Suppose the issue is free trade versus protection, and suppose my vote gives free traders a majority and thus insures the adoption of free trade. If my use of the ballot has been aggressive, some person must exist whose rights, whose legitimate freedom, have been invaded by the adoption of free trade, by my vote for free trade. But, since free trade is a corollary from equal freedom, no one's rights are violated by the establishment of free trade. If no one's rights are violated, those who vote for free trade

---

* "Principle and Method," December 1896 (XII:10, #348), p. 5.

are not guilty of any offence. When there are no aggressed upon, there are no aggressors.

It is true that the majority, by voting for free trade, force, or threaten to force, free trade upon the minority. But, since free trade simply means the absence of restriction upon trade, the majority has a perfect right, under equal freedom, to prevent the minority from imposing restrictions,—that is, from committing aggression.

How absurd, then, it is to say that there is no difference in principle between using the ballot to secure greater freedom and using dynamite! Dynamite deprives men of life and limb; the use of the ballot for the purpose of securing freedom interferes with no one's exercise of his faculties . . .

It follows that there is no objection whatever, from the standpoint of equal freedom, to the employment of the ballot for non-invasive purposes. The only objection against libertarians in party politics is that upon which I laid stress,—the danger of "impairing that force which they aim to exercise in their own distinctive work," to use Mr. Tucker's expression of my idea,—the danger of confusing the public mind and obliterating Anarchism as an independent factor in the larger political life. To repeat what I said in my previous article, non-participation in politics for libertarian purposes is not enjoined by any ethical principle; it is simply a necessary condition of successful propaganda under ordinary conditions . . .

Tucker[*]

. . . It is to be borne in mind that the question which Mr. Yarros undertook to discuss was this: Politics being, in general, what they are to-day, can a particular occasion arise when it would be advisable for Anarchists to take part in them? Now, in taking his new position, Mr. Yarros discusses, not this question, but another. In assuming the possibility of voting for a libertarian measure without at the same time participating in aggression, he discards his old premise,—politics being, in general, what they are to-day,—and virtually argues from a new one. He now tacitly premises such a transformation of politics that invasion is eliminated, and concludes therefrom that Anarchists may, on special occasions, participate in them without aggression. A very simple proposi-

---

[*] "Aggression and the Ballot," December 1896 (XII:10, #348), pp. 3–4.

tion, which nobody will deny. Unfortunately, it has not the slightest bearing on the question whether it is possible for Anarchists to non-aggressively participate in the invasive thing that are politics to-day. When voting shall have become a mere expression of opinion, recorded through the operation of a political mechanism purely voluntary in character, and leaving the minority entire freedom of secession, it very likely will prove a convenient method of practical work, of which Anarchists may properly avail themselves, not simply on special occasions, but whenever they perceive the smallest inducement to do so. But Mr. Yarros knows very well that to-day voting is nothing of the sort, and that it cannot be anything of the sort so long as Archy lasts.

Mr. Yarros cannot go to the polls to vote for a libertarian measure. Any vote that he casts, unless it be for an executive or judicial officer, must be for a law-maker. If he votes for a man who favors a particular libertarian measure, this man will vote in the legislature, as Mr. Yarros's chosen representative, not alone for the one libertarian measure, but for a thousand invasive measures. . . . And even were Mr. Yarros to cast his ballot for a man who would vote in legislature for none but libertarian measures . . . his candidate, if elected, would necessarily draw a salary out of a fund gathered by compulsory taxation. If this candidate were not elected, still Mr. Yarros' ballot for him would be counted and, probably, printed out of this same robbers' fund. And the same would be true, were this ballot cast for a constitutional amendment or for a special measure submitted directly to popular vote. In any and all these cases there would be aggression, and Mr. Yarros, by participating, would make himself an accomplice in aggression. The responsibility for the consequences he would share equally with all other voters. These consequences include the destruction of life and limb as truly (though generally not as directly) as do those of "propaganda by deed." Thus Mr. Yarros's claim that by voting he would commit no violation of equal liberty and would injure nobody is shown to be without foundation . . .

D.   "A Time to Beware of Passion"—Gertrude B. Kelly[*]

Writing shortly after the death sentence had been handed down for the Haymarket anarchists,[13] Kelly offers a characteristic and poignant example of the individualist anarchists' sympathy for the victims of state

---

* September 18, 1886 (IV:9, #87), p. 5.

repression combined with criticism of their reliance on violence. For Kelly, violence was simply misdirected, for the real bulwark of the state was popular ignorance, which could only be undermined through agitation. Here she writes specifically against the understandable desire for revenge, insisting that it would only play into the hands of reaction.[14]

If there ever were a time in which the true friends of the revolution were especially called upon to keep their reason unclouded and to possess their souls in patience, that time is now,—now, when the whole force of the hireling press is directed against the men under sentence of death in Chicago; now, when every impulse of common human sympathy tends to make us range ourselves at their side. But let not the sympathy which we feel with them in their unjust sentence make us forget for a moment that, however honest and devoted these men were (and their honesty and devotion they have proven beyond a doubt), however pure their motives, the methods by which they sought to attain their ends are not those by which the social revolution can ever really be accomplished.

O my brothers! let no blind feelings of revenge against the State and its tools lead you to play into its hands by attempting to meet force with force. Remember that the use of force must always react with most deadly effect upon us; that an economic revolution can never be accomplished by force. Remember that the employment of force leads to the redevelopment of the military spirit, which is totally opposed to the spirit that must exist in the people before anything that we wish for can be brought about. Remember that the government is really enforced, not by the bayonets by which it is surrounded, but by the ignorance in the minds of the people, and it is this ignorance, and this alone, that we are called upon to combat, and it is only as this is destroyed that success is possible. Remember that every appeal to brute force tends to retard the dissipation of this ignorance . . .

Virtuous, respectable, well-dressed, well-behaved society may now again begin its dance over the walled-over volcano, heedless of the rumblings beneath, until another explosion comes, which may take a still more deadly form than the bomb-throwing at Chicago. Are the authorities mad in their pursuit of gain and power that they do not see what a treasury of hatred they are laying up against themselves by their policy of revenge? . . .

I again appeal to you, my brothers, to let no blind feelings of revenge tempt you to aid the cause of the reaction. Now is the time above all others to stand firm in our advocacy of what is right and just, to let no fear that we may, for the moment, seem "respectable" cause us to swerve in the least from strict devotion to the highest truths that we realize, and one of these is that an *economic revolution can never be accomplished by force.*

E.   "Save Labor from Its Friends"—Benjamin Tucker[*]

The title of Tucker's editorial nearly says it all. Despite his admiration for the bravery and devotion of Alexander Berkman, the communist anarchist who attempted to assassinate the industrialist Henry Clay Frick, Tucker saw the young revolutionary as a fool. This was essentially the same way that he felt about the Haymarket anarchists and Vaillant, the French bombthrower of 1894.[15] On the other hand, he had no pity for Frick, a "conspicuous member of the brotherhood of thieves." Tucker was clearly uncomfortable both with anarchist bombthrowers and with the hypocrisy that followed their actions.[16] Ultimately, he made the same point as Kelly: violence could not bring about the revolution that individualist anarchists sought.

During the conflict now on between capital and labor, seldom a day passes without the shedding of blood. One of the most recent victims is a prominent leader of the forces of capital. The disaster that has befallen him has called out a display of grief on his behalf which, so far as it comes from the camp of labor, seems to me theatrical, and in which I certainly cannot share. Henry C. Frick . . . is a conspicuous member of the brotherhood of thieves. In joining this nefarious band he took his life in his hands, and he knew it. It is but just to say that he has accepted his fate in the spirit of a bold bandit, without a cry or flinch. His pluck excites my admiration, but his suffering moves me to less pity than I would feel for the most ordinary cur. Why should I pity this man? What have he and I in common? Does he aspire, as I do, to live in a society of mutually helpful equals? On the contrary, it is his determination to live in luxury produced by the toil and suffering of men whose necks are under his heel. He has deliberately chosen to live on terms of hostility with the greater

---

[*] July 30, 1892 (VIII:49, #231), p. 2.

part of the human race. When such a man falls, my tears refuse to flow. I am scarcely sorry that he is suffering; I shall be still less sorry if he dies.

And yet I am very, very sorry that he has been shot.

Who is his assailant? I do not know Alexander Berkman, but I believe that he is a man with whom I have much in common,—much more at any rate than with such a man as Frick. It is altogether likely, despite the slanders in the newspapers, as insincere in their abuse as in their grief, that he would like to live on terms of equality with his fellows, doing his share of work for not more than his share of pay. There is little reason to doubt that his attitude toward the human race is one, not of hostility, but of intended helpfulness. And yet, as one member of the human race, I freely confess that I am more desirous of being saved from friends like Berkman, to whom my heart goes out, than from enemies like Frick, from whom my heart withdraws. The worst enemy of the human race is folly, and men like Berkman are its incarnation. It would be comparatively easy to dispose of the Fricks, if it were not for the Berkmans. The latter are the hope of the former. The strength of the Fricks rests on violence; now it is to violence that the Berkmans appeal. The peril of the Fricks lies in the spreading of the light; violence is the power of darkness. If the revolution comes by violence and in advance of light, the old struggle will have to be begun anew. The hope of humanity lies in the avoidance of that revolution by force which the Berkmans are trying to precipitate.

No pity for Frick, no praise for Berkman,—such is the attitude of Liberty in the present crisis.

F.   "The Ethics of Dynamite"
—Auberon Herbert vs. Victor Yarros

Perhaps the most detailed discussion of violence, from the standpoint of principle and strategy, came about because of Auberon Herbert's response in Contemporary Review *to the French bombing wave of 1894. Excerpted in* Liberty, *it called forth a definitive statement from Yarros.*[17] *Herbert drew a tight parallel between dynamite and government, calling the former the child, the perfection, and the intensification of the latter, yet went on to insist that government repression of dynamiters would only escalate the cycle of violence. Yarros shared Herbert's conclusion about repression*[18]*, but objected strenuously to the parallel, suggesting that violent resistance to oppression was not theoretically inconsistent with* *anarchism. However, it had to be carefully considered* in strategic terms: *was force the best available weapon for advancing liberty?*

Herbert[*]

Perhaps I ought at once, for the benefit of some of my friends who are inclined a little incautiously to glorify this word "governing" without thinking of all that is contained in it, to translate the term, which is so often on our lips, into what I hold to be its true meaning: forcing your own will and pleasure, whatever they may be, if you happen to be the stronger, on other persons. Now, many worthy people are apt to look on dynamite as the arch-enemy of the government. . . . Dynamite is not opposed to government; it is, on the contrary, government in its most intensified and concentrated form. Whatever are the sins of every-day governmentalism, however brutal in their working some of the great force machines with which we love to administer each other may tend to be, however reckless we may be as regards each other's rights in our efforts to place the yoke of our own opinions upon the neck of others, dynamite "administers" with a far ruder, rougher hand than even the worst of the continental bureaucracies. Indeed, whenever the continental governments are reproached by some of us liberty-folk for taking possession in so peremptory a manner of the bodies and minds of the people and converting them into administration material, they may not unreasonably remark—if they happen to be in a philosophic mood—that the same reproaches should be addressed, with even greater pertinency, to their enemy, the dynamiter, who dynamites us all with the happiest impartiality on the off-chance of impressing somebody or other with some portion of his own rather mixed views. . . . Foreign governments have, however, as I think, an unavowed reason of their own for not loving the dynamiter, independent of any philosophical objection they may feel to the intellectual incoherences on his part. Conscience makes cowards of us all. Deep down in their consciousness lurks a dim perception of the truth that between him and them exists an unrecognized blood-relationship, that the thing of which they have such a horror is something more than a satire, an exaggeration, a caricature of themselves, that, if the truth is to be fairly acknowledged, it is their very own child, both the product of and the reaction against the methods of "governing" men and women,

---

[*] July 14, 1894 (X:5, #291), p. 11.

which they have employed with so unsparing a hand. . . . Our good rulers
are right to have their misgivings. We live in an age of active evolution,
and the art of government is evolving like everything else around us.
Dynamite is its latest and least comfortable development. It is a purer
essence of government, more concentrated and intensified, than has ever
yet been employed. It is government in a nutshell, government stripped,
as some of us aver, of all its dearly-beloved fictions, ballot-boxes,
political parties, House of Commons oratory, and all the rest of it. How,
indeed, is it possible to govern more effectively, or in more abbreviated
form, than to say: "Do this—or don't do this—unless you desire that a
pound of dynamite should be placed tomorrow evening in your ground-
floor study." It is the perfection, the *ne plus ultra*, of government. Indeed,
if we poor liberty-folk, we voluntaryists . . . wished to find an object-les-
son to set before those governments of today which have not yet learnt
to doubt about their property in human material, where could we find
anything more impressive than the dynamiter, with his tin canister and
his supply of horse-shoe nails? "Here is your own child. This is what
your doctrine of deified force, this is what your contempt of human rights,
this is what your property in men and women leads to."

There are some reformers by dynamite who imagine that they are on
the side of liberty. Poor liberty! As if liberty, that moves by the path of
moral evolution, that moves so slowly, just because she cannot be created
out of hand by those forms and systems which are established today and
swept aside tomorrow, liberty, that depends upon inward processes in the
consciousness of men, upon the gradual recognition by every person in
every other person of his inherent inalienable right to be himself and lead
the self-chosen life—as if liberty, in this one true sense, could have
anything to do with a tin canister filled with blacksmith's nails and flung
into the midst of a body of old and middle-aged gentlemen . . . or of
peaceful citizens sipping their coffee! Friends of liberty! No. Even the
most clear-headed of the believers in St. Dynamite understand as little
of liberty as they understand of themselves. Inventors of improved and
expedited processes of government perhaps they may be; or avengers
they may be, as fungi are avengers, when we establish the conditions that
favor decay; or, as disease may be, when we recklessly depart from the
conditions that maintain health; but don't let them dream of themselves
as friends of liberty. To be a friend of liberty is one thing; to be a
half-automatic reaction from a bad system is another thing . . .

Almost every European government is a legalized manufactory of dynamiters. Vexation piled upon vexation, restriction upon restriction, burden upon burden, the dynamiter is slowly hammered out everywhere on the official anvil. The more patient submit, but the stronger and more rebellious characters are maddened, and any weapon is considered right, as the weapon of the weaker against the stronger. . . . It is time that we laid aside this odious weapon of compulsion. More and more bitter will be the fruit of it as the years go on. Compulsion everywhere is a brutalizing weapon. . . . Force is the very weakest and most treacherous of all human implements. The history of force is the history of the continuous crumbling away of every institution that has rested upon it. . . . If we cannot learn, if the only effect upon us of the presence of the dynamiter in our midst is to make us multiply punishments, invent restrictions, increase the number of our official spies, forbid public meetings, interfere with the press, . . . if we are, in a word, to trust to machinery, to harden our hearts, and simply to meet force with force, always irritating, always clumsy, and in the end fruitless, then I venture to prophesy that there lies before us a bitter and an evil time. We may be quite sure that force-users will be force-begetters. The passions of men will rise higher and higher; and the authorized and unauthorized governments—the government of the majority and of written laws, the government of the minority and of dynamite—will enter upon their desperate struggle, of which no living man can read the end. In one way, and only one way, can the dynamiter be permanently disarmed—by abandoning in almost all directions our force-machinery, and accustoming the people to believe in the blessed weapons of reason, persuasion, and voluntary service. We have morally made the dynamiter; we must now morally unmake him.

Yarros[*]

The pseudo-individualists and the semi-individualists, the apologists of plutocracy and the stern moralists, should read Mr. Herbert's broad, philosophical, and judicious observations on the dynamite problem and form an idea of what is the proper attitude for libertarians in the premises. . . . Auberon Herbert's clear and persuasive argumentation cannot fail to have a liberalizing effect on many minds.

---

[*] "Auberon Herbert on Dynamite," July 14, 1894 (X:5, #291), pp. 3–4.

To Mr. Herbert's main proposition no exception can be taken. But certain incidental affirmations of his may be shown to be erroneous and to require qualification. For instance, in attempting to disabuse "those reformers by dynamite who imagine that they are on the side of liberty," Mr. Herbert reasons in a way which logically involves the condemnation of force under all circumstances and leads straight to the doctrine of non-resistance. But surely Mr. Herbert does not hold that any resistance to aggression is inconsistent with liberty,—that only non-resistants are true and consistent Anarchists. Mr. Herbert is not a Tolstoi Anarchist. . . . As if liberty could have anything to do with dynamite! Mr. Herbert exclaims. Why, of course, it could! Is it a violation of liberty to punish an aggression? And if it consistent with liberty to hang or decapitate or "electrocute" a murderer, why is it not consistent to blow him up? What is true of an unofficial governor,—a murderer,—is equally true of the official governors,—the kings and dictators and presidents. Those who consider them aggressors may, consistently with liberty, punish them as such. But not everything that is consistent with liberty is wise or profitable; hence, although the official governors *are* aggressors, as a rule, it is suicidal to attempt to punish them by dynamite or any other form of violence. The cause of liberty, the progress of liberty, is not to be furthered by such means, and this is the final and sufficient reason for deprecating force as a method of social reform where better methods are possible. Among such better methods are education, criticism, appeals to reason, and passive resistance to aggression. Mr. Herbert must see, in the light of these considerations, which he will not dispute, that some of the dynamiteurs might really be on the side of liberty. If they are not, the fact is not proved simply by their partiality for dynamite. It so happens that the dynamiteurs are all Archistic Communists who would restrict our liberty even more than the present Archistic *bourgeois* do. Still, a dynamiteur *might* be a consistent Anarchist. The question of method is chiefly a question of policy and expediency.

It is inaccurate to say that dynamite is the perfection of government, government concentrated and intensified. Everything depends on what the dynamite is intended for. Mr. Herbert asks: "How, indeed, is it possible to govern more effectively, or in more abbreviated form, than to say: 'Do this—or don't do this—unless you desire that a pound of dynamite should be placed tomorrow evening in your ground-floor study'?" But it is possible to say this without governing at all. To force a man to do something which he should be free to omit to do, or to forcibly prevent a man from doing something which he should be free to do, is to govern. But suppose a burglar is about to rob you, and you tell him not to do it unless he is willing to have a taste of dynamite: is *that* government? Certainly not. Now the State is a burglar, and dynamiteurs who should use dynamite as a method of forcing it to abandon burglary would not be trying to govern, but to protect themselves from government.

The foregoing will suggest the qualification needed by the statement that force must necessarily fail as a weapon against government. It will fail only where better weapons are neglected; where force is the *only* weapon, where the choice is between force and entire inactivity, force may and should be used for the purpose of acquiring the liberty of using the other and better weapons.

With reference to the actual conditions in France, it is true that the dynamiteurs are not working in the interest of liberty, and that *for* these interests dynamite is not the proper weapon. It is not because of the propaganda by deed, but in spite of it, that the French evince greater liberality and tolerance towards new ideas. No sensible revolutionist has ever claimed more for propaganda by deed than that it prepares the soil for propaganda by word, but there is danger that all opportunity for the latter will be altogether destroyed, instead of enlarged, by the former.

Notes

1. For a general discussion of individualist anarchist strategy, see Morgan Edwards, "Neither Bombs Nor Ballots: *Liberty* and the Strategy of Anarchism," in Michael E. Coughlin, Charles H. Hamilton and Mark A. Sullivan, eds., *Benjamin R. Tucker and the Champions of Liberty: A Centenary Anthology*, St. Paul: Coughlin and Sullivan, n.d. [1986], pp. 65–91.
2. Tucker, "Aggression and the Ballot," December 1896 (XII:10, #348), pp. 3–4.
3. Tucker, "Liberty and Violence," May 22, 1886 (IV:3, #81), p. 4.
4. Tucker, "The Ballot-Box Craze," September 16, 1882 (I:26, #26), p. 3. Tucker also suggested that the ballot "is neither more nor less than the paper representative of the bayonet, the billy, and the bullet." ("Mr. Pentecost's Belief in the Ballot," January 19, 1889 [VI:11, #141], p. 4.) Victor Yarros put it this way: "To vote is to govern; it is also to be governed." ("Light for a Light Bearer," December 3, 1887 [V:9, #113], p. 4)
5. Tucker, [editorial column], December 1, 1894 (X:15, #301), p. 4. See also Tucker, [editorial column], September 17, 1881 (I:4, #4), p. 3.
6. Tucker, "Up in a Balloon," November 19, 1892 (IX:12, #246), pp. 2–3. Their debate originated in #242 (see "Further Readings" for full cite).
7. In "The Twin Children of Tyranny" (March 17, 1883 [II:8, #34], p. 3), Tucker argues that dynamiters are simply out for revenge. Henry Appleton ("Dynamite, the New

Apostle of Liberty," February 28, 1885 [III:7, #59], p. 4), argues that dynamiters show "the potency of individual assertion," and have the same right to take life as do states. Yarros argues that the assassination of the French leader Carnot was an act of revenge ("Violence Breeding Violence," June 30, 1894 [X:4, #290], p. 2).

8. In the case of the American president Garfield ("Guiteau, the Fraud-Spoiler," January 21, 1882 [I:13, #13], pp. 2-3), the French leader Gambetta (Tucker, "Who Are the Terrorists in France," November 11, 1882 [II:3, #29], pp. 2-3, "Another Tyrant Fallen," January 20, 1883 [II:6, #32], p. 2), the American industrialist Henry Frick (Hugo Bilgram, "Is Frick a Soldier of Liberty?" August 20, 1892 (VIII:52, #234), p. 3), Tucker clearly indicated that the targets had it coming.

9. Tucker's early, and substantial coverage, of the Russian nihilists is the best example of this (see the appeals for aid to Siberian exiles: "To the American People," March 18, 1882 [I:17, #17], p. 1; Tucker, "Americans, Attention!" ibid, p. 2; and the serialized novel about the nihilists, N.G. Tchernychewsky, "What's To Be Done?" May 17, 1884—May 1, 1886). Much the same can be said about coverage of the Haymarket incident and subsequent trial and persecution (Tucker, "Liberty and Violence," May 22, 1886 [IV:3, #81], p. 4; "Mr. Lum Finds Liberty Wanting," June 19, 1886 (IV:4, #82), p. 5. See also his brief comment on the "justice lynching" of Leon Czolgosz, assassin of President McKinley ("On Picket Duty," August 1903 [XIV:12, #374], p. 1).

10. Tucker, "Liberty and Violence," May 22, 1886 (IV:3, #81), p. 4; "Herr Most on Libertas," April 14, 1888 (V:18, #122), p. 4.

11. A similar insistence on self-reliance is made by Sidney H. Morse (H, "The Ballot as a Substitute for Brains," August 9, 1884 [II:22, #48], pp. 4-5).

12. Tucker, "On Picket Duty," October 14, 1882 (II:1, #27), p. 1 ("the feminine mind seems to have no conception of freedom or human rights, and believes thoroughly in fiat morality"); Max [A.P. Kelly], "Max's Mirror," November 28, 1885 (III:18, #70), pp. 4-5; E.H.S. [Emma Schumm], "Female Suffrage," August 10, 1889 (VI:19, #149), p. 5; Caroline de Maupasant, "No Stilts for Women," August 11, 1894 (X:7, #293), p. 8; Lizzie M. Holmes, "The Ballot in Colorado," July 1899 (XIII:12, #362), p. 6 ("We have equal suffrage—and the invasions of equal liberty are proportionately greater").

13. See Paul Avrich, *The Haymarket Tragedy*, Princeton: Princeton University Press, 1984 for a description of the incident and trial.

14. A very similar article appeared after the execution of four of the anarchists in November 1887: J. William Lloyd, "Vengeance. An Open Letter to the Communist-Anarchists of Chicago," January 14, 1888 (V:12, #116), pp. 4-5.

15. Tucker, "Liberty and Violence," May 22, 1886 (IV:3, #81), p. 4; "Mr. Lum Finds Liberty Wanting," June 19, 1886 (IV:4, #82), p. 5; "Vaillant No Miscreant," February 24, 1894 (IX:47, #281), p. 3.

16. Joseph Labadie, a frequent contributor, made many of the same points in an article in the Detroit News, reprinted in *Liberty*: "Cranky Notions," August 13, 1892 (VIII:51, #233), pp. 3-4.

17. Tucker praised Yarros' even-handed contribution as an attempt "to explain, and to refrain from denouncing as malevolent, those acts of violence which the victims of violence commit." ([editorial column], September 22, 1894 [X:10, #296], p. 4)

18. Yarros, "Violence Breeding Violence," June 30, 1894 (X:4, #290), p. 2.

Index